CARMINE

PENCILER • PUBLISHER • PROVOCATEUR

CARMINE INFANTINO
PENCILER • PUBLISHER • PROVOCATEUR

Interviews • Jim Amash
Transcription • Brian K. Morris
Editing • Jim Amash and Eric Nolen-Weathington
Publication Design • Eric Nolen-Weathington
Cover Pencils • Carmine Infantino
Cover Inks • Terry Austin
Cover Color • Tom Ziuko
Introduction • Roy Thomas

Published by
TwoMorrows Publishing
10407 Bedfordtown Dr.
Raleigh, North Carolina 27614
www.twomorrows.com • e-mail: twomorrow@aol.com

First Printing • August 2010
All rights reserved
Printed in Canada
Softcover ISBN: 978-1-60549-025-0
Hardcover ISBN: 978-1-60549-026-7

Trademarks & Copyrights

Dedication
To my wife, Heidi, and to Keif Simon and Terry Austin. — Jim

Special Thanks
This book would not have been possible without the help and cooperation of the following people,
and we give them our most sincere thanks:

Heritage Auctions (www.ha.com)

and:

Alter Ego, David Armstrong, Terry Austin, Bob Bailey, Mike W. Barr, *The Batcave Companion*, Rod Beck, Tom Bradley, Michael Browning, Mike Costa, Ray Cuthbert, Irwin Donenfeld, Mike Dunne, Foundation's Edge, Frank Giella, Joe Giella, Tony Gleeson, Arnie Grieves, Jeff Harnett, *The Jack Kirby Collector*, Mike Jackson, Alex Johnson, Nick Katradis, Joe Kubert, Gary Land, Emmanuel Lapuente, Rob Ledford, Jim Ludwig, Dr. Jeff McLaughlin, Joe and Nadia Mannarino, Peter Meskin, Jim Murtaugh, Ken Quattro, Pat Sekowsky, Jim Simon, Joe Simon, Keif Simon, Mark Sinnott, Anthony Snyder (www.anthonysnyder.com), Roy Thomas, Jim Vadeboncoeur Jr., Dr. Michael "Doc V." Vassallo, Hames Ware, Bob Wiacek

Table of Contents

FLASH, REVERSE-FLASH ™ AND © DC COMICS.

Introduction
By Roy Thomas

Carmine Infantino defies description.

Or, to immediately turn that statement on its head, he cries out for description — only you have to keep revising, changing, updating any verbal snapshot you take of him. Because, just about the time you think you've finally got him all figured out and labeled, his strength and foibles and stylistic attributes all pinned like a radiant butterfly to some convenient wall, he'll metamorphose on you into something new and different and fly away. And you'll have a bent, blunted pin lying there on the floor, while you wait to see where he'll next alight.

In the early and middle 1940s, naturally enough, young Carmine Infantino of Brooklyn, New York, was just one of a number of undistinguished, often underage artists hanging on by his fingernails to a fledgling career as a comic book artist. At that time, he was a wannabe Milton Caniff, drawing heroes who all looked like Terry Lee and Pat Ryan and women who all bore as strong a resemblance as they could manage to Burma and the Dragon Lady.

No surprise there. During that era, nearly every adventure comic book artist wanted to draw like Caniff. Some of them even managed, with time, to render a reasonable approximation of the style of the creator of *Terry and the Pirates*. And Carmine was one of them.

Only thing is, by the time he pulled off that difficult trick, he was already on his way to Somewhere Else.

His Caniff-y Flash and Green Lantern stories of the middle and late 1940s, which became some of the best-looking that National/DC was publishing, would tack, in the 1950s, to newer winds that were blowing through the comics industry… and most particularly at DC, the company for which he produced the majority of his work.

By the beginning of the fabulous '50s, if my late auto-didactic friend Gil Kane is to be credited, it was the likes of Dan Barry that was becoming the new artistic standard at DC: work that was well-drawn, almost "pretty" rather than rugged. Look up the word "slick" in one of the weirder dictionaries, and you're liable to find a Dan Barry "Vigilante" or *Big Town* panel plunked next to it. Even though Barry himself soon moved on to illustrating a slick if somewhat antiseptic version of the newspaper comic strip *Flash Gordon*, his style continued to reign supreme at DC, influencing even the styles of more singular artists like Alex Toth and Mort Drucker, before they, too, wandered off.

And, while the echoes of Caniff could still be detected in Carmine's work on features like "The Trigger Twins" and "King Faraday" and *The Phantom Stranger*, it was a slicker, more polished, but less overtly dynamic Infantino who slowly redefined himself into one of a handful of artists who typified (and justified) the DC "house style." That's what DC wanted at the time, so Carmine had adapted like a skillful chameleon to accommodate them, hopefully fulfilling his inner needs at the same time. Like all commercial artists, he had to make a living… and DC kept him busy with increasingly important assignments.

By 1956, when he was tapped to pencil the first issue of a revived and revivified Flash in *Showcase #4*, Carmine was refining his style still further, developing some of his quirks… or rather, I should say, his personal trademarks.

It's all there, beneath Joe Kubert's fine inks, in the very first "new Flash" story, "Mystery of the Human Thunderbolt!":

A taste for modernism that put his work far more in-touch with then-current trends than was that of most of his comic book contemporaries. (See, for example, that distant yet exquisitely rendered diner at the bottom of page 4, with that rightward flare emitting from the "D" in "Diner" above the other letters of the word in a manner suggestive of the Coca-Cola logo and a million newspaper ads… note the rear-end of the car on page 6, accurately capturing the moment when the U.S. auto industry was transitioning from its long languid "postwar" look to the flaring fins that by year's end would come flying at the country in the '57 models.)

A feel for the telling detail that makes a scene seem "real," compared to the standard hero fantasies of a decade earlier. (Study that rumpled cardboard milk carton on page 2, complete with pull-back plastic top and bent straw… the repeating of near-identical scenery and angles on page 6, panel 2, and in the first panel on page 7, a reminder that only instants have gone by since a bullet was headed straight for Iris West's perky head.)

And the skylines. Perhaps, more than (and symbolic of) everything else, the skylines.

Jack Kirby's New York-style cities had been all tenements and Lower East Side and Upper West Side, which was perfect for his world… while those of most (no, not all) other comic artists tended to be relatively nondescript, as if they'd been requisitioned from the props-and-scenery department of a lesser movie studio like Republic or even Monogram.

Carmine's cityscape backgrounds were composed of towers of steel and glass and sky-reaching spires, straining for the stars—and half convincing you that they might just reach them. They rise above the nighted street down which Barry Allen races while first discovering that he's received the gift of super-speed... they're visible behind the aforementioned diner and above the verdant treetops behind it... they look on while the Flash races down the front of one of their number in his first true defiance of gravity... they're there when he's racing across the bumpy waters of the river/harbor, and as he carries the defeated Turtle Man back toward the justice that awaits amid those bastions of modern civilization.

Superman artist Wayne Boring, I suppose, had pioneered some aspects of those backgrounds with his own cityscapes, but it was Carmine who made the mega-city — whether it was called New York or Central City or later Gotham City or Metropolis — into an eternally looming yet quietly beneficent presence. Somehow, it just didn't seem likely that some dark, primitive force like evil was going to triumph while those sleek architectural marvels stretched across the horizon from border left to border right, subtly reminding the reader that the story he was reading was taking place in a world that was, ultimately, civilized.

Over the next few years, as *The Flash* swiftly (how else?) became one of DC's best-selling and most influential titles, Carmine continued to refine his style. Other artists even emulated his skylines, but the days when one had been likely to confuse Infantino's work with that of Kane or Anderson or any other artist were pretty much over with. Only that fact that fate (in the shape of his editor Julius Schwartz) decreed that he rarely inked his own work kept his hallmark style from being even more distinctive. And when he was allowed to apply his own pen to those graceful yet dynamic pencils, as in the early "Elongated Man" stories in *Detective Comics*, we had a fleeting glimpse of an Infantino that was, if anything, even more impressive.

Not even a few minor false steps — like those disruptive hands he sometimes liked to draw jutting out from the sides of captions, pointing this way and that, to the distraction of at least this reader—stopped Carmine's upward march.

For he had ideas — ideas for covers, ideas to make DC a more dynamic company, to compete with the growing competition coming by the mid-1960s from the upstart Marvel Comics a few blocks uptown.

Thus, by the mid-1960s, he had transmuted himself into a cover art director for a company that hadn't even known it needed a cover art director. And DC's covers achieved a new drama and liveliness they hadn't had in years. He both art-directed and inspired other artists — Nick Cardy comes particularly to mind — to some of the finest cover designs of their careers.

And Carmine still wasn't done. Okay, so perhaps it fell into his lap that he had the chance to move from cover art director to publisher and head honcho of the entire company, as few artists or writers ever do. No matter. Personally, since my teenage years, I've felt my life has been very much influenced by the so-called "position play" of chess grandmaster Aaron Nimzovich, who wrote an influential chess book called *My System*. You develop your pieces... move them into strong, unassailable positions... you keep your eye on what's going on all over the board... and then you wait for things to happen, things you can make use of. I think this is what Carmine instinctively did... and it served him, and for that matter DC, very well indeed.

When I was acting as Stan Lee's associate editor at Marvel, and later as his editor-in-chief once he'd gotten himself kicked upstairs to publisher (Stan clearly had a lot of the same instincts as Carmine did), he and I could tell when DC began to abandon its relatively static look of the early '60s and achieve some of the same dynamics and pyrotechnics that artists like Jack Kirby, Steve Ditko, and John Romita had brought to Marvel.

It was a cross-town shoot-out during the latter 1960s and early '70s... Stan Lee and his merry Marvel crew against Carmine Infantino and the creators (mostly artists originally) to whom he applied a loose yet encouraging rein — the likes of Cardy, Neal Adams, Joe Kubert, Bernie Wrightson, Dick Giordano, the deceptively under-appreciated Joe Orlando.

And I'd like to think that everybody — fans and pros and even the comic book industry — was the better for it.

Thanks, Carmine. Thanks for being there... as artist, as inspirer, and yes, even as imperator of the Distinguished Competition.

It's been a wild and woolly ride, these past several decades...

And you, as much as anyone, are the one who paced us all.

Roy Thomas has been a writer and sometime editor in the comics field, mostly for Marvel and DC, since 1965. In the 1970s Carmine Infantino tried to hire him away from Marvel to oversee Superman and other books at DC... and such was the strength of Carmine's siren call and Roy's respect for him that it took a writer/editor situation to keep him at Marvel after 1974. Roy's always wondered what might have happened if he had moved to "Earth-C"....

CHAPTER 1

Education Comes First

(below) Chester Gould created the *Dick Tracy* newspaper strip in 1931, just a few years after Carmine was born. This strip, which ran March 1, 1934, is from around the time Carmine would have first started reading and copying Gould's work. Gould's style hadn't quite evolved to the classic *Dick Tracy* look yet, but he was getting close.

COURTESY OF HERITAGE AUCTIONS (WWW.HA.COM).

©1934 TRIBUNE MEDIA SERVICES, INC.

JIM AMASH: *You were born May 24, 1925, a few years before the Great Depression started. What was the neighborhood that you grew up in Brooklyn like?*
CARMINE INFANTINO: I lived in a mostly Jewish neighborhood, one or two black families, some Irish... it was a very poor neighborhood, but clean. I remember we had a trolley car going around in the middle of the street. We lived near a cross-section. There was a playground for kids on the corner called Central Avenue which had gates on one corner. One of the boys I grew up with went to the [electric] chair. There was a pool parlor across the street where we used to hang out as kids, and that's where I met some of those tough guys. I remember they were quite honorable, but you didn't cross them. [*laughter*] I knew many of them quite well. One guy, I was the godfather of one of his children, all of whom went to jail, I think. We weren't tight friends; we just knew each other casually. I had no real close friends there, because I went to school and started meeting guys like Frank Giacoia and other guys interested in art and cartooning. My neighbors did not have the same interests as I.

I must have been about seven or eight years old when I started drawing. Dick Tracy was my favorite character. One time I copied him from one of the strips and my father didn't believe I didn't trace him. My uncle berated him for that. My uncle was Mexican and was married to my mother's younger sister. We lived in a four-story walk-up tenement, and on the third floor, my mother, father, my brother and I had three rooms with a bathroom in the hall. My aunt and uncle had the other three rooms in the back with their bathroom in the hall. And we paid the enormous sum — it was a cold water flat, you know — of $18 a month, which many months my father couldn't afford. It was my grandfather's house. He was a real jerk, my mother's father. He'd demand the rent sometimes knowing we didn't have it; it was terrible. This was the early 1930s. I worked as a shoeshine boy at five or six years old, and when I was twelve I worked for my uncle in a food store, carrying orders to people up and down the stairs, to help the family income.

We had an oblong kitchen — quite small. There was a sink in there, but no place for a shower. There was no such thing as a shower. You'd have to sit in the sink and bathe yourself. I remember my father getting up in the morning, putting coal in the stove to get the place warmed up, because you're freezing. It was not fun. We had a dining room and a bedroom. My brother Jimmy and I slept in the dining room. There was a dining room table and a foldaway bed. My folks had the bedroom. It was very wide open.

My aunt had the largest apartment down there. She had five children. One boy died at 16, and that was very sad. In those days, Jim, they'd keep the body in the living room... open caskets. Very bizarre.

JA: *Did you play any sports?*
CI: I played baseball a little bit. Highland Park was nearby. We used to walk up there, over a mile, to play. One of the guys was Phil Rizzuto. He was wonderful; a hard-assed little guy, but

nobody thought he'd make it because he was so small. But he came from that neighborhood. He was very good, and the range he had as a shortstop was incredible. But I was not that good. Most of the guys weren't that good, but Rizzuto became a star shortstop for the New York Yankees. Highland Park was where the scouts saw him play.

Baseball was the only sport I played. I didn't like any other sports. I preferred first base. I was a New York Giants fan in Brooklyn. Figure that one out. I don't know why. As a kid, I was a fan of Carl Hubbell and Mel Ott. A couple of times my father took me to see the Dodgers at Ebbets Field, and the guys that hung around with me were pissed as hell. But I was a little kid, you know? I'd be screaming, "Kill him! Kill him! Kill him, Carl!" And the guys in the stands wanted to kill me. One guy says to my father, "What's wrong with your son?" My father says, "What can I do? He's that way." [laughter] Isn't that cute? We went to a couple of games, not that many; we couldn't afford it. But in those days, hey, you'd get in for 15 cents or a quarter.

JA: *I think a quarter would get you in the bleachers back then.*
CI: My father would pay for that, then he'd tip the guy a dime and we'd get the top seats, but not the top seats in the first row there. I remember Carl Furillo, Carl Erskine... all the Dodgers and Giants players. I saw Jackie Robinson; he was incredible to watch. He was genius. He'd go up and down that baseline, back and forth; he drove the pitchers nuts. He got them so crazy that they didn't know what to do with the ball. And he was fast, I mean fast! You've got to be to steal home plate. Even though I hated the Dodgers... I hated them because I was a Giants fan, but I had to respect Robinson.

JA: *Tell me about your parents.*
CI: My father was a musician. He taught himself to play the alto sax, the clarinet, and the violin. Do you remember Harry Warren? My father was fronting his band; they were friends. Warren wrote the song "Chattanooga Choo-Choo," as well as music for some Judy Garland films, and *The Lullaby of Broadway*, the famous stage play. But it was a really bad depression, and in those days you had to go to the five-and-ten and play your music all the time, all hours of the night and day. My mother didn't like that. She didn't want to be home alone. She made him stop playing music and he began working on houses, which he hated. How do I know that? Because as a kid, I used to go to work with him and help him. It was terrible, cleaning toilets and all that crap. Anyway, it bothered him all his life. Some

days, my father would sit by a window and play a mournful tune on the saxophone. I'd just sit and listen to him, not knowing how bad things were. It was so sad. That man never complained, but his heart was broken. And then I went out shining shoes to make some money.

JA: *What happened when you got interested in art?*
CI: One of my uncles came over when he heard that I wanted to be an artist, and he told my father, "What are you, crazy? All these guys end up painting houses." He tried to talk my father out of it. That's one uncle. The other uncle — Harry, the Mexican uncle I mentioned earlier — encouraged me and told my father, "Leave him alone. Let him do whatever he wants." The other guy who kept telling me to paint houses, his own son ended up in advertising. [laughs] Isn't that wild?

My father didn't talk much, but he was trying to discourage me from going ahead with this. And I said, "I want to draw. I'm going to the School of Industrial Arts on 42nd Street." I didn't care what anyone thought. I was going — period! They couldn't stop me. That was the end of it. My mother said, "Get a city job. You'll make a living for life and you won't have to worry." Could you imagine me in that? [Jim laughs] Thirty-five dollars a week in those days. Well, that's how people thought then. They thought you should get something steady where you work steady.

JA: *Did your mother work?*
CI: Yes. She used to make pants in a factory, so I didn't see her much. She lived with my grandmother a lot. But the good part of that, she always spoke Italian, and I learned to speak Italian.

(above) Harry Warren *(right)* and Al Dubin *(left)* were collaborators in the 1930s and wrote music for such films as *42nd Street*, *Gold Diggers of 1933*, and *Moulin Rouge* (all of which were made in 1933). Warren — born Salvatore Antonio Guaragna — was the son of Italian immigrants, as was Carmine's father, Pasquale Infantino. It couldn't have been easy for Pasquale to give up being a professional musician, but then to see Warren — his friend and someone with whom he shared a common background —sign on with Warner Brothers in 1932 and become a huge success in Hollywood must have filled him with regret.

JA: *How good was your Italian?*

CI: It's pretty good now. At the beginning, I used to laugh at her. "Aah, I won't need that stuff!" She'd say "Someday, you're going to need it," and she was right. When I got to Italy, I needed it. [*laughter*]

JA: *What was it like when you celebrated holidays or birthdays?*

CI: One Christmas… it was very awful. I'll never forget that. We didn't have the money for food, so I went out with a shoeshine box, and that money I brought home. My father had to wait for it to go shopping for Christmas, and the poor man felt castrated. Can you imagine that kind of a thing? It's terrible for a man to have to go through that. I didn't think of it that way, but he did. A terrible situation. I think I never got over a lot of that stuff.

So my mother got a job, and my father became a plumber, but there wasn't any work. He went to places like the Democratic Club to see if they could him find a job. His name was Pasquale and he was told at one place, "Listen, mister, with that name, you'll never get a job" — meaning his name was too Italian. We talk about discrimination now, but it was there then, too.

So he changed his name to Patrick. It didn't help much, but he changed his name anyway.

JA: *Well, Infantino is not exactly an Irish name.*

CI: I know, but the first name… they thought he could get by with it, but it didn't help.

JA: *The woman usually ran what went on in the household. Is that true of your house?*

CI: My mother wasn't there. I grew up with my grandmother, you see? She lived on the first floor and we were on the third floor. My grandfather had a bootblack parlor, a shoeshine spot. He used to block and clean hats. He and his wife lived in the back of the store, and my aunt lived on the middle floor. In the one room, there was a guy who lived there. He worked for Trommers Beer. In those days, it was big stuff in Brooklyn.

My grandmother couldn't speak English. I loved her. We used to tease her, "Grandma, why don't you learn how to speak English?" And she used to say to me, "Someday, you're going to be happy you learned the language."

JA: *My feeling of you was that, basically, even as a kid, you were a loner, weren't you?*

CI: Very much so, yeah.

JA: *Carmine, why do you think that was?*
CI: I don't know, Jim. I didn't fit in with the rest of the crowd. I don't know. Some of them were gangsters, as I said. Some of them were pretty good at baseball, football, and everything else, and a lot of stickball. We played stickball, but I wasn't that good at it. I really wasn't that good. I was *good*, but not *that* good.

JA: *Do you think being an artist — because you were drawing already — maybe had something to do with it? Because a lot of artists are loners.*
CI: It's very possible. I liked to be by myself a lot. I knew that. But I can't tell you why. I felt I was different than the other people in my neighborhood. Maybe it was because I felt inadequate. Who knows? I've always kept to myself.

JA: *It's a common feeling many artists have. Artists are sensitive people. They tend to suffer from low self-esteem at times, and maybe too much self-esteem at other times.*
CI: No, it was low self-esteem on my part. I was a little chubby as a kid and very shy around women. And there were these young guys: the

women used to fall all over them. I had no problems like that. I wasn't that lucky then. I changed, though. [*laughter*] I was very shy. I'm still shy, by the way. I'm not very open with people — you know that. I was never an extrovert — ever.

JA: *What kind of student were you?*
CI: Not the tops. When I graduated from junior high, they wrote, "Bored by education." You know when the teachers evaluate you? That's what they wrote about me. Isn't that wild? I sat there drawing a lot. Talking and drawing. [*chuckling*]

JA: *So you drew in class when you should have been taking notes.*
CI: Yes. In those days, I got a basic education, that's it. I drew a lot of *Smilin' Jack*, and then *Terry and the Pirates* came on the scene and, boy, I went crazy for Milton Caniff. I loved *The Phantom*, too. I didn't pick up on Harold Foster until a little later. I couldn't wait to get the newspapers to look at that stuff.

JA: *DC started publishing comic books in 1935. Did you buy them?*
CI: I did when I could afford it, which wasn't that often. I didn't know I wanted to be an artist at that point. I just enjoyed copying those characters.

JA: *Jack Cole's brother, Dick, once told me that Jack was always a dreamer. Would that definition fit you?*
CI: You know what happened? My love for architecture started to come on very early. I wanted desperately to be an architect. I used to look at buildings, I'd try to reshape them, redesign them, and then I tried to go to school for that. And, of course, that was out of the question.

JA: *But you did go to the 1939 World's Fair.*

(above) Carmine "went crazy" for Milton Caniff and his *Terry and the Pirates* strip. He certainly wasn't the first or the last comic book artist to show a strong Caniff influence in their work. Caniff's bold blacks and cinematic layouts worked very well in the rapidly evolving medium. Shown here is the *Terry and the Pirates* strip for June 11, 1937.
(left) Another favorite of the young Carmine was *The Phantom*. While Lee Falk created and designed the character and wrote the strip — which still runs to this day — Ray Moore was the artist during the time Carmine would have first become a fan. Shown here is a panel from the May 3, 1938 *Phantom* strip, by Lee Falk and Ray Moore.

(above) This photo appeared in General Motors' 1939 New York World's Fair booklet, *Futurama*. GM's "Futurama" exhibit was designed by notable industrial designer Norman Bel Geddes, and was approximately 36,000 square feet in size.

CI: Yes, and I went nuts for the General Motors section. Of course they had "Cities of the Future" there, with the flying cars and strange roadways. I went there four or five times, I believe. I kept going back there all the time.

These were models... do you know how big they were? It was a whole city they had there. I would say it was about a half-mile around, the whole thing. You wandered on this treadmill, and you go around the whole thing. There were lines around the block for that thing.

JA: *You were in high school when you decided you wanted to draw comics.*
CI: Basically. I worked hard to learn how to draw. I wanted to get better so I could make a living at it. At 16, I was trying to get a job, and I got an offer from Al Capp to come work for him. My father said, "No way. You're not quitting school." I would have had to move to Boston, and my father said, "If the job is there now, it'll be there later." I was very disappointed. My father was right, though. The education comes first.

JA: *How did you get the idea to go to Al Capp?*
CI: I didn't. He saw some drawings I did. I used to visit artists to see what I could learn, and one of them was Morris Weiss. He was a terrific cartoonist and very nice to all the young people in

the industry. Anybody who'd call, he'd spend time with them and he'd give them his time and energy and everything. He was just a nice man. I went to him many times to show him my drawings. Apparently, I'd done some drawings and left them with Morris, who showed them to Al, and he contacted me.

Morris was one of my first contacts. I called him very timidly and said, "Do you think I could come see you?" He said, "Of course," and he was wonderful. So was a guy named Charlie Flanders, who drew *The Lone Ranger.* I used to go to Charlie's studio. He was across from Grand Central Station in those days. I'd sit and look and talk to him. He let me do some backgrounds or some background figures on *The Lone Ranger.* I was 16 or 17 — still in high school.

After school, I'd go running around to see these people. I was very tight with Frank Giacoia. We went to junior high school and high school together at the School of Industrial Arts. After school, we'd go around to the companies. I got my first job from Victor Fox, who was in the same building as DC Comics. It was one of those cheap, little outfits. They gave me a story to do, I brought it in, and they rejected it. It almost broke my heart. I kept plodding along.

JA: *But Joe Simon gave you and Frank a "Jack Frost" story to draw.*

CI: Yes, but that was after I had been to Fox. I inked it, and Frank penciled it. Frank was always a very slow penciler. His inking was pretty slow, too. Frank didn't really enjoy working that much; he was too easily distracted. That was his biggest problem.

JA: *Do you think he was afraid to pencil?*
CI: I think so. I think he was afraid, because he had some newspaper strips. He had *Sherlock Holmes* — I penciled a number of those for him — and *Johnny Reb* — I did some of those for him, too. I wasn't the only one. He had everybody work for him.

JA: *Jack Kirby, Mike Sekowsky, I think Gil Kane, too.*
CI: True, but Frank was a sweetheart. He just came home to talk rather than work. He had a television over his drawing board. How can you work and look at television? He was always late on his jobs. Later on, as a publisher, I used to give him raises all the time, thinking that would encourage him to work, but it didn't do a bit of good.

I was about 15 when I met Frank. He was reading a comic book, and I went over to him and said, "Can I look at that?" He said, "No." [*laughter*] I gave him a dirty look... he was just kidding around. We started talking, then we got very friendly. We both got a quarter a day from our parents. Fifteen cents was for food, and ten cents was car fare back and forth from Brooklyn. A nickel to go and a nickel to come back. We'd go to this old restaurant and buy one order of scrambled eggs and potatoes — the coffee was free — for 15 cents, and we'd split it. And we'd buy a comic book with his money one day and then the next day buy a comic book with my money. We did this for a long time.

JA: *Was he the first friend you made who read comic books?*
CI: No, but he read them carefully. All the kids, when I was in Brooklyn, bought comics and traded them.

JA: *What was Giacoia like as a young kid?*
CI: The same way as when he was old — the same attitudes. He had a teacher who was an old woman. He got pissed off at her; I think she yelled at him or something. As she's coming up the stairs, he threw a chair down at her. He could have killed her, you know. I didn't think it was funny. I yelled at him. "Frank, for Christ's sake, she's an old lady. What's the matter with you?"

JA: *Was he a real talkative guy when he was young?*
CI: Not so much. I heard he talked a lot at the end of his life. He used to repeat this phrase: "That guy better wise up, everybody gotta wise up." He was the only one that had to wise up, you know what I mean? He used to love to say that to me, "Wise up, wise up." He was a smart one. Look at how he ended up. He didn't take his own advice.

JA: *Who got the idea of going around to the comic book companies?*
CI: I don't know which of us did. We did it together, I know that. Well you know why? We were the only cartoonists in the class, I think, so we hung out together. And then we decided go visit the comic book companies. We made pests of ourselves and then went up to see Simon and Kirby at Timely.

JA: *How did you know they were at Tudor City? Was that common knowledge?*

(above) Unfortunately, no one — not even Carmine himself — is certain as to which "Jack Frost" story was Frank Giacoia and Carmine's first professional work. However, noted Golden/Silver Age comic art expert, Dr. Michael J. Vassallo — along with Jim Vadeboncouer, Jr. — has determined that the "Jack Frost" story from *USA Comics* #3 — the splash page of which is shown here — is the most likely choice of three possibilities. Also, George Klein may have touched up this story.

COURTESY OF MICHAEL "DOC V" VASSALLO.

JACK FROST ™ AND © MARVEL CHARACTERS, INC.

(above) Carmine stayed in school and graduated, and he had the cap and gown to prove it.

COURTESY OF *ALTER EGO* MAGAZINE.

(right) Carmine's high school friend and fellow comic book professional, Frank Giacoia, as pictured in the 1975 *Mighty Marvel Comic Convention* program book.

COURTESY OF *ALTER EGO* MAGAZINE.

(below) Though Frank Giacoia was the credited artist on the *Sherlock Holmes* strip, many other artists penciled for him, including Carmine. This title panel from a 1954 Sunday strip was likely penciled by Mike Sekowsky.

COURTESY OF HERITAGE AUCTIONS (WWW.HA.COM).

©1954 NY HERALD TRIBUNE, INC. & THE ESTATE OF ARTHUR CONAN DOYLE.

CI: No, someone told me. I don't know who the guy was that told me, but we tracked 'em down. When you're a fan, you track down your idols.

JA: *Did you show your work together in the same portfolio?*
CI: No, we showed our work separately. Joe Simon looked at our work and asked, "Who's the artist here?" And Frank said he was. Joe said to me, "You're the inker, I assume." "Yeah." I didn't care. I wanted any kind of work I could get. Frank said he was the penciler, that was it. That was the only job we ever did where he penciled and I inked.

JA: *Did you help Frank on the pencils at all?*
CI: No, no. He did them himself.

JA: *I've seen that story, and there's a little bit of the Simon and Kirby type of line work in your inks.*
CI: You see that, huh? I'm sure that was intentional. I was trying my best, but I know we both did a lousy job. It was my first real job in comics. I was scared to death. But Frank had balls; he did all of the talking. He didn't care. I give him credit for that. We got along, but personality-wise, we were not alike.

JA: *I assume you and Frank went together to turn the job in.*
CI: Yes. Joe looked at the pages, but he didn't say that much. Then he offered us a job. Frank said, "Yes," and I said, "I don't know. I have to talk to my father." Well, you know my father wouldn't let me quit school. Frank quit school and took the job.

JA: *Did you ever do* Young Allies *at Timely for Joe Simon?*
CI: I think I did. I think I did that with Frank Giacoia. He must have gotten us that job. By the way, I remember seeing Stan Lee there then. He was like an office boy.

JA: *What was your parents' reaction when you became a professional?*
CI: My mother used to say, "I would love to see you get a city job, because you'll get paid regularly and retire with a pension." They worried about things like that because of the Depression. I told her, "Mom, I cannot do that kind of thing." So she said, "Well, I'm sorry you're going to be an artist. I'm not happy with it." I said, "I'm sorry, but I'm going to do it anyway." My father didn't say anything. He never said a word. He was very strange that way.

JA: *If you had done what Frank Giacoia had done and quit school, what would your parents' reaction have been?*
CI: They wouldn't have been happy at all. My father didn't get to go to high school, because his family needed money, so he had to help support them. He would not have been happy if I had quit. He didn't want me to be an artist, either.

JA: *What would you have been if your parents had their way?*
CI: I probably would have had a city job and be dead by now, because I would have killed myself. [*Jim laughs*] No, I mean that. I'd have never stood it.

Making the Rounds

JA: *You were still living at home when you became a comic book artist. Did some of the money you earned go to supporting the family?*

CI: [*chuckles*] Oh, all of it went to support the family. My father didn't have too much luck in business, not at the beginning. Later on, he became a city plumbing inspector, and he enjoyed that. I told you how his heart was broken when he couldn't be a musician anymore.

JA: *Well, when you're creative, then you're doing something non-creative...*

CI: I think that's the thing that stuck with me. I understood it. So when I did well, he never said a word, but I knew he approved.

JA: *Your brother Jimmy was how many years younger than you?*

CI: He was seven years younger.

JA: *Was he interested in being an artist because of his big brother?*

CI: No, Jimmy had just came out of the Army. He was out on Governor's Island with John Romita. When Jimmy came home, I called Joe Simon. "Joe, my kid brother's looking around for work. He can't find any work. Do you think you could use him?" Joe said, "Absolutely. Send him over." So Jimmy went there and started working. He worked with Simon and Kirby, he worked with Mort Meskin and a bunch of guys, and he had a good time. Then he reached the point when he said, "I've got to go," and Joe called me. "Carmine, he's gotten so good. He'd be a hell of a cartoonist." I said, "Joe, I can't interfere with that, I'm sorry."

JA: *Why do you think Jimmy was interested in being an artist, and why did he lose interest?*

CI: I have no idea. We never discussed it. Can you believe it? The only thing I know is he didn't want to be a cartoonist. Maybe he didn't want to compete with me. It's very possible, you know. Jimmy was a hard worker. He became an advertising artist with some big agency — I don't remember their name now, but he worked pretty hard there. Long hours.

JA: *Maybe he didn't like working at home?*

CI: You're right. He did not enjoy working at home, but he liked the advertising business better than cartooning.

JA: *How did you meet Ken Battefield? He worked for Harry Chesler's shop.*

CI: You remember that name? Oh, my God. He was working at Chesler's when I met him. He was like the wise, old sage. One time, he said to

(below) Jimmy Infantino worked for the Simon and Kirby shop from 1952-58, penciling mostly back-ups for various Atlas comics, including this one from *Wyatt Earp #16*, likely written by Hank Chapman.

COURTESY OF BOB BAILEY.
©1958 INTERSTATE PUBLISHING CORP.

(above) Jimmy Infantino (standing in back with glasses) during his days with the Simon & Kirby shop in the early 1950s. Left to right, Joe Simon, Jack Kirby (standing), Mort Meskin, Jimmy, and Marvin Stein. On Joe Simon's board is what appears to be a drawing of Jimmy.

me, "Don't even think of trying to make a future in this business, because there are guys in it now who won't even make it. Kid, you've got not even a ghost of a chance." He used to batter us down all the time, and you know why? Because he didn't have it. He said comics were dying. I remember he had no future there, but who knew at the time?

JA: *You had a chance meeting with him in a coffee shop, and he took you over to Chesler's. How did you run into him in the coffee shop?*
CI: I was going to the School of Industrial Artists on 40th Street and I was having lunch. Battefield was sitting there while I was reading a comic book. He sat next to me. He told me how he worked for the comics, blah, blah, blah, blah. Then he mentioned Harry Chesler: "Why don't you come up and talk?"

Now, Harry had a terrible reputation. In all fairness, when I went up there, he said, "Come up any time, sit here, watch the guys," and he used to give me five bucks a week to do that, which was very nice of him. I loved just sitting there. I watched them all work. He had done the same thing for Joe Kubert. Chesler was very nice to young kids. I heard he was a mean man at times, but not to me.

A few years ago I was trying to find the place on 42nd Street. It was a four-story building, and it had a rickety elevator. When it opened up on the fourth floor, Harry sat there with his greasy hat at a desk, smoking a cigar. And right behind

him was a Milton Caniff original. It was so impressive to a young kid. You walk in there into a little room where he sat, and next door was a small, open room with about six artists working. Battefeld was there, and there was this Russian guy, a real Communist: Dan Zolernowich. He used to preach at me all the time. Mort Lawrence was there, and there was a guy, Joe something. He went into commercial art after a while. I don't remember his name any more.

JA: *What do you remember about Mort Lawrence?*
CI: We got to be very friendly, and then later on I shared an office with him. We had an office just below Bernard Baily's, I think, he and I together. We, of course, were in the Dixie Hotel. We used to pick up women there. We'd come into town and wave at them. He was married to a beautiful red-headed woman at the time.

JA: *Did Chesler give you any advice?*
CI: No.

JA: *He was expecting the other people to do that.*
CI: Yes. He never said a word. Just come in, sit, and watch Mort, and watch these guys draw. I would sit with a piece of paper and just sketch and sketch and sketch for a couple hours after school. This was around 1940, while I was in the ninth or tenth grade. And that five dollars was cash money. That was important to me.

JA: *While you were watching the artists, did you do any work around there? Did you erase any pages?*
CI: No, that came later at Quality Comics.

JA: *Owned by publisher "Busy" Arnold. But that was a summer job, wasn't it? You went to Chesler's during the school year.*
CI: Yes. Maybe Harry suggested it, I really don't remember. But I did end up there. It was a tough job. There's another one, Will Eisner's ex-partner... the Jerry Iger shop. I worked for his place there for a while, but I don't remember anything about him. I met Ruben Moreira there, and Nick Cardy. He was "Viscardi" in those days. He lost some "Vis" in his name. [*Jim laughs*]

JA: *When you went to Quality, how much did they pay you a week?*
CI: About ten bucks, but I'll never forget a couple of weeks there: I killed myself. I rubbed my fingers to the bone erasing pages, and they screwed me on the money a couple of times.

And you couldn't fight it, because it wasn't worth it. I kept my mouth shut, because I was looking at Reed Crandall's *Blackhawk*... Eisner and Lou Fine's work... all those guys were great artists.

JA: *Were there many people in the Quality offices?*
CI: There were a couple of editors. The artists didn't work there, though. No artists worked there. I didn't get to meet any of them.

JA: *During that time, George Brenner was an editor, Gill Fox was an editor. Was John Beardsley there? They were all three of them there at one point.*
CI: Yes. I think John ran it, if I'm not mistaken. I remember seeing Gill Fox there. John was the editor in chief, I think. He hired me. He said, "I can't give you a job drawing, but I need somebody to do clean-up work." I said, "I'll take it." I didn't have that great of an impression of him, and I barely remember Brenner. I used to run up to all these places to visit.

I whited out the ink lines that stuck out of the panel borders. "Busy" Arnold didn't like those little lines. Nobody gave me art tips, but I absorbed those pages. They were beautiful. I studied the drawing, the storytelling, the way lines were made... everything! I'd go home and try to practice what I was learning. But I did no drawing up there. And then I worked at the Binder Studio for two summers, doing backgrounds.

JA: *Didn't you do some "Spy Smasher," which was published by Fawcett? That company was Binder's main account.*
CI: I guess I did, but it doesn't really ring a bell. I did do a little penciling there, so maybe "Spy Smasher" was what I did. I didn't draw much there. Binder was okay; he didn't talk much and he didn't pay much. The shop was a big, empty loft with desks lined up all over the place, and he sat in the corner someplace. It was like a sweatshop there with maybe 20 people crammed in there. That wasn't for me, but I needed whatever work I could find.

JA: *After that, you went to work for Charlie Biro.*
CI: I did a lot of backgrounds for him on his *Daredevil* comic. I also worked for him in 1946, '47 on *Crime Does Not Pay*, some *Daredevil*, and a Western called *Desperado*.

We used to go to his house, me and Norman Maurer. Norm did some inking, and I did some backgrounds. We'd work all night long. It was tough, because I had to go to school in the morning. Charlie was always behind in his schedule. This was when I met Norman.

Biro was tough, but good. He ended up at NBC, in the Art Department. When I did this particular work, I worked at his house. A few years later when I worked for him, I worked at home, penciling stories for him. I didn't ink that work.

JA: *So you never dealt with Bob Wood?*
CI: No. I met him; he was very nice, quiet, but he was a drunk. He didn't talk very much. Charlie ran the show, pretty much. I don't think Bob Wood got enough credit for what he did. *Crime Does Not Pay* was his idea, and he was a hell of a good writer. So were his brothers, Dick and Dave. They were drunks, but they were good writers.

Charlie had a larger than life personality. He could be very charming, and people liked him. Bob Wood was quiet, hard to know.

JA: *Since this is one of your earliest jobs, was Charlie giving you art advice while you were doing his backgrounds?*
CI: Yes, he helped me. He used to push storytelling. He was very strong on that.

(above) While Carmine was erasing pencil marks from inked pages for publication and learning the ropes of the comic book business at Quality Comics, he was studying the work of the many great artists who worked for them, such as Reed Crandall. This cover for 1948's *Modern Comics* #78 was produced a few years after Carmine had left Quality, but you can see why Crandall's work was worth studying.

COURTESY OF HERITAGE AUCTIONS (WWW.HA.COM).

ARTWORK ©1948 COMICS MAGAZINES, INC. BLACKHAWK © AND ™ DC COMICS.

(above) *Top Spot Comics* only lasted for one issue, but Carmine was there. Here is his opening splash panel for back-up feature, "The Menace," done through Bernard Baily's shop.

COURTESY OF KEN QUATTRO.
©1945 TOP SPOT PUBLISHING CO.

I was freelancing in those days. I think I met Gil Kane there, if I'm not mistaken. Baily paid hardly peanuts. He was very sweet; he just didn't pay you much. You live and you learn because you do a lot of stuff. That's where I met Charlie Voigt, the old-timer. Mac Raboy was there, too. He was a genius. He was very sweet and he was so slow. He used to paste up stuff from his old work and then draw around it until he put the book together.

I penciled for Baily. Some stuff I inked, too, but it was mostly penciling. I remember he needed production. That's all he cared about: getting the stuff out.

JA: *Do you remember how many people worked there?*
CI: Quite a few people worked there. It was a big office. I was there about a year or two.

JA: *Do you remember if your Timely work was packaged by Baily, or did you get that work yourself?*
CI: It probably happened both ways, because I remember editors Vince Fago and Al Sulman, and I did work for Baily during part of that time.

JA: *And since you were inking backgrounds, did he discuss positive/negative shapes?*
CI: No, he didn't. That came much later when I was in school.

JA: *But he would at least discuss line weights with you, and textures.*
CI: That he would talk about. Biro treated me very nicely. He loved Norman, by the way. He thought Norman was a genius. I always thought Norman was a very bright man.

After I left Biro, I graduated to drawing full stories on my own. I think Bernard Baily's shop was my next stop. I couldn't get work elsewhere.

JA: *Did Baily have an assistant?*
CI: Not that I know of. I believe he ran the shop by himself. If anyone helped him, I didn't know about it.

JA: *His wife didn't help him?*
CI: I don't think so. I don't remember seeing her.

JA: *Did Baily provide your art supplies?*
CI: No, I supplied my own paper. Paper, pencils — that was simple. The only thing he provided was a desk. It was a sweatshop over there.

(right) It's difficult to say exactly how much work Carmine actually did for Timely in the mid-'40s. It appears he was the primary penciler for this seven-page "Human Torch" story which ran in *The Human Torch* #25, but there are at least two different pencilers at work here. Thanks to Jim Vadeboncoeur, Jr. and Hames Ware for the identification.

COURTESY OF MIKE COSTA.
HUMAN TORCH, TORO © AND ™
MARVEL CHARACTERS, INC.

JA: *Would he try to mentor you in any way?*

CI: No, he never bothered me. Maybe he should have, but he didn't. He wanted to grind out material. That's all he cared about. He wanted to get as much material as possible out.

Then I shared an office with Mort Lawrence. He was a very nice man. He eventually moved out of town. I don't know where he moved to, but I don't think he did comics any more. He did something else.

JA: *I know he did comics up into the early to mid-'50s.*

CI: I didn't know that. I lost track of him for some reason. And we were very close at one point.

JA: *I don't know if this is true, but someone told me that they thought "Lawrence" was not his real last name.*

CI: As far as I knew, it was. I never questioned that.

JA: *Marvin Levy told me that when he worked for Bernard Baily, Mort Lawrence was drawing* Captain America, *because he occasionally would do some backgrounds on that feature for Lawrence.*

CI: If he said so, it's true then. I don't know a thing about that. I don't remember Mort drawing *Captain America* at all.

JA: *Well, he probably just did some filler things, because Captain America appeared in so many titles for Timely.*

CI: Okay, that's probably what it was.

JA: *Do you have any personal stories about Mort Lawrence?*

CI: No, but we were friendly. He had a gorgeous wife. They were very nice, and I'd sometimes spend weekends with them. They were very sweet people, the two of them. He looked like Clark Gable, by the way. A big, tall, handsome guy; a nice, lovely personality. He was talkative to a degree. You had to know him first. He was interesting.

JA: *I have you drawing some funny animal comics in '42 for Timely.*

CI: Yeah, I did some of those for Vince Fago. I would have done anything to make a living, period.

JA: *Also, in 1943, I have you as doing "Captain Wonder" for Timely.*

CI: That rings a bell. I did a lot of work, didn't I?

JA: *Did you draw a few "Human Torch" stories in 1945?*

CI: I think I did some of those — a couple of them. I didn't enjoy them, though. I worked with Fago there. He had a bad eye, I think. It looked off in one direction or something.

JA: *Do you remember drawing "The Angel" in '45 and '46? He had a pencil-thin mustache, yellow-and-blue costume.*

CI: No, I don't remember that at all. But as you know, I did a lot of work that I don't remember.

JA: *In 1946, I have you as drawing "The Patriot" for Timely.*

CI: That rings a bell, but why, I don't know. I think I did that for Al Sulman. I don't remember working for Stan Lee at all.

JA: *Why did you do so few stories for Timely?*

(above) Page five of Carmine's story for *The Human Torch #25.* Carmine probably did most of the penciling on this page.

COURTESY OF MIKE COSTA.

HUMAN TORCH, TORO © AND ™ MARVEL CHARACTERS, INC.

CI: I guess they fired me, I don't know. Maybe I moved on... who knows?

JA: *For Holyoke, you did "Commandos of the Devil Dogs," pencils and inks, in 1945, and in 1944 you did "Hell's Angels," pencils only. For Lev Gleason, I have you doing "Daredevil" in 1947, and a feature in the early '40s called "Hero of the Month," as well as some Westerns around '44.*
CI: There was another company in there I did work for, because I met John Giunta there.

JA: *Was it Magazine Enterprises? You did some war stories for them.*
CI: That's the one, yeah. That's where I met John Giunta. I was very tight with him.

JA: *So all this is around the same time. At this point, I don't think you can separate which came first, can you?*
CI: No, I went back and forth, back and forth all over. I don't remember, myself.

JA: *You didn't care — you were happy to be working. I can understand that. We'll start with Holyoke.*
CI: Milt Cohen was the guy that got me to Holyoke. He was a friend of Lou Fine, and Lou Fine did a strip called *The Cisco Kid* that Milt was trying to sell and couldn't. I think I met Lou through Gil Kane.

JA: *Cohen, who later changed his last name to Caine, was Lou Fine's agent for a while. I think they met at the Johnstone and Cushing art service. So how did you meet him?*
CI: Cohen? He used to hang around all over the business. I ran into him at Baily's.

JA: *Leonard Cole was the editor. Do you remember anything about him?*
CI: Nothing, literally nothing. He wasn't there that much. Milt Cohen and I were there most of the time in their office at the Times Building. That's where they were based.

JA: *There was a woman who did some editing there by the name of Ray Hermann.*
CI: That rings a bell. I think she was big, tall, chubby blonde. She was very nice, though.

JA: *So they handed you a script, and you penciled and inked it. Did Cole want to see your pencils before you inked them?*
CI: No, but you know what? Milt Cohen inked all of that stuff. That's how I got to work with Milt Cohen. I didn't ink them. In other words, he got the work for us. Milt was a lousy inker, by

(below left) Carmine penciled and inked the four-page "No Ice Today" back-up strip for Aviation's *Contact Comics* #4, cover-dated January 1945.

(below right) Meet Hell's Angels. Carmine penciled their first adventure for Holyoke's *Sparkling Stars* #1, cover-dated June 1944.

COURTESY OF JIM VADEBON-COEUR, JR. AND *ALTER EGO* MAGAZINE.

"NO ICE TODAY" ©1945 AVIATION PRESS.

HELL'S ANGELS ©1944 ET-ES-GO MAGAZINES, INC.

the way. One of the worst! He was a letterer, too, and I think he lettered the stories we did. They didn't pay us much.

JA: *In 1944, I have you at Magazine Enterprises, which may have been through Bernard Baily. Magazine Enterprises was owned by Vince Sullivan.*
CI: He didn't like me or my work. I did a little, not much.

JA: *Let me ask you about a couple of other small companies. One is called Spotlight Comics. In 1945, you drew something in* Jeep Comics — *a feature called "Captain Power" — for R.B. Leffingwell, "Golden Eagle" for Aviation, "Prince Ra" and "Ted O'Neil of the Commandos" for Feature Comics, and "Jiu Jitsu Joe" for Cambridge House.*
CI: All of that was through Bernie Baily. Bernie packaged for a lot of little companies, and I often didn't know where my stuff was going to be printed. We worked for Bernie, and then he paid us.

JA: *In 1946, right before you started working for Shelly Mayer, you began working for Hillman Publications. At this point, you hadn't set on a style yet.*

CI: No, I was not comfortable with any style, but I was still into Caniff, wasn't I? There was Foster in there, too.

JA: *Frankly, I also see a little bit of a generic comic book look in your style at that time, but many artists of the time were influenced by Milton Caniff. You had not stylistically broken out, so things like "The Flying Dutchman" that you did for Hillman doesn't look like your later work.*
CI: No, a lot of it doesn't. You're right, it was generic. I was still trying to find my style.

JA: *When I look at a couple of things you did for Hillman, it looks to me like a man who's learning, and yet I don't see a super-definable style.*
CI: Yes, that's true. I did "The Heap." The editor, Ed Cronin, really pushed me to write, and if it wasn't for him, I wouldn't have learned how to do it.

JA: *What made Cronin think you could write?*
CI: He'd say, "Son, I know you can write." I said, "I've never tried." He said, "What? You're going to write it." He forced me to write. He said, "You're going to have to learn to do everything." He used to push that on me constantly. "When

THE SINISTER SURGERY INCIDENT

IT'S NOT VERY LIKELY THAT YOU-'VE HEARD OF THE LITTLE TOWN OF ALGOYA, SOMEWHERE IN SOUTH AMERICA, BUT CHANCES ARE, YOU WILL! WHEN THE HISTORY OF THIS WAR IS TOLD, EVENTS WILL SHOW THAT ONE OF THE MOST AMAZING AND INSIDIOUS PLOTS WAS HATCHED IN THE TINY TOWN, UNDER THE VERY NOSES OF ITS UN-SUSPECTING POPULACE!

CARMINE INFANTINO

LET US HAVE A LOOK INTO THE CANTINA OF PEDRO DIEGO VALDEZ! IT IS A HOT AFTERNOON......

PEDRO'S CANTINA

...AND MOST OF THE GOOD CITIZENS OF ALGOYA ARE ENJOYING THEIR SIESTAS!

you find yourself looking for work, it helps your chances if you're a writer as well as an artist." He was right.

I brought a couple of story ideas in, he didn't like them, and I had to re-do them. Then I wrote one he liked and he said, "This is fine. Draw it." I thought, "What's this guy doing to me? He's driving me nuts." "The Heap" was the first feature I wrote. Then I did "Airboy" after that.

JA: *You did "The Flying Dutchman" before you did "The Heap," so you probably just drew that.*
CI: I just drew that one. Hillman was publishing a gangster book called *Wanted*. I wrote and drew a story called "The Finger Man." I also drew a character called Rackman. And before you ask, I supplied my own paper. [chuckles]

JA: *You did "The Flying Dutchman" first, then "Airboy," which you wrote and penciled.*
CI: Wasn't "The Heap" before that?

JA: *I have "The Heap" as 1948 and "Airboy" as '46 to '48.*
CI: Then I must have written "Airboy" before I wrote "The Heap." I wrote all of my "Heap" stories.

JA: *You penciled "Gunmaster" for Cronin in 1948. You also drew "Link Thorne, The Flying Fool."*
CI: I did that after Simon and Kirby did. I remember seeing them there.

Cronin lived in Connecticut and came in to work every day. He was a very strange man. He loved you one minute, hated you the next.

JA: *A couple of people told me that when he counted the pages, he'd count them over and over when you brought them in. He'd go, "One, one, one. Two, two, two. Three, three, three."*
CI: You know why? His mind would wander, and he seemed very nervous and timid sometimes. Despite all of that, he was a nice man, very conservative in nature and posture.

JA: *What did he say when he was criticizing your writing?*
CI: First, he'd assign me a story. Say he'd give me a crime story to do. He'd say, "Go home and do it," so I would. I'd bring it in and he'd say, "It stinks. Do it over." [chuckling] I'd say, "Why?" He'd say, "Think about it. Why would I want to read that thing?" "What's with all the whys?" He'd throw these "whys" at you. "Why? Why? Why?" You started with those and have to answer the whys yourself. That's when I got the message.

AFRICA!! THE DARK CONTINENT WHICH HAS ALWAYS SPELLED ADVENTURE... WHERE GOOD MEN AND BAD MEN HAVE LEARNED CERTAIN LESSONS WELL...WHERE FLYING CREATURES ARE SURPRISINGLY BIG-AND THE ELEPHANT IS A VERY "IMPORTANT GENTLEMAN" AS AIRBOY FINDS OUT...!

AIRBOY COMICS, published monthly by Hillman Periodicals, Inc., at 4600 Diversey Ave., Chicago, Ill. Executive and Editorial Offices, 535 Fifth Avenue, New York 17, N. Y. Edward Cronin, Editor. Vol. 3, No. 8, September, 1946. Printed in the United States of America. Price 10c a copy, subscription rate $1.20 a year in United States, possessions and Canada. Copyright 1946 by Hillman Periodicals, Inc. Entered as second class matter October 26, 1945, at the Post Office at Chicago, Ill., under the Act of March 3, 1879.

JA: *So he didn't pick apart your stories and say, "This doesn't work," or, "That doesn't make sense"?*
CI: No, but it was better his way. Think about it: he says, "Why?" It makes you think. You see my point? It's terrific.

JA: *When you brought him a story, did you have it all written out?*
CI: I had to write a synopsis first.

JA: *When he approved a synopsis and you went home, did you write it as you drew it?*
CI: No, I had to write it and bring it in first, and then go back and draw it... except when I did "The Heap." By then he felt I was in my prime. That was interesting. I came in, showed him the story — boom! — he let me go with it. He trusted me completely.

JA: *Why didn't you ink those "Heap" stories?*
CI: Cronin didn't ask me to. [chuckles] I was

(above) Opening splash to Carmine's "Airboy" story in *Airboy Comics* vol. 3, #8 (September 1946). Carmine may have written this story, too.

COURTESY OF MIKE COSTA.

©1945 HILLMAN PERIODICALS, INC.

(facing page) Another of Carmine's stories for Holyoke — *Captain Aero* #26 (August 1946). This time he also inked the job, and the difference is clear. His inking is finer than was typical of this period, and most likely influenced by fellow Baily shop artist, Charles Voigt.

COURTESY OF JIM VADEBON-COEUR, JR. AND *ALTER EGO* MAGAZINE.

©1944 CONTINENTAL MAGAZINES, INC.

HOURS LATER...THE DAWN...

WELL, YOU'RE ALL FIXED, BIRDIE! NOW TO GET OUT OF HERE!

LATER...

I'VE BEEN OVER THE VELDT FOR AN HOUR AND STILL NO SIGN OF THAT ELEPHANT AND GIRL! I'LL BE COMING OVER THE JUNGLE SOON AND WON'T BE ABLE TO SEE ANYTHING!

TWENTY MINUTES LATER..

THERE'S A NATIVE VILLAGE BELOW. MAYBE I'D BETTER GO DOWN AND SEE IF I'M ON THE RIGHT TRAIL!

IS THE TRIBE OF THE ELEPHANT WORSHIPPERS NEAR HERE?

NO, MWAMBA! NO! DO NOT HUNT FOR THAT TRIBE! IT MEANS DEATH!

TURN BACK, MAN-BIRD! TO GO TO THE NORTH IS GREAT DANGER!

OH! THEY'RE TO THE NORTH, ARE THEY? THANKS!

AS AIRBOY WINGS AWAY, A RUMBLE COMES FROM THE DRUMS IN BACK OF HIM...THE JUNGLE "TELEGRAPH" IS IN OPERATION!

MAN WITH WINGS COMING! KILL!

KILL! KILL!

(above) Carmine penciled and wrote this "Heap" story for *Airboy Comics* vol. 5, #3 (April 1948). Though his name appears first in the credits, Leonard Starr, known primarily for his *Mary Perkins, On Stage* newspaper strip, was the inker on this story.

(facing page) Page 6 of Camine's "Airboy" story in *Airboy Comics* vol. 3, #8. The influence of Milt Caniff is fully on display here.

(above) This photo was taken during a National Cartoonists Society tour in Germany in 1956. Pictured from left to right are Mac Miller (a caricaturist), Carmine, David Pascal (a gag cartoonist), a model (the NCS tours always travelled with a model for the soldiers to ogle at), Bill Holman (writer and artist of the *Smoky Stover* newspaper strip), and fellow comic-book artist Jerry Robinson.

writing and penciling, and he said that was enough for one guy to do. As for story ideas, I used to go to the public library a lot and read. I read about World War One, thought about Baron Von Immelman [the character who became the Heap], and I created what I thought would make a good story. I watched a lot of movie serials and would get ideas from them sometimes.

JA: *Some people who worked for Cronin said that he often co-plotted the stories.*
CI: What he would do is inject ideas in my ears, but he never co-plotted. Not with me, anyway. What he would say is, "Carmine, how about in here you bump up this piece," or this or that, but that's about it. But he would discuss it with you. You'd say, "Well, I don't think —" "Well, then why?" He made you think all the time. "Now how do I do this?" He'd question certain things and if you had the right answer, okay. If you didn't, you had to fix it. He was a good editor and you didn't get away with just anything you wanted to write.

JA: *Hillman didn't pay as well as DC, did it?*
CI: No, but the experience was worth a fortune. You couldn't beat that.

JA: *By this time, you were working in comics full-time and making a living. Did this alter your parents' attitude about your career choice?*
CI: They didn't say very much. They were happy the money was coming in, because I helped support the family, and they were very happy about that. I was so thrilled when I got the job at DC, but it went right over their heads. They didn't think that much about it. They didn't care so long as I was working.

JA: *How old were you when you moved out of the house?*
CI: I was in my late twenties, I think. I stayed at home quite a while, because my parents needed the money. I couldn't move out.

JA: *You were born in 1925. Why weren't you drafted into military service?*
CI: I had a gall bladder operation during that time, and by the time I got out of the hospital, they didn't need me any more. In those days, gall bladder problems were very serious, and they didn't know what the hell I had for about two years. The pain was so excruciating. First, they thought I had cancer... they didn't know. But I doubled up in pain and they finally gave me morphine to ease the pain until they discovered my gall bladder was the problem. When I recovered, I tried to join the service, but they wouldn't take me because of my gall bladder problem. I used to go back there every month, but was always rejected.

But I did a lot of traveling with the Army for the National Cartoonists Society in the 1950s. In fact, they gave us titles, a GS-17, for that. I went to Europe, I went to Asia. When they wanted me to do artwork for them, I did, for free. I did whatever I could to make up for the fact I couldn't join the service.

CHAPTER 3

Settling in with DC

JA: *While you were working for Ed Cronin, you started working for DC and Shelly Mayer.*

CI: He was my mentor. I was a young kid and was very impressed with him. I always tell a story about him. Frank Giacoia and I went up to DC Comics. Eddie Eisenberg, who was in production, looked at our work and said, "We can't use you," and sent us to Shelly. "Tell him I sent you. Show him your work." Now Shelly's in this little cubicle with half-glass windows, the old-fashioned ones, and the rest of the place was all artists working at tables. We're sitting there and he's looking at our work. The door was behind us, and from there we heard someone yell, "En garde!" And little Irwin Hasen jumps in with a T-square in his hand. Well, Shelly drops our pages, picks up a T-square, and they start fighting over the desk, back, forth, around... dueling. Finally, at the end, he touches Irwin in the stomach. Irwin stops, kisses him on both cheeks, leaves. Shelly comes right back to his desk and picks up our pages like nothing happened. I looked at Frank. "What kind of madhouse are we in here?" [*Jim chuckles*] You're laughing. It was hilarious at the time. It was weird, you know. They were good friends.

JA: *I take it you never dueled with Shelly.*

CI: No, no, no. After that, he said to me, "Your stuff is not bad, but you need more schooling. I could give you a job now, and you'd end up like some of the artists who don't fulfill their destiny. Go away for a year and study — really study — come back in a year, and I'll give you a job." He knew I was working at Hillman. Shelly said to me, "A guy named Sheldon Moldoff had the same potential, but he got into copying other people's work, and now he can't do anything else." I did what he said, and he eventually hired me. Frank said he wasn't going to school, so he went elsewhere and got work. If Frank had taken Shelly's advice, he'd have been a better artist and probably had more confidence in his penciling. A tragedy, really, for Frank. He suffered by going for the quick buck.

I think the very first feature I did for Shelly was "Ghost Patrol." In those days, 64 pages gave the companies room to train you. They'd give you an eight-pager here and there, until they thought you were ready for the important features. "Ghost Patrol" was a crazy feature, not very impressive... well, it was stupid. But Shelly

(below) The Ghost Patrol goes down for the count — literally! The story these panels are from was written off by DC and never published. Carmine drew several "Ghost Patrol" stories, beginning in *Flash Comics* #86, the same issue he took over the new "Black Canary" feature. Most of his "Ghost Patrol" stories were written by John B. Wentworth and inked by Bob Oksner, though this one was probably inked by Bernard Sachs.

(right) A 1945 photo of editor/cartoonist Sheldon Mayer, which originally ran in *Amazing World of DC Comics #5*, taken by DC production man Sol Harrison.

COURTESY OF *ALTER EGO* MAGAZINE.

©1975 DC COMICS.

(below) Another panel from an unpublished "Ghost Patrol" story, likely inked by Bernard Sachs.

COURTESY OF HERITAGE AUCTIONS (WWW.HA.COM)

GHOST PATROL ™ AND © DC COMICS.

liked what I was doing and moved me on to more important characters.

Shelly was tough because he wanted me — all of us — to do better. He taught me to move the camera around. He kept insisting, "The camera's got to move. The camera's got to move." He pushed me into seeing good films. That was very important to him. In fact, the English films were the ones he pushed me toward. "Go see the English directors, because they're the best at making the camera work." I would go sometimes two, three times a week to see an English film.

JA: *Would he make you redraw pages or panels?*
CI: No, he only made minor corrections. Shelly would take a page and stand it up onto the desk and say, "You see this character on this page here? Where is he in the next panel?" I'd say, "Gee, I think he's in the background." He'd answer, "How am I supposed to know that? Am I supposed to read your mind?" He was really very rough about it, you know. But he would also say to you, "This is what it should have been. This should have been that." And I said, "Well, I'll change it." He said, "No, I don't want you to change it up. I want you to *remember* it." That was his point. Once I started getting what Shelly wanted, he lightened up. He always wanted you to push yourself to do better and think more. He did that to Alex Toth and Joe Kubert, too. Storytelling was the most important thing to him. Draftsmanship — figure drawing and

drawing correct perspective — was important, but not as important as telling a story clearly and concisely. He made us better artists.

Shelly would pit me against Joe against Alex against Frank. He'd say, "Look at what they are doing." He wasn't trying to create competition between us so much as he was trying to inspire us to do better. Alex, Joe, and me were, in a certain sense, his "children," and he wanted us to grow up together. I doubt he really thought of it quite that way, but it's what it amounted to, more or less. He set us up to become the next wave of artists — he told us that, and that he expected us to come through. He knew DC needed new, brighter blood and decided that's what we were going be. Alex, Joe, and I owe a part of our success to Shelly Mayer.

JA: *You also knew Gil Kane. What was he like then?*
CI: The same way he was when he got older. He was rather tall. I think I gave him the right name: "The Don Quixote of Comics." He was always fighting windmills. He was very dramatic. He used to sit sometimes at his drawing board with his jacket and tie on, with his sleeves rolled up, because he saw the famous Cole Porter write songs that way. He loved show business. He should have been in show business. He was fun. He had the old nose when he was young.

JA: *He changed his appearance, and that suggests a man who's unhappy with himself.*
CI: I would assume that, yes. He changed his name, his appearance, everything. He got very solemn after he changed his nose. He was a fun, happy guy before that.

JA: *When you knew him, you knew his name was Eli Katz. Did you call him that?*
CI: Yeah. Eli.

JA: *When did you start calling him Gil?*
CI: I didn't. After a few years, we didn't see each other any more. When he became "Gil Kane," I didn't know him. We weren't friendly. I mean there was nothing that happened, any big fight or anything. We just weren't friendly.

JA: *DC was where you guys met each other.*
CI: All of us were friendly. Around 1948, Joe Kubert began renting space from photographer Brad Smith, and he started a studio. I remember Alex Toth shared space there for a while. So did a few other guys. Irwin Hasen used to go there — Frank Giacoia, too. I didn't share space there, but I'd go and visit. I worked at home.

I needed to work alone. I needed my own space. I was concentrating on improving my work, drawing every bone, every muscle, every nerve in my figures, just trying to decide what looked good. Joe Kubert loved his own work, Alex Toth loved his own work, but I was never a fan of my own work. I always felt there was something wrong, not quite good enough, always not good enough. Maybe they felt the same way and never said it. One time, Jack Kirby told me that the minute you're satisfied with what you're doing, you're no good any more. I didn't want that to happen to me.

JA: *Did you guys ever discuss the idea that Shelly was trying to create a little competition between you?*
CI: We never said a word about that, but we talked to each other. Like, if I saw something Alex did, I'd say, "Alex, this is terrific what you did on this page," and vice versa. We talked to each other a lot. We met at DC a lot. We'd meet at Brad's, too.

JA: *In those conversations, would you discuss the state of comics, would you discuss your work? What was being discussed?*

CI: Girls! [laughter]

JA: *Naturally! Well, you're all artistically starting to grow in this period. You've got one man who's watering you. Yet all three of you developed differently.*
CI: I think Shelly did that purposely. He was certainly sharp about it, I know that, because he would keep us apart. None of us ever copied the other's work. We were fans, we loved each other's work, but that's about all. We were encouraged to be our own men, to have our own personality reflected in our work. And that's what we did.

JA: *Did you feel that you had to compete with other artists?*
CI: Oh, yes, because you knew — *you knew* — everybody was trying to get your job in the old days. So you had to work hard and not fool around. Joe, Alex, me — we all kept studying, studying, studying.

JA: *How much of that came from the fear of losing work or the fact that you felt that you had to improve yourself?*
CI: I think it was a little of both.

JA: *What I'm trying to get you to tell me is what drove you?*
CI: Fear, maybe, I guess. I don't know what it was.

JA: *Was it fear because you lived through the Depression?*
CI: It could well be, because Jack Kirby had the same feeling, you know. Jack and I used to talk about that during the *Charlie Chan* days. We were all having coffee, and Jack noticed me, I guess. He said, "Carmine, you've got my problem." I said, "What the hell is that?" He said, "The fear. You never lose that fear of the Depression. As long as you live, you're going to have that. No matter how successful you get, you will never lose that." And he was right. I never felt successful because of that. Never, never at any point.

(below) A panel from an unpublished "Dr. Mid-Nite" story probably intended for *All-American Comics* #110 and drawn circa 1949.

(above) Irwin Hasen, best known for his work on DC's "Wildcat" series and his newspaper strip, *Dondi*; Keif Simon; and Carmine share a moment at the 2007 New York Comic-Con.

the boat, he finally realized he had been fired. He said that he was falling behind us — there was a new wave coming in, and he was part of the old wave, I guess. Maybe it's true, I can't say. He did a lot of comic book work in his time, and Shelly and Alex were big fans of his work. What Irwin lacked in technical skill, he made up for with warmth and charm. He was insecure about his work, but so was I.

JA: *What was Alex Toth like when he was young?*
CI: I know his personality went through some mad changes later, but back then he was a nice, quiet, young guy and a nice-looking guy, too. He talked when he had something to say, but he didn't go on like Gil Kane would. Later on, I tried to work with Alex to keep him at DC, but it didn't work out. He became difficult to work with. You know the story about Joe Kubert rejecting Alex's "Enemy Ace" story? Alex changed Kanigher's story into one of his own. Joe sent it back to him — an entire story. That was the right thing to do. It was disrespectful to Joe. You don't do that to your editor. I'm sorry he became an unhappy man. Alex was one of the all-time greats and he could have done even more than he did... Well, it was a shame to see him not use his talent. There was nothing beyond his capabilities. You know that — you were his friend for years.

JA: *Not even in your publishing days?*
CI: Never! And Jack was right then. Jack and I were very close. We were very friendly.

JA: *But now, looking back, don't you feel like you were successful?*
CI: No, now it belongs to some other guy I'm not related to. [*Jim laughs*] But I don't like to talk about this business, either.

JA: *I do know that.*
CI: And especially the artwork. Ugh, forget it.

JA: [**chuckles**] *But still, the Carmine Infantino who broke into comic books could have hardly imagined he would have become the publisher at DC Comics.*
CI: No, no, I never had that in mind, and that was a freak circumstance.

JA: *Irwin Hasen told me that one of the reasons he quit doing comic books in the 1950s was that he felt like he'd fallen behind people like you, Joe Kubert, and Alex Toth.*
CI: But he was fired, too. He tells that famous story, remember? Whit Ellsworth told him to go take a trip, a vacation, and then when he got on

JA: *I know.* [pauses] *Well, let's move on. Would you go to the newsstands and check out the books when they came out?*
CI: I don't think so. I was too involved in my work, except for when I'd see what the others were doing when I was in Shelly's office or at Joe's studio.

JA: *You didn't collect your own work?*
CI: No, I thought it was all crap.

JA: *In this early period, you never thought about getting your originals back?*
CI: No, I didn't think it was any good. I didn't want to see it once I was done, because I was into the next story, trying to get it done, and get it done as best as I could.

JA: *How fast an artist were you in this period — '47 to '49?*
CI: I was always about the same speed. I was not that fast. I put long hours in. You know, two pages in twelve hours; that's a long time. I'd draw until 1:30, two o'clock, two or three in the morning.

I used to warm up a little before I started the day's work. I'd turn a page over and do all my warm-ups. All my stuff had sketches all over the back. I drew good-looking women and idealized men.

JA: *So you weren't exactly solving drapery problems and stuff like that when you were sketching on the backs.*
CI: No, I drew figures, mostly, although I was doing a lot of different things. One morning, I got up, I was into cars. I'd design cars of my own invention. Another day, I'd draw houses, another day, people — women, men — something different. I'd do this for about an hour.

JA: *When did you start building a reference file?*
CI: Early on. Ed Cronin stressed that — so did Shelly Mayer. I'd clip out Robert Fawcett's work from magazines... Noel Sickles, too. And then I'd go to the genius that Jack Kirby and Mort Meskin loved: Edd Cartier, who had drawn illustrations in the *Shadow* pulps. Mort learned quite a bit about the use of light and dark from Cartier's work. So did I. Shelly once said, "Your characters' clothes look like they came out of the Middle Ages. When you buy your paper in the morning, cut out the damn fashions, please, and

look at them." So I started doing that. *National Geographic* was great because they had photos from around the world. I clipped stuff out of other magazines and newspapers, too.

JA: *What do you remember about John Belfi inking your work?*
CI: I don't remember John doing that. But Belfi, Frank Giacoia, and I went to the same school and were in the same class together. Belfi and I graduated. Frank quit school, as I've said.

JA: *John told me that you dug into the paper a little and used a hard pencil lead.*
CI: Then he did ink me, because that's the way my pencils were then. You know, I continued to work for Hillman for a while, but DC paid better, and I decided to stick with them solely. I was working my brains out. Wherever I could get the job, I would take it and do it. I was working long hours, long hours. Page rates weren't great back then. Shelly started me out at $15 a page for pencils.

I was drawing "Johnny Thunder," which was really not much of a character. I suppose he could have been better, because his Thunderbolt was interesting, but the situations they were in were pretty juvenile. Bob Kanigher wrote those

(below) These sketches were drawn on the back of a "Detective Chimp" page for *The Adventures of Rex the Wonder Dog* #21 in 1955.

(right) This page is part of a "Black Canary" story originally intended for *Flash Comics* #112, but the title was cancelled with issue #104, and the story didn't see print until 1970, in the pages of *Adventure Comics* #399. You may have noticed lines in between the tiers where the board was cut into three pieces. For years it was common practice at DC to destroy original artwork when they were done with it. Luckily, whoever cut up this page did so very carefully so that it was able to be reassembled.

COURTESY OF TERRY AUSTIN.

©1970 DC COMICS. BLACK CANARY ™ AND © DC COMICS.

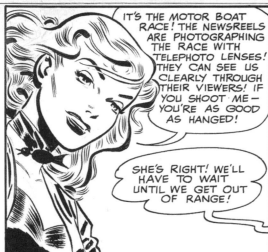

stories, and he had no respect for the characters. The stories were nowhere near as good as the "Flash" stories. DC knew it — they knew "Johnny Thunder" was a loser, so Kanigher and I brought the Black Canary into the series. Immediately, she got a good response, and it was, "Bye, bye, Johnny Thunder." Nobody missed him.

JA: *When you drew "Johnny Thunder," your pencil lines tended to be shorter than they were before. I don't want to use the word "choppy," but they were blunter.*
CI: They were choppy. I was always choppy. That was my style. Always blunt — short, blunt lines.

JA: *The Black Canary is really your first comic-book creation. When it came time to create Black Canary, did you have to submit a character sketch first?*
CI: No. When Kanigher gave me the script, I said, "How do you want me to draw her?" He said, "What's your fantasy of a good-looking girl? That's what I want." Isn't that a great line? So that's what I did. I made her strong in character and sexy in form. The funny part is that years later, while in Korea on a National Cartoonists trip, I met a dancer who was the exact image of the Black Canary. And I went out with her for three years.

Bob didn't ask me for a character sketch [for the Black Canary]. He had a lot of respect for me, I must say that. He always trusted my work.

He never once had me bring in a sample, ever. He was tough on everybody, but if he didn't trust you, you didn't work for him. I don't think he was tough on Joe Kubert; they seemed to get along okay. I drew war stories for Kanigher. He would just say to me, "Here's the story. Do it." Anyway, Bob loved my Black Canary design.

JA: *When you started drawing "The Flash," Lee Elias was drawing it, too. For a long time, E.E. Hibbard was drawing it. Elias was keeping to the Hibbard style somewhat, although his figure work was not as stiff as Hibbard's. Your visual stylization on "The Flash" is a little bit different than on the "Johnny Thunder" and "Black Canary" stories. Were you asked to conform to the Flash look?*
CI: No, Shelly left me alone. "Do it any way you want to."

(above left) Black Canary made the cover of *Flash Comics* #92 when her solo series debuted, replacing "Johnny Thunder."

COURTESY OF HERITAGE AUCTIONS.

©1948 DC COMICS. BLACK CANARY, FLASH, HAWKMAN ™ AND © DC COMICS

(above right) A 2000s quick sketch of Black Canary.

COURTESY OF KEIF SIMON.

BLACK CANARY ™ AND © DC COMICS

JA: *But you did draw it in that style.*

CI: In the back of my mind, [the Elias and Hibbard styles] probably did influence me, I'm sure.

JA: *But you still gave him those thick eyebrows Hibbard had given him.*

CI: Well, that was the look of the character. You couldn't change that. Shelly said, "Stay with the character. The rest, do what you want." We had to stay with the character they created all those years ago.

JA: *I've noticed that the work you did elsewhere right around that time, and afterwards, was more like Carmine Infantino.*

CI: Well, don't forget I sort of matured then. At this stage, I think I was really into Milton Caniff, and, yes, that would be the major influence. Although, Hal Foster's panel compositions were marvelous. That was what I studied the most when I looked at his work. Of course, Lee's stuff was very Caniff-ish, but that's what influenced me the most: Caniff and Hal Foster. Elias did good work, and I liked it. He drew a good Flash for the time.

I knew Lee Elias. He was a fantastic violin player, I mean incredible. And he was a nice man. I got along very well with him. We had coffee

out together a few times. I never saw any of these other crazy antics people have described.

JA: *When you and Lee Elias drew "The Flash," you guys really helped invigorate the series.*

CI: We did, Lee and I? It's very possible. We did the best we could. We also had good writers: Bob Kanigher, Gardner Fox, and John Broome.

JA: *Your Flash looked like he was running much faster than when other artists drew him.*

CI: Yeah, I was changing him slowly. Even Lee used to say to me, "What the hell do you do with him? Your Flash runs faster than mine." I said, "I put Vaseline on his feet." [chuckling] It was very funny. But I was doing much of this by instinct, too. I thought about how a man with super-speed would look when he ran. I positioned his body so he looked like he was running fast. I tilted his helmet with the wings so it wouldn't look like it would fall off when he ran.

JA: *You worked for Shelly for about a year or so, right?*

CI: Something like that. That wasn't really DC then, though. Shelly's office was down the hall in All-American Comics at that time.

(below) The Golden Age Flash as drawn by E.E. Hibbard (a splash page from *Flash Comics* #72) and Lee Elias (the cover of *All-Flash* #30).

ART COURTESY OF HERITAGE AUCTIONS (WWW.HA.COM).

FLASH ™ AND © DC COMICS.

The panel on the left comes from a story intended for *Flash Comics* #106, which went unpublished, while the panel below comes from Carmine's last published Golden Age Flash story (*Flash Comics* #104, February 1949). Carmine kept Flash's face pretty close to the model established by Hibbard and Elias before him, with thick, bushy eyebrows and a lantern jaw, but the postures he used gave his Flash a greater sense of speed and fluidity.

JA: *But DC and All-American had merged into one company.*
CI: Yes, but they were still kept separate, because we went *down* the hall. We weren't allowed to go *up* the hall. We didn't feel like we belonged [at DC proper]. [*chuckles*] Yeah, we all felt that: Frank, Alex, Joe.

JA: *Do you think Shelly felt that?*
CI: I think he felt the same way. He didn't ever like being an editor, you know. He wanted to be an artist again, or they pushed him out. I don't know what was going on.

JA: *Shelly told me that, one day, he was in his office and there were a couple of artists out there. One of them says, "What are you doing here?" "I'm here to see the old man," meaning Shelly. Shelly was like 28 years old and Shelly didn't like being thought of as an old man.*
CI: *But he was, compared to us.*

JA: *But the thing is, Shelly told me he realized that he didn't want to grow old in that job, and that's the reason he went back to being a cartoonist.*

CI: Oh, that's interesting. I can believe that. He loved being a cartoonist, I know that.

JA: *So now you're doing a major book, really for the first time. How did that make you feel?*
CI: I guess I was comfortable there. I was comfortable.

JA: *But did you feel a certain excitement?*
CI: Maybe just a little, not much. I was happy to be working on a major feature. "The Heap" and "Airboy" were Hillman's big features, but they weren't as big as "The Flash."

JA: *Did you get more money when you graduated to drawing "Flash" stories?*
CI: No, nothing changed.

JA: *Then you did some "Justice Society" segments in All-Star Comics.*
CI: I drew some covers, too. Shelly put me on the covers right away. Even though I didn't like the Green Lantern — it was a dumb costume — I did enjoy drawing the Justice Society. It was a nice break from "The Flash." They were well written stories. I could understand why kids liked them.

JA: *How did you work with Shelly on the covers?*
CI: He'd say, "Give me a cover on the Justice Society," and he'd give me the script to read. "Pick out something." I'd pick out one idea, he'd say, "No, I don't like it. How about this one?" Then he'd pick something else, so I'd do the one he wanted.

JA: *Did you have to give him a sketch first?*
CI: Yes.

JA: *How critical would he be of the sketch?*
CI: Very much so, just like I told you earlier. That was one thing about Shelly: He knew how to provoke you to do better and better and better. He was making professionals out of kids, and you couldn't beat that.

JA: *But this was not anything more than a boss-to-free-lancer kind of relationship, was it?*
CI: It was more than that. [Alex, Joe, and I] loved him. We knew what he was doing, so even when he was rough, we knew he was doing the right thing. Many years later, when I was running DC, Shelly saw me and said, "Jesus Christ, I created a monster." [*laughter*] That's funny. But he added, "I'm proud of it." That meant a lot to me.

Somewhere around the same time, some executives from Warners asked, "What is this guy [Shelly] on the payroll for?" Shelly had a lifetime pension plan. I said, "This guy was an important editor here for a long time, and he deserves some respect." Well, they hemmed and hawed and then said, "Well, alright. Keep him on." I kept *Sugar and Spike* going so they couldn't give me a hard time about Shelly. Then when the book was canceled — Shelly felt that they killed his book — he was still on the payroll, still on the health plan. He was a sick man. They didn't want to keep him on. I went upstairs and said, "If it makes you feel better, I'll pay for it. Take it out of my salary." [*grumbles*] They let it alone, but I never told him. It would have made him very upset if he knew all this was going on. He was so good to me. Why shouldn't I reciprocate? He deserved it for all he did for DC.

(below and facing page) Carmine may have thought Alan Scott wore "a dumb costume" in his Green Lantern guise, but that didn't stop him from drawing a story of *Green Lantern* #39. Unfortunately, the title was canceled before the story — pages 1 and 8 of which are shown here — could be published.

WRECKING THE GOTHAM LIMITED IS THE ONLY CRIME MENTIONED OUTSIDE THE CITY ITSELF! I'LL COVER THAT— JUST IN CASE!
IN A SHORT WHILE...
THE GOTHAM LIMITED! UNHARMED!
SUDDENLY...
A ROBOT PLANE— FIXED TO EXPLODE ON CONTACT— HEADING STRAIGHT FOR THE TRAIN!
ZOOOMMM!
I'VE GOT TO MAKE IT CHANGE DIRECTION!
GREEN LANTERN'S POWER RING DIVERTS THE ROBOT CONTROLLED PLANE FROM STRIKING THE TRAIN...
SUDDENLY, THE DISTURBED ROBOT MECHANISM CAUSES THE PLANE TO EXPLODE, NOT HARMING THE TRAIN— BUT HURLING GREEN LANTERN TO THE GROUND!
WHAM!
8
WRITTEN OFF

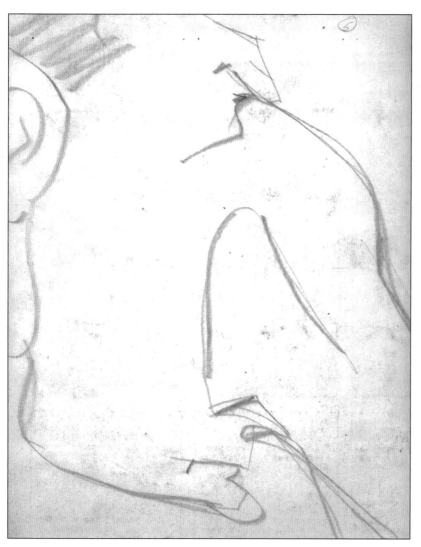

(above) Carmine drew this caricature of Julie Schwartz in 1967 on the back of an "Elongated Man" board.

COURTESY OF BOB BAILEY.
©1967 CARMINE INFANTINO.

JA: *When Shelly was the boss, was he very friendly to you?*
CI: Yes, but never *that* friendly. He didn't let it get beyond a certain point. That's another thing I learned from him. When you're the boss, it's a different situation.

JA: *How did you learn that Shelly had quit editing?*
CI: I went in one day, and he said, "Come on with me. See this guy? You're going to be working with him [Julie Schwartz] from now on." Julie looked up, stared at me, and went right back to what he was doing. I went back with Shelly to his office and asked, "What's going on?" He said, "I'm going to leave. I'm going to do my own drawing. I want to do my own stuff.'"

Well, I was very upset. I said, "Shelly, we're so used to working with you." He said Alex and Joe felt the same way. I didn't want him to leave in the worst way. He said, "Listen, I've got to be happy, too. You guys are happy and I want to be happy." What are you going to say? So I started working with Julie, but I really kept my distance with him, and we were not friendly.

Before this, Julie had only worked with the writers, editing copy. That's why I didn't know him before then.

JA: *You told me that Julie didn't like your work in those days. Did Julie tell you that or could you just sense it?*
CI: I sensed it, but one time, many years later, I brought a job in that I had really worked my tail off on. I said, "What do you think?" He says, "You got paid, didn't you?" [*Jim chuckles*] I never asked him again. Julie expected you to be a professional and treated you like one. He expected you to act like one. Mostly, he was all business.

JA: *When Shelly left, you were working for Julie directly. But Kanigher was editing, too. Did they edit books together?*
CI: No, but they shared an office. They didn't like each other that much.

JA: *But you worked for both of them at the same time.*
CI: Every once in a while Bob would say, "Carmine, I need a job from you." And I'd look at Julie, who always said, "Go ahead," sometimes grudgingly. And that would be the end of it, although Julie once said to me, "Don't make a habit of this." [*laughter*] You know what that meant.

JA: *If Julie had said no, what would have happened?*
CI: Then I couldn't have worked for Kanigher. The DC editors had their own little kingdoms and they didn't want their guys working elsewhere — even within the same company.

[Julie and I] hardly spoke back then. I'd come in, drop off a job, he'd give me another script, I'd take it and leave. Sometimes he'd ask me to make minor changes, which I did. Julie was always a "cross the t's and dot the i's" type. He was cold and distant in those days.

JA: *In this time period, was the way Julie did covers with you similar to the way you did them with Shelly?*
CI: No, it was strictly the old-fashioned way. He'd pick something out of the script and tell me to draw that scene, most of the time. I'd do a rough sketch that he'd have to approve first. So in some ways, it was done the way I had worked with Shelly, but with little conversation.

JA: *You also drew "The Atom" in 1948.*
CI: I didn't like that character.

JA: *I believe you redesigned that costume. Julie would have asked you to do that, right?* [*Carmine agrees*] *They were trying to save the character; he had had a dull costume. He was revitalized — a new costume and he was made stronger.*

THE **FLASH** FOLLOWS THE TAXICABS TO THE RIVER WHERE...

THERE'S THE ROCKPILE THAT GEORGIE IMAGINES IS A CASTLE. IT'S DESERTED OF COURSE. NOT A SOUL AROUND.

CI: I did design that costume. I guess Julie wanted to re-introduce him, because it was a different character when he originally started.

JA: *How did you feel when you found out "The Flash" was canceled?*
CI: Well, I was fine by that time. [*chuckles*] We were worried, because the books were dying. We started doing science fiction, romance, Westerns... just trying to find something that would sell. We were very worried, all of us.

JA: *What reason were you given for* Flash Comics *and* Green Lantern *being canceled?*
CI: They didn't sell, simple as that. I don't know if it was a surprise to me. The stories were getting tired. The whole thing was getting tired. We had begun to repeat ourselves, so we tried moving into other genres.

JA: *Did you feel like you were losing steam on "The Flash"?*
CI: If I had continued on it then, maybe I would have. It did start to get boring. I think the original Flash was a good character, but he was starting to look outdated. Same thing with the Green Lantern.

JA: *In 1949 you drew a couple* Boy Commandos *stories.*
CI: Yes, I did some for Jack Schiff, I believe. He was very bland... innocuous. I shouldn't say that.

JA: *Well, if that's how you felt, then that's how you felt. Did you like drawing* Boy Commandos?
CI: No. I didn't like war stories — not those or the ones I later did for Kanigher. It wasn't my thing.

JA: *Why didn't you ink your own stuff at that time?*
CI: They didn't want me to. DC didn't want me to do much inking; they wanted the penciling out of me. They'd give me occasional stories [to ink]. I'd have done fine on my inking if I'd

gone on. There was a house style, and I was not the house style.

JA: *During this time, you started working for Joe Simon and Jack Kirby on* Charlie Chan. *You drew it in the Simon and Kirby style.*
CI: Sure. I was imitating Jack then.

JA: *Why did you feel the need to imitate Jack? You didn't do much of it on* Boy Commandos. *Were you asked to imitate Jack?*
CI: No, Jack never said a word to me, but I watched his every move. I imitated him, perhaps by instinct, mostly by choice, though. I thought if I worked in his style, I'd learn how he did what he did. He was the best comic book artist there was. Jack and Joe paid less than DC, but I wasn't interested in the money so much as I was in learning from Jack. It was hell for me, though, because I did that work after my DC work. I was burning the candle at both ends, but I wanted to work in their studio.

(left) The Flash is just a blur of motion in this unpublished panel intended for *Flash Comics* #106.

(below) On top of drawing a couple of *Boy Commandos* stories, Carmine also penciled the cover of *Boy Commandos* #33. The inker is unknown.

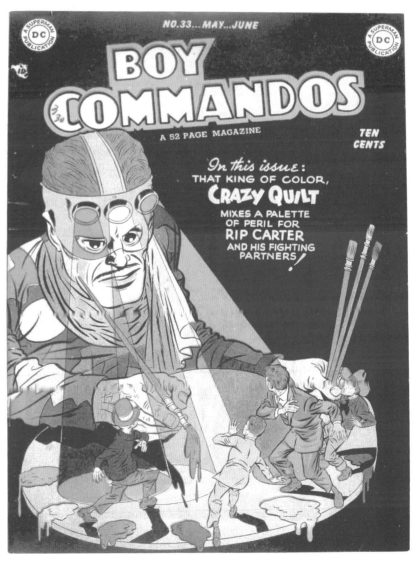

(above) Jack Kirby (pencils) and Joe Simon (inks) cover art for *Charlie Chan* #3 (Oct.-Nov. 1948).

COURTESY OF *THE JACK KIRBY COLLECTOR.*

©1948 CRESTWOOD PUBLISHING.

(facing page) Carmine drew four stories for *Charlie Chan* #1 (June-July 1948), and he even signed them. As shown in this splash page from that issue, Carmine was trying to evoke the Simon & Kirby style.

COURTESY OF *ALTER EGO* MAGAZINE

©1948 CRESTWOOD PUBLISHING.

It amazed me that Jack never laid out his panels ahead of time. He'd just start drawing the figure from the leg down. Incredibly scary. I never saw anybody else ever do that. And he drew fast. Jack could draw four or five pages a day. He was a thinker, though. Everything he did, he thought out.

When I was drawing a scene on *Charlie Chan*... I had done a scene where these two guys beat up an old lady, so I drew it. Jack looked at me and he says, "Carmine, would you mind a suggestion?" I said, "Absolutely not. That's why I'm here." He said, "Rather than showing them beating up the old lady, have one of the villains on the couch smiling, and on the wall behind him, draw a shadow of the guy belting the old woman. That way the imagination takes over. It becomes a far worse situation." He was right. That's the kind of thing I learned from Jack. He taught me how to be more cinematic.

I studied how he drew folds and feathered the fold lines. I saw how he spotted blacks in backgrounds and on the figures. I learned how to get more animation in my figure drawing. Nobody drew more animated figures than Jack Kirby, and I needed to learn how to do it better.

JA: *When Jack worked —*
CI: He smoked a whole cigar. [*laughs*] That cigar never left his face. When he was finished with it, he'd light up another one. He didn't talk very much. If you asked him a question, he'd answer.

Otherwise, he wouldn't say anything. Jack would pencil, I think, five to six pages a day, and then Joe would outline them and Jack would go back and fill the blacks in.

JA: *When Jack drew, did you see him write the scripts?*
CI: I saw him do some writing. Sometimes he wrote as he drew. Sometimes he had a script, but he didn't always follow it.

JA: *Would he write scripts and then draw it?*
CI: No, if Jack had a pre-written script, then it was probably done by someone else. I remember him writing in the copy on the pages. If he didn't like something in a script, he would change it. That, I know he would do, no question about it. Jack came up with many, if not most, of the plots for the stories. But they used other writers, too. Jack Oleck wrote a lot of stories for them.

JA: *Did you see Joe writing? What did Joe usually do in the office?*
CI: He was a businessman. Joe took care of the finances. He had to, because Jack wasn't equipped to do that. I saw Joe do some inking, but sometimes Jack would ink, too. Sometimes Joe would ink the outlines, and Jack would do the rest. Sometimes they had other guys pitching in with the inks.

But don't forget that Joe was a very sharp writer. People don't give him much credit for that. His idea was to take classics and turn them into comic book stories. Remember the *Boy Commandos* story with the Trojan Horse? Joe did that sort of thing all the time. He'd take a classic, twist and turn it around, and use it, and it would be great. He was very clever. I don't think he got enough credit for his whole process. But that's not to take anything away from Jack, obviously — the combination was magic. They really worked hand-in-hand easily. It was a full and equal partnership.

We didn't socialize that much. We'd talk every once in a while. Joe used to love to buy and sell houses and build houses. So weekends we'd go out together looking at houses, he'd buy a house. He and my father were very close — my father knew plumbing and he knew construction — and on weekends we'd go look at houses, and if they liked it, they'd get the plans and they'd build it.

JA: *I remember Jack Kirby telling me that at one point — on Long Island — he and Joe lived across the street from each other.*

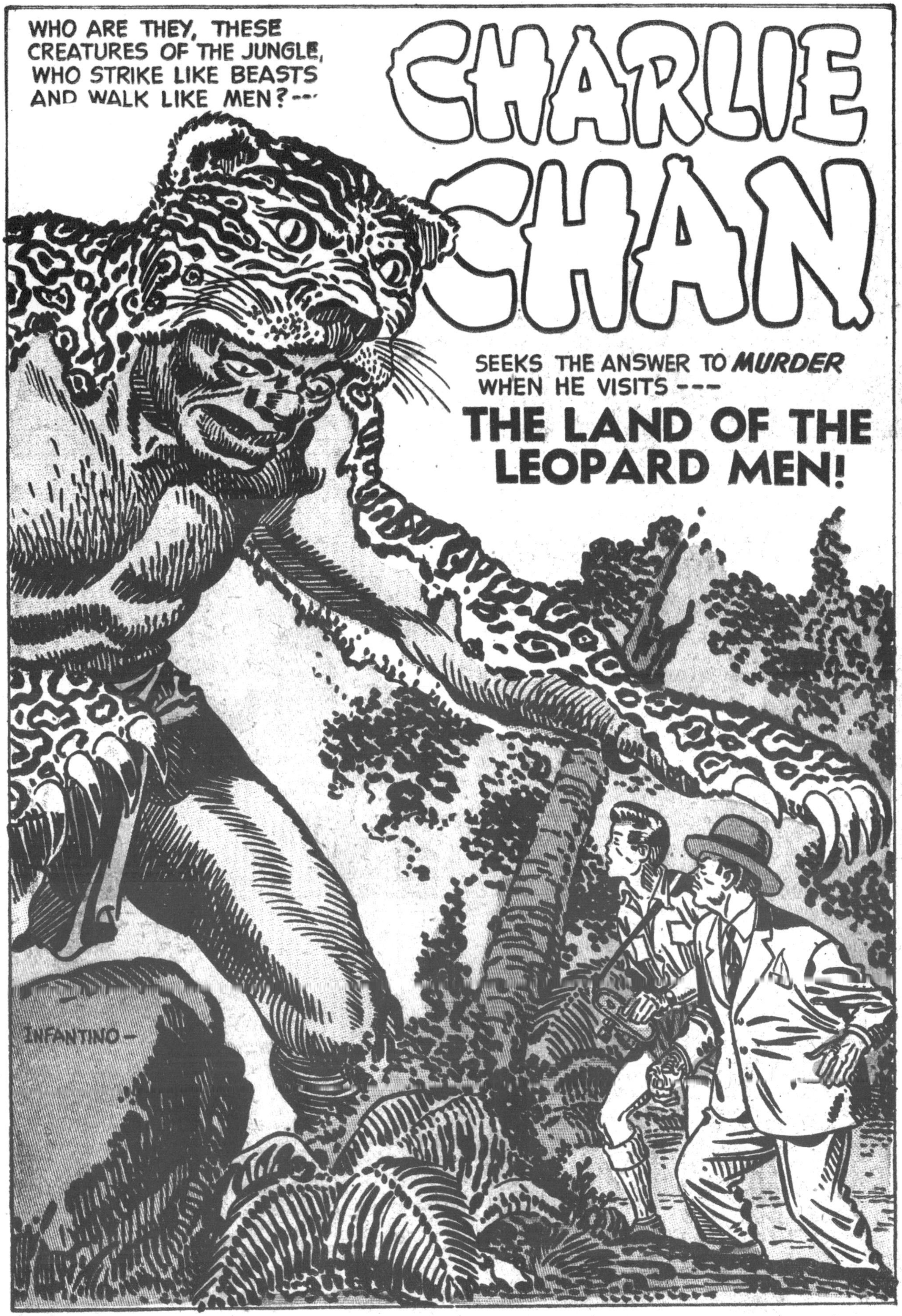
WHO ARE THEY, THESE CREATURES OF THE JUNGLE, WHO STRIKE LIKE BEASTS AND WALK LIKE MEN?---
CHARLIE CHAN
SEEKS THE ANSWER TO MURDER WHEN HE VISITS ---
THE LAND OF THE LEOPARD MEN!
INFANTINO-

YOU ARE GUILTY OF MANY CRIMES-- I SEE *TROUBLE* COMING YOUR WAY IN THE FORM OF---

CHARLIE CHAN

(above) Another of Carmine's splash pages from *Charlie Chan* #1. Joe Simon did the inking only on this one page of the story.

COURTESY OF *ALTER EGO* MAGAZINE

©1948 CRESTWOOD PUBLISHING.

CI: They did, in Westbury, but actually it was a different — right across the street was over the line. One lived in Nassau, one lived in Queens, and they were right across from each other. Nice houses, nice. They worked very closely in those days.

JA: *When they had the studio and they had other people there —?*
CI: You mean in Crestwood. The office was about 20 feet wide, and Jack would be in the corner. Mort Meskin would be next to him. Marv Stein and Howard Ferguson were there, and two other guys — I can't remember their names right offhand. I had a spot in the corner on the other side of the room, but once in a while I'd get up and go watch Jack.

JA: *Can you gauge — just at that time period, meaning post-war — their popularity in terms of sales and with other professionals?*

CI: All I know is that Jack Liebowitz was very upset that they didn't come back to him and do more books for DC. Joe and Jack were getting a piece of the action at Crestwood, but I think Liebowitz would have given them that, actually. So he was quite upset they didn't give him a chance to make an offer. He loved 'em. They made a lot of money for DC. *Boy Commandos*, the "Manhunter"...

JA: *Did you do anything else besides* Charlie Chan *for them?*
CI: No. No, at that point I couldn't do it any more. I said, "Joe, I can't. I just can't keep up the pace." He understood, and we remained friends.

JA: *Outside of the newspaper strip that you and Jack tried to do, you never inked Jack. Would you have liked to?*
CI: It would have been interesting. I'd have probably been too nervous.

JA: *Tell me a little more about Mort Meskin.*
CI: Yes, I knew him quite well. He was a terrific guy. I loved him. He was a genius. I wanted him to come back to DC when I took over. He came up, and I gave him a script. He came back about a week later and returned the script. "I can't do it, Carmine. I can't do it." I figured, emotionally, he felt he couldn't handle it. He said, "There's too much going on here," meaning he was busy doing storyboards for BBDO [Batten, Barton, Durstine & Osborn — one of the world's foremost advertising agencies].

JA: *When you knew him back in the late '40s at Simon and Kirby, were you aware that he had any emotional problems?*
CI: You could feel it. In the morning, he would come in and talk. Other days, he wouldn't say a word, so I knew something was going on. I knew him, but I minded my own business.

One day, he came to my apartment — this was when I tried to get him back at DC — and I said, "Morty, how many years were you in analysis?" I think he said ten or 20 years. I said, "What did you learn?" He looked at me for a couple of minutes and said, "Carmine, don't dig too deep. It's a sewer down there." That was scary.

JA: *Joe Simon and Jack Katz both told me how they used to draw circles on Meskin's pages before he could start drawing them.*
CI: When Kirby came in during the morning, he'd do it right away — just draw a couple of lines. Mort would come in, and he'd start to

(left) Mort Meskin at his drawing board.

COURTESY OF PETER MESKIN AND *ALTER EGO* MAGAZINE.

JA: *Were you ever afraid of a blank page?*
CI: Never. Thinking about Mort now, I remember he had drawn "Johnny Quick," and he really made that character move. He was better at that than I was. He had a flow I didn't have.

JA: *He also spent more time drawing multiple images than you did.*
CI: That's probably where I got it from then. People give me credit for that, but he did it first — and better. I must have gotten the idea from him. Where else would I get it from? It must have stuck in my brain somewhere, because I didn't consciously try to follow what he did.

JA: *Tell me about Howard Ferguson.*
CI: Yes! He was a crusty, old bastard. [*chuckles*] He was one hell of a letterer. He was a fat, older, German guy — very tough. Jack used to say, "Don't pay attention to him. He's all right." He smoked cigarettes like a train. He had a daughter to take care of, because his wife left him. He had a chip on his shoulder all the time, but he could letter. His logos were the best!

(below) When drawing Johnny Quick in motion, Meskin would often show him in multiple places at once, fully inked with no connecting speed lines. Carmine rarely used this technique during his stint on *Flash Comics* in the '40s, but when he did, he would blur the figures. In this panel from *Flash Comics* #104 he cut away parallel diagonal lines to show the figures are not entirely "there." He took this concept one step further in the '50s with *The Flash*, drawing loose, incomplete ghost images of the hero running.

work. But if it was a blank page, he couldn't do a thing. A couple of times he said, "Carmine, do me a favor. Put some lines down to help me, would you?" He needed something to get him rolling, and that could do it for Mort. But he was such a talented man, my God. He really knew how to draw and tell stories.

One time, my brother Jimmy was working at the Simon and Kirby studio, and he said to Mort, "Do you mind if I watch you?" Mort says, "Yes." [*Jim laughs*] He and Mort became good friends later.

THERE'S THE CRUISER, MR. HARKNESS--BUT MAY I ASK WHY YOU'RE STARING AT ME?

SORRY-- IT'S JUST THAT YOU'RE SO EASY TO LOOK AT!

SURE--SHE WAS LOVELY ENOUGH TO STARE AT--BUT I HAD ANOTHER REASON!...

THAT RING-- CARVED OUT OF CORAL--TOM JANSEN HAD IT ON THE DAY HE SAVED ME!

THAT NIGHT I SPOTTED ANOTHER PIECE TO FIT IN MY PUZZLE...

SO THE BOSS AND VICKY TAKE MOONLIGHT STROLLS. HOW ROMANTIC AND INNOCENT IT LOOKS-- BUT VICKY'S WEARING TOM'S RING AND THAT TELLS ME I'M GETTING WARM!

THE NEXT MORNING, FEYDA SHOWED UP WITH SPECIAL PASSENGERS--AND SPECIAL EQUIPMENT.

WHAT'S ALL THIS DIVING GEAR FOR, MR. FEYDA?

YOU'RE PAID FOR PILOTING-- NOT ASKING QUESTIONS! SET YOUR COURSE FOR MANGO ISLAND--THE EAST COVE...

HOURS LATER, ANCHORED OFF MANGO, WE LOOKED LIKE ANY OF THE NEAR-BY IDLE CRAFT--BUT WE WERE PLENTY BUSY!...

PORTABLE OXYGEN TANKS--THAT AVOIDS PUMPING AIR OR ATTRACT-ING NOTICE--AND THERE ARE NO AIR LINES TO LIMIT THE DIVER'S WORKING RANGE ...

WE KILLED AN HOUR FISHING, UNTIL THE DIVERS CAME BACK-- BUT NOTHING HAD HAPPENED...

WHERE TO NOW, MR. FEYDA?

NOT FAR. WE'LL LAY FARTHER OFF AND TAKE LIFE EASY UN-TIL DARK--THEN WE'LL MOVE FAST!

JA: *I'm curious if you have any thoughts on this, because those of us who work in this business know how high-pressured it can be with deadlines, and trying to find work, and keep a job. Do you think that's what caused a lot of those guys, back then at least, to be drinkers or smokers?*

CI: Well, smoking and drinking were thought to be something you did when you were an adult. To some people, it meant you were being a grown-up. I became a drinker — a heavy one — when I was a publisher, and that was one of the reasons I was glad to be gone from the job, actually. I started drinking in the morning at one point, it was so rough. The tension is heavy, because you worry. But as a freelancer you live check-to-check... you've still got to pay your rent, you've got obligations, and you've got to get paid. Some of the smaller companies didn't pay much, and some would stiff you. You'd bring in a job and wouldn't know if you'd get another one or go home empty-handed. You learned to live with the empty feeling that your future was not in your hands. Some editors played with you because they could — it was a power play with them. They held your fate in their hands; they're still like that. We all felt the tension. Some people dealt with it by drinking, and nearly everybody smoked. It was a release for some.

JA: *But do you feel like being a freelancer in the '40s was tougher than, say, being a freelancer in the '60s?*

CI: For me it was better later, because I was a better artist. I was a prime artist for DC, so it was no problem for me in the '60s. I had all the work I wanted.

In the 1940s, it was very tough. In a way, we were lucky, though, because with 64 pages in a book, they could hide weaker or developing artists. You don't have a place to go now, because there are no anthology books. You can't develop anywhere now, except maybe at small black-and-white publishers. You have to develop on your own. You don't have it? Then you won't make it. I wonder how many guys who could become good with a good editor to help them never get a chance?

JA: *I want to get back to the late '40s at DC. We started to talk about the transition from super-heroes to Westerns and other genres. You did a lot of stuff. You did "Foley of the Fighting Fifth," "King Faraday"...*

CI: I loved that one. Kanigher was ahead of his time on that character. Faraday was like James Bond.

Shown are Carmine's cover for *Danger Trail* #3 (above left), as well as a page from one of his two stories in that issue (facing page) and the splash page for his "King Faraday" story in *Danger Trail* #5 (above right). Though Bob Kanigher came up with the idea for King Faraday, both stories shown here were penned by David Vern. Both stories and the cover were inked by Joe Giella.

COURTESY OF ROD BECK.

KING FARADAY ™ AND © DC COMICS.

(above) The splash page of "Kit Colby, Girl Sheriff," from her debut story in *Jimmy Wakely* #1 (Sept.-Oct. 1949). Inks by Frank Giacoia.

(right and facing page) Carmine enjoyed drawing the "Pow-Wow Smith" strip in *Western Comics*, perhaps in large part because he was often allowed to ink his own work, as in this panel from issue #73 (Jan.-Feb. 1959) and this page from the final issue, #85 (Jan.-Feb. 1961).

JA: *You drew "Pow-Wow Smith."*
CI: I really liked him. That was written by my friend Eddie Herron. Yeah, that was lovely. We started him in the Old West, but they moved him up to the present day.

JA: *You also drew romance comics.*
CI: I didn't like those; I hated them. The stories were stupid. It was the same thing over and over again. Phyllis Reed was the editor there, and Kanigher was writing the stories.

JA: *But Phyllis Reed was not the first romance editor. Zena Brody was before her. Ruth Brandt edited for a brief time in the 1950s, too.*
CI: I remember Zena Brody, but not Ruth Brandt. Phyllis Reed was a lovely lady, rather mannish looking — dark hair, tall, slim. A nice person — delightful. I did some romance stories for Julie, too, by the way. Bob wrote them, so I got most of my direction from Bob, even though Phyllis was the editor. Kanigher used to brag about their romance.

JA: *I know. She told me.*
CI: She did? Really? I didn't know she'd tell you that.

JA: *I knew her. She was honest and sweet, and I liked her. I don't think she cared that I knew. I mean, she didn't brag about it, but she didn't hide it either. In fact, I didn't bring the subject up — she did. She knew I was taping and was unconcerned that anyone knew. Well, it was in her past, so it was of no consequence to her at that point.*
CI: You know Bob had a big mouth. He told everybody about their relationship. I told him one day, "Bob, it's a personal matter. I don't want to hear about it." He shouldn't have done that. I don't believe in that stuff. He had no manners.

JA: *You did "Kit Colby, Girl Sheriff."*
CI: Oh, crap. Did I really?

JA: *I'm afraid you did. You did "Lady Danger."*
CI: Ugh! [*Jim laughs*] I kept working, anyway.

WARM DELIGHT FILLS THE HEART OF PRETTY *FLEETFOOT*, DAUGHTER OF THE SIOUX CHIEF, *THUNDERCLOUD*...

TONIGHT BEGINS THE FEASTING OF THE *COURTING COUPLES!* *POW-WOW'S* PROMISED TO BE HERE FOR IT...

AFTER THE FINAL CEREMONY TOMORROW NIGHT *;Sigh;* WE'LL BE OFFICIALLY ENGAGED! BUT *POW-WOW'S* LATE! WHAT CAN BE KEEPING HIM?

AT THIS MOMENT, THE REDSKIN SHERIFF IS GALLOPING ALONG THE TRAIL TO THE SIOUX CAMP...

MASKED MEN -- ROBBING THE *REDWOOD STAGE!* Hmmm -- I'M LATE FOR THE *COURTING COUPLES CEREMONY*-- BUT STILL, I HAVE MY DUTY TO PERFORM ...

CHARGING IN AT THE HOLDUP, THE LAWMAN RIPS OFF A SHOT AT ONE BANDIT, AS HE LEAPS FOR THE OTHER...

KRAK!

LOCKED IN A HAND-TO-HAND STRUGGLE, THE INDIAN DRIVES HIS OPPONENT BEFORE HIM, WHILE BEHIND HIM...

GOT TO RECOVER MY GUN -- GET THE SHERIFF... WHILE HIS BACK IS TURNED...

2

Look, I wouldn't have even mentioned the business with Phyllis, but it wasn't a secret.

JA: *He spent a lot of time trying to prove himself to everyone.*
CI: Too much time, if you ask me. He took up fencing to show how much of a man he was.

JA: *Did you think he was insecure?*
CI: Oh, very — I think so.

JA: *Did you have many conversations with Phyllis?*
CI: Not too many, no. Kanigher really gave me the scripts, and she wouldn't say very much. But she was very sweet, and I liked her. I must be honest, there was something wrong with him, but I liked him. I got along with all of them.

JA: *What was Kanigher like as your editor?*
CI: Perfect. He never bothered me, but I understand he ripped some of those guys to shreds. I heard he was brutal to Mort Meskin. He never did that to me, ever. Maybe he respected me.

JA: *But you were friends beyond the work, weren't you?*
CI: Well, friendly, but not friends. I'm not that big on semantics, but you know what I'm trying to say.

JA: *Did you prefer working for him over working for Julie?*
CI: No, but he was a warmer personality — very creative. Look at the Flash ring he created. That was his idea.

JA: *When you quit doing the super-heroes, did you miss them?*
CI: No, really, not at all.

JA: *Did you like drawing Westerns?*
CI: Not particularly. I don't know why. Everything was monotonous at that point. You know why? There was nothing really standing out. We were doing Westerns, we were doing science fiction — we didn't know what the hell was coming next. We were worried about getting work, that's what we were really worried about.

JA: *When you went into Julie's office, you never knew what he was going to hand you next, did you?*
CI: We didn't know what was going to come, or if *anything* was going to come. I was happy to have work, so if Julie wanted me to draw Westerns, then that's what I'd do. I built up a good reference file on horses. The Eadweard Muybridge book on horses was of great help to me. I got a lot of movie stills. There was a place in New York where you could buy movie stills. I think they were a dime apiece or something. They were great, though. I had all the reference I needed to draw the West.

JA: *You once told me that Jack Kirby had written a script for a Western newspaper strip, and you drew it. Which of you went around trying to sell it?*

'BUDDIES'

CI: I did. Then I did one called *Sam* about an old guy who's out in the Village and told his story. I did one called *Hometown*, based on Thornton Wilder's kind of writing, around the mid-'50s. When Joe Kubert wanted to sell *Tor* as a newspaper strip, I wrote it for him. I tried everything in creation. I tried to move a humorous thing like *Friends*, three guys and a girl. [*Ed. note: The feature was called* Buddies.] Nothing I did sold.

JA: *Why do you think you couldn't sell one?*
CI: I don't know why. I went nuts trying. I'd do them every night. I'd work on a different strip every night. I did work on *The Phantom*, but that was only a few days worth in 1961. And let's see... I penciled some *Dondi* dailies for Irwin Hasen once. I can't remember when I did that, though.

JA: *You worked for Dan Barry in 1955 on* Flash Gordon.
CI: I drew very tight roughs, but Dan stressed out over them. He inked them. He was ticked off, because I did them so fast. Dan was slow. He was a strange guy.

We were always on a tour together for the Army, and he kept telling me he was a boxer. We were doing these NCS shows, and he kept bragging about how he was a boxer. One time, we're getting on the bus together and there was

this model coming with us. I was sitting down, she sat down next to me, and he grabbed me by the shirt. I got mad and said, "I've had enough of you." I got up and belted him a good one. I started yelling at him, and he backed off. "You said you're a boxer. Now prove it!" After that, he was like a little baby around me, "Oh, you know I was just having fun" — all that nonsense. I'm not proud of losing my temper, but I didn't like being grabbed like that.

JA: *I don't blame you. Speaking of newspaper strips, there was a time in the late 1950s — maybe early '60s — when Al Capp wanted you to move to Boston and pencil Li'l Abner for him. Did he remember you from the first time he had an interest in you?*
CI: That's an interesting question. I don't know. I saw him at the NCS meetings. He offered me $300 a week, but I didn't want to move to Boston, and things were going well at DC, so I didn't feel the need for the change. By this time, I was more secure about my future at DC. He had Frank Frazetta working there, but I'm not sure how well they got along. Capp could be difficult, and I didn't need the hassle of dealing with him.

JA: *Did you know Milton Caniff?*

HOMETOWN

HOMETOWN

HOMETOWN

HOMETOWN

CI: I met him. He was my idol. I was just like a kid: you go up and talk to him like he was Jesus Christ. Hal Foster didn't come to the NCS meetings much, but it was great to see him because I admired him so much.

JA: *Okay, so things were tightening up in the business by 1950, and you started working for other companies besides DC. For Avon, you did Jesse James with Joe Kubert, you did some science-fiction stories, and a feature called "Turano the Conqueror." You also drew a horror story or two, and something called "Attack on Planet Mars."*
CI: I vaguely remember that last one. It was a tough period for many of us. That's why I worked so hard at doing newspaper strips.

JA: *Sol Cohen was your editor. Do you remember him?*
CI: Not well. He was bland, slightly oddball. The offices were just as bland. They only paid about $10 a page. I did that work as fast as I could. Take the *Jesse James* stuff Joe and I did. I penciled a story in one day, and Joe inked it in one day. Now Joe says we each did our part in two days. Well, maybe he did, but I penciled it in one. I know it was quicker than two days, because I had guns in different hands at all times.
JA: *Who got that job? I was trying to figure out why did you pencil and Joe ink? You guys had to be teamed up for a reason.*

CI: I don't remember. It was just an outside job. Joe knew Sol Cohen, so maybe he got the job for us. Joe was doing whatever he could, too, during that time. I did a couple of science-fiction jobs for Standard Publications, too.

JA: *Of course, you didn't tell anyone at DC you were doing this.*
CI: Oh, no. They would not have been happy about it.

JA: *Also, in '51 to '53, you worked for St. John Publications. You did "Desert Eagle," Hollywood Confessions, "Joe Barton," some jungle stories, some romance, and* Son of Sinbad. *Joe Kubert was there, too.*
CI: Joe was everywhere! I must admit that I don't really remember that stuff.

JA: *Did you ever meet Archer St. John, the publisher?*

(above) A splash panel and full page from "Gunplay at Gallatin" (*Jesse James* #5, Nov. 1951), penciled by Carmine and inked by Joe Kubert.
COURTESY OF TERRY AUSTIN.
©1951 AVON PERIODICALS, INC.

(facing page) Carmine loosely based his *Hometown* strip on Thornton Wilder's 1938 Pulitzer Prize-winning play, *Our Town.*
©1975 CARMINE INFANTINO.

(left) The opening page from Carmine's back-up story in *Son of Sinbad* #1, Feb. 1950, the only issue of the title produced. The inker is unknown. Joe Kubert also drew a story for the book, as well as its cover.

(above and right) In addition to Westerns, Carmine also drew some horror stories for Timely/Atlas. Shown here are panels from "Don't Try to Outsmart the Devil," the lead story from *Adventures into Terror* #13 (Dec. 1952), penciled by Carmine and written by Stan Lee.

CI: No. Joe worked with Norman Maurer there. They did that 3-D stuff.

JA: *Did you work for Joe there?*
CI: No. It must have been someone else.

JA: *Did you meet Matt Baker there?*
CI: I may have, but I don't remember. It was side stuff, and it didn't mean much to me.

JA: *Did you ever try to get work from EC Comics?*
CI: No, isn't that funny? I never thought of working for them. They were like a little clique of their own. They were like a private club, but I wasn't invited.

JA: *You also worked for Ziff-Davis, drawing romance, science fiction, and Westerns.*
CI: Yes, I think I did. It wasn't particularly good artwork, was it?

JA: *Were you rushing it?*
CI: No, it just wasn't that good yet — but the stuff was still growing. You know, I was learning, changing, developing.

JA: *Was Jerry Siegel your editor?*
CI: No, I never met Jerry — or Joe Shuster, either. Apparently Jerry was working there at the same time, but I don't remember who my editor was. That company is mostly a blank to me now. I was working wherever I could, because DC may have been steady, but there was no telling when that would or could change.

JA: *You drew crime comics for Timely in the 1950s, and you said that some of them that are listed with your brother's name, you did.*
CI: Yeah, I drew some of them. Jimmy drew some of them, but not all. [Comics historian] Michael Vassallo isn't as sure as I am; we have a friendly argument about that. I used Jimmy's name because I knew he wouldn't care, and it kept DC from knowing what I was doing. I don't remember who I worked for on these. I know it wasn't Stan Lee or Al Sulman.

JA: *Don Rico?*
CI: I don't think so. I knew Don later on, when I lived in California. A nice man. That's my memory of him.

JA: *Do you remember drawing* The Adventures of Alan Ladd *for DC in 1949?*

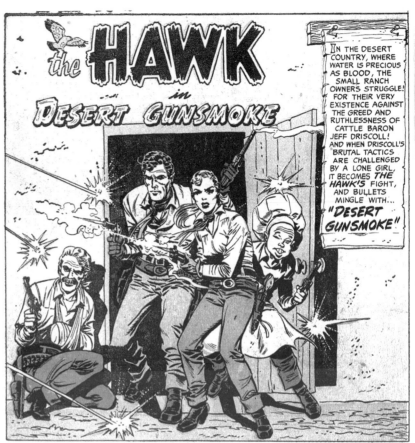

CI: I don't think I did that, unless it was back-up stories in the book.

JA: *And you drew* Jimmy Wakely *for DC, too.*
CI: That, I remember. Alex Toth drew those, too. He hated it. So did I. A very dull character.

JA: *Didn't you like doing a feature that was based on a real person's likeness?*
CI: That had nothing to do with it. The stories were dull. I did try to capture [Jimmy Wakely's] likeness, but I don't know if I succeeded very well. I think Frank Giacoia inked those stories. I'm not sure.

JA: *And of course, in '52, you drew some* Rex, the Wonder Dog. *Did you like that character?*
CI: No, but the chimp I liked. I loved that. *Rex* was dull, dull, dull. The stories were forced and repetitive.

(above) Carmine's splash page from Ziff-Davis' *The Hawk* #2 (Summer 1952).

COURTESY OF JIM VADEBON-COEUR, JR. AND *ALTER EGO* MAGAZINE.

©1952 ZIFF-DAVIS PUBLISHING COMPANY.

JA: *You drew The Phantom Stranger in '52 and '53. Did you like that character?*

CI: Yes. John Broome wrote those. I did like them. I liked designing the character; I thought he looked good. It was a little different than some of the stuff I was doing at the time. The stories were much more timid than some other companies would have done, but DC wasn't about to go in that direction.

JA: *I know Julie did not like your inks, so what did it take for you to get Julie to let you ink some stories?*

CI: I demanded it. Every once in a while, Julie knew I had to get a "release," so he'd let me ink some stories. But he told me he didn't like my inking. He preferred Murphy Anderson's tight, slick look over my stuff. I can understand that. Sy Barry was good over my pencils, and Joe Giella was also very slick, so he got to ink my *Flash* stuff. My favorite inker was Frank Giacoia, as you know.

JA: *What about "Detective Chimp" did you like?*

CI: Everything. The stories were funny, charming, and I loved drawing that little chimp. It's my favorite series in comics.

JA: *You also drew* Danger Trail *and "Captain Comet."*

CI: *Danger Trail* was fun. That was written by Dave Wood and Kanigher, too. "Captain Comet" was for Julie. I drew the first stories, and I designed his costume, but it wasn't much of a series. We didn't have but a few pages to work with; there was no chance to develop the character. I drew Kanigher stories for *All-American Men of War.* I hated it, but at least I got to ink a few of them.

JA: *You started "Detective Chimp" in '52 with John Broome.*

CI: I inked those, too. Julie didn't want me to ink it.

JA: *Was that the first thing you inked for Julie?*

CI: Yeah, and then he said, "No more." I argued with him on that. That's when I was getting more confidence. I could have gone anywhere to work, so he was afraid to lose me. He didn't want me to ink any of my stories. I was unhappy about that.

"AS BOBO YANKED HARD, HE UNINTENTIONALLY FIRED THE ARROW FROM THE BOW..."

HE'S A TRICK-SHOT ARTIST! HE HIT THE GUN OUT OF MY HAND!

KOO!

D-DID I DO THAT?

"THE EFFECT OF THAT SHOT ON THE CROOKS WAS DEVASTATING..."

WHAT ARE WE GONNA DO, BOSS? WE CAN'T GET THE PLANE OFF THE GROUND--

AND WE HAVEN'T GOT A CHANCE AGAINST THAT SHARPSHOOTIN' CHIMP!

"IN THE CONFUSION, BOBO CAUTIOUSLY INCHED CLOSER TOWARD THE GANG..."

WATCH OUT! HE'S GOING TO FIRE AGAIN!

DON'T SHOOT! WE--WE GIVE UP!

I DON'T GET THIS, BUT WHO AM I TO ARGUE WITH HUMANS?

"AND SO, WHEN WE FINALLY TRAILED THE GANG FROM THE CAVE, BOBO HAD THE SITUATION COMPLETELY UNDER CONTROL..."

BOBO, YOU'VE CAPTURED THE PHONY PIRATES! HOW CAN WE EVER REPAY YOU?

JUST KEEP ME IN MIND WHEN YOU'RE HANDING OUT THE PRIZES FOR THE BEST COSTUME, MR. MAYOR!

"WE DISCOVERED THE REAL 'PIRATES' WHERE THEY HAD BEEN LEFT, TIED HAND AND FOOT BY THE GANG THAT TOOK THEIR PLACE..."

WE HAD NO CHANCE, YOUR HONOR! THE GANG JUMPED US--AND STOLE OUR UNIFORMS!

THEY WOULD HAVE GOT AWAY WITH THE GOLD TREASURE--IF NOT FOR BOBO!

"LATER THAT DAY..."

AND THE PRIZE FOR THE MOST ORIGINAL COSTUME GOES TO BOBO--AS LIGHTNING ARROW!

YAAAAHEEEE!

GOSH! NOW I'LL NEVER GET THAT OUTFIT OFF HIM!

The End

⑥

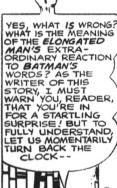

JA: *What did you dislike about the war comics?*

CI: Everything. Lots of fussy details, and it all had to be accurate. I wasn't that good on that stuff. I felt stifled. Russ Heath was very good at that stuff. I saw that guy draw a circle for a head, an oblong for a tank, and with a brush, he literally drew that whole thing out in detail. I couldn't believe it. He was so good at that.

JA: *Did you get to know John Broome or Gardner Fox very well?*

CI: John, I saw in the office. John was not the type who would socialize very much. Neither would Gardner, actually. So they came in, they worked directly with Julie, and didn't socialize. Neither did Julie in those days.

John didn't talk much, but he was the kind of a guy who would bleed over one page for days at a time, and he would sometimes be very late. We'd have a few words, now and then, and if he'd tell me he liked something, he say, "Julie liked the '[Detective] Chimp' story we did," or, "He liked this 'Elongated Man' story," and that was it. That was the most he'd ever say. He always reminded me of Gary Cooper: tall, lanky, and quiet.

Julie played pinochle with Milt Snappin [a staff letterer] during his lunch hour. That was a sacred time for him. That's why Alex Toth had that fight with Julie. Alex came in at lunch time and asked for his paycheck. Julie told him to wait until he'd finished lunch. Now, everybody knew not to bother Julie during that time, but Alex didn't care. He wanted his money now. Julie could have given Alex his check; it'd only have taken a moment of his time, but he didn't

want to do it. He wanted to play cards and have lunch and be left alone. I think there was tension between them anyway. Alex hated drawing *Jimmy Wakely*, and he wanted to draw only what he wanted to draw. Well, you couldn't take that attitude with Julie. He was the boss and didn't put up with a lot of nonsense. So they had a fight, and Alex walked out. Both of those guys were stubborn.

JA: *How did you get to be friends with Ed Herron?*

CI: We met in the office. We just clicked and we were good friends. I loved him. He used to tell me, "Never settle for any job you've got. Never! Keep shooting, looking up, looking up." He's the one that pushed me on. He was the head of

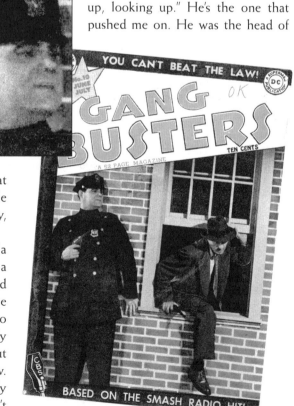

Stars and Stripes during World War Two, you know. Editor in chief, that's some job. Then he blew his whole career. But that's something else. He did a lot of *Captain Marvel* writing in the early 1940s. Everything he wrote was good. John Broome was a brilliant writer, but Eddie was my favorite.

He died of cancer at the Veterans Hospital down on 23rd Street. I was there a day or two before he died. That broke my heart. He ended up a terrible drunk. I still feel bad when I think of how he ended up. I miss him.

JA: *Julie sure rewrote a lot of Gardner Fox's scripts.*
CI: I know. I think it hurt Gardner and inhibited his work, because he knew Julie was going to rewrite everything he turned in. I can't explain how they worked together, because I wasn't with them when they plotted stories. When I came into Julie's office, they'd be sitting there working on scripts. They'd go to lunch, and when they came back Julie and I would go over what I had brought in. Gardner would wait until I finished with Julie, and once I left they'd go back to writing.

JA: *Most of the time, you didn't sign your name. Did you care?*
CI: Well, the comics were in a bad light, publicly. The public didn't like comics, and we were almost ashamed of what we were doing. I told you what I did. I used some pseudonyms: "Rouge Enfante," which means "Carmine Infantino," and other times, "Cinfa." But the "Rouge Enfante" was funny, because Julie, sometimes he got nasty letters. "What the hell are you doing, hiring this guy 'Rouge Enfante,' when he's copying Infantino? Why don't you get rid of the bum?" [*laughter*]

JA: *What led you to use that name?*
CI: I loved it, and when Julie talked about it, I used it even more.

JA: *When Dr. Wertham and Senator Estes Kefauver started attacking the comics —*
CI: Maybe that's why we hid our names. We were ashamed of what we did.

JA: *You really were ashamed?*
CI: Oh, sure, because you hide your head. The concept was that comics were killing kids. Supposedly, some were jumping out of windows and cutting off heads. You know, that kind of talk was embarrassing as hell, so we'd never say what we did.

JA: *Were you afraid the comics were going to shut down because of the Senate investigations?*
CI: We were very worried, and don't forget the sales took a nasty beating. Oh, Jesus! They took a beating you can't believe. We had to take page cuts.

JA: *DC cut your rate?*
CI: By two dollars, which was more money then than now. "It's either that or we're going out of business." The inkers took a dollar cut, pencilers took two dollars, and the writers took a two-dollar cut.

JA: *Who informed you of the pay cuts?*
CI: That was Julie. He said, "Take it or leave it." What else could I do?

JA: *When did you start getting raises again?*
CI: Oh, man, it took a couple of years. We were angry about that. The story they gave us was

(above) Carmine began signing his "Elongated Man" stories starting with *Detective Comics* #350 (Apr. 1966). He confused some fans by signing his name as "Rogue Enfant" on this "Elongated Man" splash from *Detective Comics* #354 — the only such case of him doing so in the series.

ELONGATED MAN ™ AND © DC COMICS.

either we'd do it or they'd kill the books, so we had no choice. I don't believe that was true, but that's what they told us.

JA: *Did you discuss that with other artists very much?*
CI: We all talked about it. We were all very pissed about it. But later we got raises.

JA: *Were they just small raises?*
CI: We got two dollars, three dollars a page at a time.

JA: *Did you have the top rate?*
CI: At the end I did.

JA: *You mean by 1966?*
CI: Yes, I made $18,000 a year then. That was good money then. Do you know what I was getting? Thirty dollars a page, just pencils. Fifty when I inked the story, too.

JA: *Did you ever have any dealing with co-owners Harry Donenfeld or Jack Liebowitz?*
CI: None. I used to see them in the hall once in a while. They didn't talk to us.

JA: *What about Whitney Ellsworth?*
CI: I met Whitney once. He saw my work once and told Julie, "Give this guy a raise." That, I remember. He saw the work, and then I dealt with Whit later on.

JA: *But he was Editorial Director in the '40s and '50s. You didn't deal with him much?*
CI: No, he didn't deal with anybody much. He was like the token goyim. At least, that's what I was told. He was hired to be the token goyim, because Julie's the one who ran his books.

JA: *Do you think Julie, Kanigher, and the other editors had to deal with Ellsworth all that much?*
CI: No, because Ellsworth got busy with *The Adventures of Superman* television show. Whit would look in every once in a while, not that often. But sometimes I'd be sitting, working with Julie. He'd come in, look, he'd say, "How are you?" and then walk away. That's about it. But Julie would be shaken a little bit when he'd come in.

JA: *So the editors were pretty autonomous.*

CI: Oh, yes.

JA: *Did you ever meet editor Bernie Breslauer? I know you didn't work for him.*
CI: That rings a bell. Yes, a nice man, a lovely man. I met him only in passing.

JA: *What do you remember about Ray Perry?*
CI: A colorist, a wonderful, very lovely man. He had white hair. He showed up every day, did his work.

JA: *When I've interviewed people and they talk about when they went to DC looking for work, Ray Perry was the man who usually looked at their work.*
CI: No, I thought it was Eddie Eisenberg, who worked under Sol in production. It was Eisenberg who first looked at my work when I came in looking for a job.

JA: *Did you deal with Ray Perry much?*
CI: I talked to him once in a while, that's about all. I'd look at his coloring work, say hello, goodbye, and that was it. I was not Jack Adler or Neal Adams, if that's what you mean, nothing like that. I didn't get friendly with the production people. I dealt with Julie. If there was a correction to make, I'd go into the production room and say hello to somebody there, make the correction, and leave.

(above) With the decline in the popularity of super-heroes in the late '40s and early '50s, crime and horror comics moved to the forefront. DC followed the trend just like every other publisher, though their "mystery" books — whether of a science-fiction or supernatural bent — were much tamer than most of the fare to be had, so they were spared the brunt of the Kefauver hearings. Covers to *Mystery in Space* #6 (Feb.-Mar. 1952), inked by Joe Giella, and *Phantom Stranger* #4 (Feb.-Mar. 1952), inked by Cy Danzji.

(facing page) Sketches drawn on the back of a "Detective Chimp" page in 1955.

CHAPTER 4

Lightning Strikes Again

JA: *How did you find out that there was going to be a new Flash?*

CI: One day I was delivering a job, and Julie says, "Carmine, we're going start doing super-heroes again." I said, "Aw, no!" I didn't want to do them. I figured it's old hat all over again. And he said to me, "No, no, you don't understand. We're going to do the Flash, but we're going to do a new version of the Flash." Bob Kanigher sat in on that meeting, and said the same thing: it was to be different, exciting, blah, blah, blah. Julie said, "We're changing everything about him. I'd like to see some sketches from you for the Flash."

Later, Kanigher was over at my apartment

(below) Meet the Flash! An all-new Flash sped onto the scene in the pages of *Showcase #4*. This opening splash page was a play on one of Carmine's cover sketches for the book, and showed off a sleek, new speedster.

FLASH ™ AND © DC COMICS.

and saw the Flash sketches I had done. He liked them. My Flash costume was designed to emphasize the fact that he was a runner. The old costume didn't really do that; it wasn't as skin-tight as mine. I added the lightning accents to the costume for identification and because I knew I could do something with them when I drew the Flash running.

JA: *How often did Kanigher come to your house?*

CI: Oh, quite a bit. He used to stop by every couple of weeks. He'd stop in, we'd talk, kid around. I lived about six, seven blocks away from DC. He loved to talk. When he wasn't in the office, he was a different guy. He could be fun. We never talked business though, isn't that strange?

JA: *Had a script been written when you had this meeting with Julie and Kanigher?*

CI: I don't believe so, not yet. Julie said, "When you come in next week, Bob said we'll have a script ready." And Julie added, "Bring some sketches in for covers." I said okay, but by the time I'd come in, Bob has his own cover sketch, and that's the one they took.

JA: *Kanigher gave you the idea for the film strip cover [Showcase #4].*

CI: Yeah, it was his idea. I did three different rough versions of that cover, but they were all variations of the same idea. One of them was of the Flash running towards the reader, breaking through a page. Another had Barry Allen in the background, with the costume coming out of the ring. And the third had the film strip, which, of course, we used. But it was really Kanigher's basic idea, and

that's the one that Julie wanted. It was a good idea, and as it turned out it's a classic cover.

JA: *Do you think Julie picked you to be the artist because you were his "number one" artist or were you picked because you had been the last artist to draw the Golden Age Flash?*
CI: I don't know. I never thought about having been the last Flash artist or whether or not that influenced Julie's decision to have me draw the new Flash.

JA: *Julie also chose the last "Hawkman" artist — Joe Kubert — to do the new "Hawkman" series. He couldn't use the last "Green Lantern" artists — Alex Toth and Irwin Hasen — to revive that character, because they were no longer working for DC.*
CI: That's right. I'm sure all of that entered into Julie's thinking. And he put Mike Sekowsky on the *Justice League* because most of the original "JSA" artists were either not at DC or too busy on other books. I'm glad I didn't have to draw the *Justice League*. That was a busy book! I was busy enough with Julie's other titles.

JA: *When you're going to draw the new Flash, because you had been the artist of the old Flash, you're not the same person, you're not the same artist any more.*
CI: I didn't feel that way in the way you phrased it. I didn't even think of it that way. I don't think they did either... I don't know.

JA: *But you knew that you were different, that your work was changing.*
CI: I knew that I was different.

JA: *When you were thinking about, "How am I going to draw him running?" thinking about what Mort Meskin did with "Johnny Quick," thinking about what you had done on the Golden Age "Flash"... what were your thoughts?*
CI: My immediate thought is, "Think animation here, think animation." That was my basic thought. How could I get more movement? I didn't want it to look like the old Flash, and neither did anyone else. That was the key, and my basic aim was "get movement here." If we

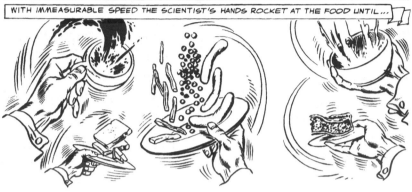

didn't accomplish that, we weren't going to accomplish anything. There wasn't much real movement in the old Flash. He was a little stupid-looking with that hat.

JA: *So what did you do to create more movement?*
CI: Well, I used multiple figures. I tilted the Flash's body when he ran. Don't forget, when a

(above) Barry Allen discovers he has super-speed when a falling plate of food seemingly freezes in mid-air before his eyes. From *Showcase* #4. Written by Bob Kanigher, with inks by Joe Kubert.

FLASH ™ AND © DC COMICS.

(above) This panel from the final page of *Showcase* #8 was the first instance of Carmine using multiple images of the new Flash to depict his speed.
(left) Wide horizontal panels helped Carmine give the Flash a sense of movement.

COURTESY OF HERITAGE AUCTIONS (WWW.HA.COM).
FLASH ™ AND © DC COMICS.

figure's running, the head and torso lean forward. The body takes almost an elbow-shaped angle. I drew the last figure first and the first figure last. That created more motion, but I didn't explain a lot of this to Bob or Julie — I just did it. They liked it, but they didn't know why they liked it. It was a lot of work to draw it that way, but it worked!

JA: *What was your initial impression when you read the first script?*

CI: I loved the part with the costume in the ring and the part in the restaurant where the waitress spills the soup. That was all Bob's thinking, and, again, he was creating as much motion as he could in the scripts. Every story element he used was promoting motion. He was very

sharp that way. I give him a lot of credit. He and I thought in the same direction. Of course, I brought it in, he said, "That's it. I love it." He didn't talk that way, ever. Praise for others was not common for him, but it made me feel good this time.

For some reason, Julie took Kanigher off the book after that lead story. Something happened there that I wasn't privy to, but when I went in to get the next story, I saw that John Broome had written it. I looked at Bob; he looked at me and shook his head.

JA: *Actually, Kanigher wrote one story in each* Showcase, *and Broome wrote the other. Kanigher didn't write* The Flash *when it first became a series, though he came back years later.*

CI: Okay. But no matter what, Bob did not like losing the series or sharing responsibility for writing the stories. This I know absolutely! And you can't blame him, because he did the hard work of recreating the Flash, and then, all of a sudden, there's John Broome writing what Kanigher felt was his series. Well, Julie and Bob didn't like each other, I think.

JA: *There's no question they disliked each other. But years later, Kanigher did write some Flash again. I know that Kanigher wrote a story [#161] in the mid-'60s. Julie had a story idea about the Flash giving up his costume, and he had Gardner Fox and Kanigher each write a story based on that idea.*

CI: I created the cover for that idea, and they had to invent stories around that, right?

JA: *Right. And in the letters page on one issue, Julie said that Kanigher was the originator of the Flash.*

CI: Really? I'm surprised by that.

JA: *Around '69 or '70, John Broome retired from comics, and Kanigher wrote some Flash stories again, including the 200th issue. In issue #201, Kanigher wrote a new "Golden Age Flash" back-up that Murphy Anderson penciled and inked.*

#8 May-June

11

As the beautiful reporter returns to her vigil... FLASH is about to streak off when...

HERE I GO--COVERING THE REST OF THE CITY AGAIN!--NO, WAIT! MAYBE THAT'S JUST WHAT THE "BRAIN" BEHIND THIS WANTS ME TO THINK! THAT THE THIRD CRIME WILL BE COMMITTED ELSEWHERE!

WITH EVERYONE'S EYES FOCUSED ON THE BOX--NO ONE WOULD NOTICE WHAT WAS GOING ON--UNDER HIS VERY FEET! HMMM--?

BANK

UNSEEN BY HUMAN EYE, FLASH ROCKETS PAST THE EXTRA GUARDS OUTSIDE THE CENTRAL CITY BANK...

GETTING WINDY, ISN'T IT?

BANK

DOWN TO THE UNDERGROUND BANK VAULT RACES THE SCARLET SPEEDSTER...

SO YOU FINALLY FIGURED OUT MY CHINESE PUZZLE BOX CRIME BLUEPRINT, FLASH! HA! HA!

THERE ARE THREE OF YOU! WELL, MAYBE YOU WON'T FEEL LIKE LAUGHING IF YOU LEARN YOUR BROTHERS ARE ALREADY IN JAIL!

BUT, EVERY TIME FLASH TRIES TO COLLAR THE LAUGHING CRIMINAL ...

I FORGOT TO TELL YOU--

--I'M WEARING A LIVE WIRE SUIT!

HA! HA! HA!

This is what Julie told me: Irv Novick lived a block or so away from Kanigher, and sometimes Novick would drive over to Kanigher's house and give him the pages. Then Kanigher would bring them in to Julie. So one day there're no pages. Julie went to Kanigher and asked, "Where are Novick's pages? They're supposed to be in today." Kanigher coldly said to Julie, "Novick is your problem." That was the last straw for Julie.

CI: I never heard that story. What book was Novick doing?

JA: *He drew The Flash for a long time, but he also drew Batman for Julie.*

CI: His *Batman* work was terrific. You couldn't get much work out of him. He was very slow. He used to do a lot of advertising in between comics stories. That's why he couldn't get the work done on time.

JA: *Of all the Flash writers...*

CI: Bob and John were the best. Gardner wrote pretty nicely, but Julie rewrote his stuff so much it was like Julie wrote it himself. It was really overdone, I thought.

JA: *What do you feel that Gardner Fox's stories lacked that John Broome's had?*

CI: Warmth. John was much more creative, slow. But Gardner was very academic.

JA: *Contrast an Eddie Herron script with a John Broome script.*

CI: They were very different. John's stories were more light-hearted. Eddie was not light-hearted. It was good, hard, solid stuff, but he could be funny, too. They both wrote detailed scripts.

JA: *You didn't like having scenes described in that much detail.*

CI: No, I didn't pay attention to them anyway. [*laughs*]

JA: *It took a while for the Flash to get his own book.*

CI: Well, what happened is they put out four issues in *Showcase*. When the first sales figures came in on "The Flash," they couldn't believe them because they were so high. Then the second one came in, and they were even higher, and the third and fourth were higher still. They knew they had a hit.

JA: *Do you have any idea why they started the numbering at 105? It was a continuation of Flash Comics' numbering from the 1940s.*

CI: Is that what it was? Maybe they had a thing about starting with issue #1? They probably wanted the distributors and the fans to think this book had a history. People don't always want to try new stuff. These were conservative times. That's my guess.

JA: *How did you feel when you found out that The Flash was going to be a regular series?*

CI: Well, they didn't tell you very much, you know. I came into the office one day and Julie said, "The Flash is going to be a regular series." He said nothing else. I didn't have any feeling one way or another. It was work, and, after Senator Kefauver and Doctor Wertham's witch hunts, that's all I cared about at the time.

I know this is off the subject, but I want to interject something here. Comic books today show and tell everything. There aren't many boundaries now, and I don't like it. There was one good thing about the Comics Code, though I didn't realize it at the time. We weren't allowed to do some

stuff, and though I don't like censorship, that censorship forced us to be more creative in a way. We had to imply what we couldn't show. It forced us and the readers to use our imaginations.

JA: *How good were you about meeting deadlines?*

CI: I was perfect. I never missed a deadline in my whole life. One time I had to go to the hospital for an operation. I called Julie and said, "I'll get your work done before I go in." Julie said, "Carmine, you need to take it easy." I said, "No, no. I'll get the work done." I had someone deliver the work for me, but I got it in on time.

There were a few guys who were notorious for blowing deadlines. Julie didn't like having his schedules disrupted and would get upset sometimes. We considered those guys to be unprofessional.

JA: *Did you have any input with the scripts once you started drawing the stories?*

CI: No, I never did that.

JA: *Not even on an artistic level? For instance, if you had a page that called for five panels, would you ever stretch it to six?*

CI: No. I always adhered pretty closely to what I was asked to do. [pauses] Well, sometimes I might have added a panel. I didn't make a habit of it.

JA: *There was never a time when you said to Julie, "This plot point doesn't make sense"?*

CI: No, no. I never saw a need to do that. Julie always edited very tightly. At times there was more rewriting on the scripts than what originally had been written. The only person Julie didn't rewrite was John Broome.

JA: *Did you ever think about writing your own stuff for Julie?*

CI: No. I did write my own stuff for the newspaper strip ideas I had, but only then. I was too busy

drawing to even consider writing. The one time I did, Julie said, "I've got my own writers. I don't want anybody else." And since John Broome was so good, how could I compete with him? My fate was just to pencil for Julie, except when I could talk him into doing a little inking. I had to demand that with "Detective Chimp" and "Elongated Man," and got my way then.

JA: *Did you feel as though Julie was more enthusiastic about doing the science-fiction comics as compared to his other books?*

CI: Absolutely. If you read his super-hero stories carefully, you'll see he always had a lot of science-fiction in them — *Batman* being the exception. But Julie worked just as hard on the Westerns as he did on the science-fiction. Julie was diligent; he worked very hard to make his

(above) Julie Schwartz, of course, came to DC Comics from the field of science fiction, having been an agent for many successful SF authors. It made perfect sense for him to edit titles such as *Mystery in Space* and *Strange Adventures*. Seen here are an opening splash panel from *Mystery in Space* #39 (Aug.-Sept. 1957) and a page from *Mystery in Space* #14 (June-July 1953).

COURTESY OF JIM LUDWIG AND TONY GLEESON.

©1957 AND 1953 DC COMICS.

(right) The Charles and Dorothy Manson House, designed by renowned architect, Frank Lloyd Wright, who in the early '50s became one of Carmine's biggest influences.

(above and right) Carmine studied for two years at the Art Students League, under the guiding hand of William C. McNulty. It was during this time that Carmine's work took a dramatic change, moving away from illustration and further into design. McNulty (1889-1963) was a painter and print-maker best known for his etchings of buildings and cityscapes. Shown here is a print of "In the Fifties (Whirlpool)," a 1930 etching of New York City.

©1969 PETER A. JULEY & SON.

books the best. Julie knew what he wanted and what worked. That's what made him so good. And he began to like what I did, so I was in good shape. When I was in his office, he made me read the script before I left. He said, "Read the script. If you have any problems, tell me about them now." If there was a problem, we'd talk it out, but generally there were no problems.

And later, when we did "Strange Sports Stories"... I'm not sure, but I think Irwin Donenfeld wanted a sports book, so Julie came up with this idea. Julie called me and said, "I want this to look different." I came up with those silhouettes in the captions to make it different. I always tried my best to please Julie, and he respected me. We had a good rapport after a while.

JA: *So your relationship with Julie started changing?*
CI: A little. He started asking me to come up with cover ideas with which he'd base stories on. That's when I knew he was starting to come around. He said, "Why don't you do covers for me, and I'll build stories around them? You'll get more work that way." I'd bring in two or three cover layouts about the size of typewriter paper, and he'd pick out which ones he wanted. Sometimes, he'd take the whole three at a shot.

JA: *Before we get further into the* Flash *discussion, I want to talk about your artwork and how it was changing.*

CI: That started in the early 1950s, I feel. I studied under William C. McNulty at the Art Students League, and he said to me, "Have you ever read anything about art?" Of course, he saw some of the stuff I'd been drawing. I was putting backgrounds in the scenes. "So why are you doing that?" I said, "I like to draw the whole scene." He said, "Why?" I said, "I like to balance everything out." So he showed me a Frank Lloyd Wright book. I went nuts over it and went out and bought my own copy.

JA: *Is it fair to say that in the '40s — your first decade of work — that most of the art you were doing was more intuitive rather than studied?*
CI: Yes, absolutely.

JA: *So this was mostly work from your gut. You were not analyzing your work.*
CI: No, no, not at all.

JA: *Joe Kubert told me he was the same way then.*
CI: Really? I didn't know that. That's interesting. Well, McNulty tore me to shreds, and then he rebuilt me. I was drawing my brains out on the figure, every nut and bolt. He says, "What are you doing?" I said, "I'm drawing realistically." [*chuckles*] He said, "You're making photographs when you do that. And photographs can do it better than you can, so why bother?" That comment made me tear the drawing to shreds. Then he says, "I want you to rethink," and thus, he taught me to think. So I said, "Well, that's easy." "No," he said, "That's

64

not easy. What I'm telling you to do is not easy. I'm telling you to restructure your thinking. You're a designer, but you don't know it." He was tough. He was good. I studied with him for about two years, three times a week, because I so admired him.

JA: *As far as I can tell, it looks like you must have been studying there around '51 or '52.*
CI: Yeah, but my comic book work got very bad because of my studies. Julie says, "What are you doing here, for Christ's sake?" I was changing rapidly, the stuff was going through a whole metamorphosis, and Julie was really upset with the new stuff I was turning in. He said, "You're turning in crap, you know that? Don't you want to work any more?" They didn't know what I was doing. I didn't explain it either. Julie wasn't an artist and couldn't understand what I was going through.

JA: *Well, this was the first time you started thinking about positive and negative shapes, deep focus in space, and the way shapes work with each other. Because you were just drawing by rote before then, this was the first time you really analyzed what you were doing.*
CI: By rote, yeah, and I didn't do that any more, thanks to McNulty. He'd sit down with me and say, "Why this shape? Why this? And why are you putting this shape against this shape?" Then he would say to me, "You put a figure on a page, right? About one-quarter of the page — make everything point to that figure." When I did that, I saw what he was talking about. You build up all your backgrounds, pointing to that bigger figure, and it works. It started to work, but it took a while to understand this. I had never thought about positive and negative space before.

JA: *This is where you really start to become a designer. Would you agree?*
CI: Yes, but Julie, he hated the stuff when I began changing. When change happens, you're a nothing in between the changes, you know what I mean? I was stopping the drawing. I was literally dropping all the drawing. I didn't care about it any more, and the designing was taking shape and form, and it overtook my drawing.

JA: *Was Kanigher saying anything to you?*
CI: He liked what I was doing, Bobby did. Isn't that funny? He used to say to Julie, "Leave him alone, leave him alone. I like what he's doing."

JA: *Alex Toth told me that in the late '40s, early '50s, Sol Harrison used to be on his back all the time.*

CI: Oh, he was a pain. He didn't like me. He hated everybody. He promoted himself as the Art Director at DC Comics, but he wasn't. He was the production man, period.

JA: *Alex told me — I'm talking late '40s, early '50s — that he would show Sol his work, and Sol would say, "It's very nice, Alex. But you don't know what to leave out." Did you ever hear stuff like that?*
CI: No. He never talked to me like that.

JA: *So when your art was changing, there was silence.*
CI: Not a word. I never even went near [Sol Harrison]. I didn't bother him at all. Alex used to look for comments from everybody. That was the difference. He went to him, he went to Jack Adler, he went to everybody. I didn't care. I did my own thing, so I didn't care what anyone else thought. That's the loner in me. [laughs]

JA: *In late '40s, early '50s, Alex, Joe, and Jack Adler told me that DC set up a modeling session one night a week where they drew from a model.*

(below) Jack Potter (1927-2002) was a successful illustrator with an impressionistic style, who made his name with a series of ads for Coca-Cola in 1956-57. Not long afterwards, he left the world of commercial art to become a teacher at the School of Visual Arts. He developed a class called, "Drawing and Thinking," which he taught for 45 years until his death.

©1957 COCA-COLA.

(above) On the left is "L'Absinthe," 1876, oil on canvas, by Edgar Degas (1834-1917), a French painter and one of the founders of Impressionism. On the right is "Seated Nude," 1916, oil on canvas, by Amedeo Modigliani (1884-1920), an Italian-born painter and sculptor who primarily worked with figures and nudes.

CI: I didn't go. I didn't have a need for it, I felt. I was going to the Art Students League, and then I went to the School for Visual Arts. I was getting my education from trained professionals.

JA: *Did you go to Visual Arts after the Art Students League?*
CI: Yes. I needed more, and I studied with Jack Potter.

JA: *What did Jack Potter do for you?*
CI: He was a brilliant designer. He really pushed me further into design. Whatever I was doing in design wasn't enough. He would really elongate the figures more. He stretched them like rubber. He'd look at my work and say, "See these figures on the paper? They've got no purpose. Do three figures or four or five." "I don't see why." He'd answer, "Just do it. Do it." And I'd draw the three figures, or five figures there, depending on what the eye would see when the figure's in a certain position. I did this for about two years. After that, I was through. I never had another teacher. I was on my own then. I think I had developed by that time what I wanted to do. I was at a point then that I knew where I was going with this stuff.

JA: *In the past, we've talked about how Modigliani and Degas had influenced you.*
CI: William McNulty put me onto Modigliani, Giacometti, Degas, and Frank Lloyd Wright. The shapes that Wright used in his house designs greatly influenced me. It was his work that got me to thinking about how to draw houses and place them in a scene. I took his ideas about shape and design and did my own version. There was drama in his style, and I incorporated that drama into my work.

JA: *What did you learn from Degas' work?*
CI: Design. He, like Modigliani was a designer. Degas used his shapes beautifully. There's a beautiful painting he did of the absinthe drinker. He's sitting there with the prostitute, having a drink, and, if you notice, the table begins on the far right and turns right into the picture, takes you right into the picture. That's designing. And then Degas had his figure bent forward, his arm is holding the drink; every part of the figure is posed to lead your eye down to the drink. The girl is bending forward into the drink and pointing up to him. Everything points to him, but he does it very

feminine in style. I shouldn't say "feminine," just "softer," but Giacometti's work was harder. If you combine the two styles, it makes a wonderful figure and a wonderful look.

JA: *Let's tie this in with* The Flash. *By the time you were drawing the series, your approach to page and panel composition was changing.*
CI: Yes, I wanted to emphasize his speed and used long, stretched-out panels for that effect.

JA: *Your emphasis on horizontal panels rather than the standard vertical helped create the sense of speed, but, also, it caused you to think differently about spatial relation-ships of forms.*
CI: There're two things involved: I was using negative space all of a sudden and using long panels for speed effects. It was a matter of using both or one opposed to the other... anything to create contrast.

JA: *As far as the captions were concerned —*
CI: That was my idea. When I was a kid, I never once read a caption. No one did. So I figured, "I'll fix that." I took the caption — it was one big piece — and broke it into three sections. I put the pointing hands on the boxes, and everybody liked that.

JA: *What gave you the idea to do that? You didn't do that before, so why now?*
CI: Jim, I didn't read them myself. I started thinking, "Why don't I read them?" Because they were boring! All of a sudden, I saw the captions as a detriment. I figured, "Let's make them part of

(left) A 1910 self-portrait, oil on canvas, by Swiss painter Giovanni Giacometti (1868-1933), who was strongly influenced by the French Impressionists.

(below) In this panel from *The Flash* #116 (Nov. 1960), Carmine combines several techniques to give the drawing a sense of motion: multiple incomplete images of Flash running, connected by speed lines; a long, stretched-out panel shape; and negative space. Flash seems like he is almost falling into the white space above the silhoutted skyline.
FLASH ™ AND © DC COMICS.

subtly, very gently, and your eye goes there without realizing what you're doing. That's designing.

JA: *And Degas' approach to drawing human forms?*
CI: Again, the same quality. If you look at his stuff carefully, there's no real design there, no reality to his clothing designs or the folds in his clothes. It's all basic shapes — that's all it is. Where there's clothing, there's just one, big shape with touches of shadow. Same thing with his figures. It's so simple, it's frightening.

JA: *What did you learn from Giacometti?*
CI: He had a real raw quality about his work, which is contrasted with Degas, who was

AS *FLASH* DARTS ACROSS THE CITY, QUESTIONS AND THOUGHTS PILE UP IN HIS MIND...

IF THE STORY IS TRUE... THEN THE FUTURE IN THAT *PHOTO-SYNTH*.

SHOWED ME RUNNING ACROSS TOWN JUST LIKE THIS

...DIRECTLY TOWARD M.ODRIEX'S ESTATE

...WHERE HE WAS WAITING WITH A GUN TO SHOOT ME!

BUT *HOW* CAN I ESCAPE MY *FATE?*

(right) In the "Strange Sports Stories" features, such as this one from *The Brave and the Bold* #49 (Aug.-Sept. 1963), Carmine made extensive use of small silhoutte panels — sometimes even alternating between silhouettes and traditional panels. Inks by Joe Giella.

©1963 DC COMICS.

(below) In order to draw attention to often skipped caption boxes, Carmine used little tricks like drawing hands coming out of the boxes. He usually reserved this treatment for splash pages with lots of text. *The Flash* #145 (June 1964). Inks by Joe Giella.

FLASH ™ AND © DC COMICS.

the composition. Readers would pay more attention to them if I did." Everything I did there was for the sake of the composition.

JA: *When you penciled it, did you place the balloons?*
CI: Oh, yes. Every word balloon, I placed specifically. Balloons are part of the composition, and I would get pissed the first couple of times they screwed around with me there. I said to Julie, "I'm going to stop doing this thing if they don't follow my balloon [placement]. The shape is part of the picture." Julie got wise to what I was saying and said, "Okay, I understand that." They followed [my placements from then on].

JA: *When you roughed out the panels on a page, did you consider each panel as a separate drawing, or the whole page as one drawing, as one piece of art composed of separate drawings?*
CI: Sometimes I added panels on my own and sometimes I combined panels; I had that liberty from Julie. I was thinking, "If I was a reader, what would please me more?" The whole page was always a unit, and one panel would flow to the other. Then, of course, I did three across the top. The third one would always point towards the next one down below. I drove the reader where I wanted him to go.

JA: *When you were laying out a page, were you laying it out abstractly?*
CI: Abstractly. I laid the whole story out from beginning to end. But after I laid out the whole story, I went back and, if there were some areas I didn't like, I reinforced or changed them. Sometimes I changed whole pages or threw whole pages away if I felt that what I did wouldn't work. Once that was done, I was satisfied; then I finished them off. Some artists thought page by page, panel by panel. I didn't think that way. I thought of the page as a whole shape, one big package.

JA: *Then drawing line directionals to make the eye travel smoothly across a page was intentional.*
CI: Always. It was very important, I thought.

JA: *Around the mid-'50s, you started using more silhouettes, too.*
CI: Yeah, that was the "Strange Sports" stuff; that was done purposely.

JA: *Yes, but you were doing it before that.*
CI: To a degree, but not like that. That was special with the sports stories.

JA: *What led you to drawing more silhouettes?*

CI: It's a different approach to a drawing. I always tried to get a different approach. Every issue, I tried something different.

JA: *Your backgrounds versus your foregrounds — usually the foreground is what the viewer sees first unless you design otherwise.*

CI: If I wanted the reader to look into the background first, I'd use a very simple shape in the foreground. Let's say there's a guy's head; I used the most basic shape I could, and all the detail would be in the background stuff. You've got to look there first.

JA: *More often than not, your backgrounds were designed, but it was the way you spotted blacks. You saved your blacks, it seems, for the important areas.*

CI: I used them as sparingly as possible, especially for *The Flash*. I didn't think *The Flash* needed much black. I believe that very strongly, because large, negative spaces keep the panels wide open. It's not a *Batman* story where blacks close things in. *The Flash* was much lighter; it had much more flow. Once you get dark and heavy, you lose the kind of space I wanted the stories to take place in.

JA: *"Adam Strange" had a little more black in it.*

CI: Not much, but he was a different kind of character. The space scenes took more black. But then the other settings went to the reverse. Dark on the planet, and open on the space: I took all kinds of chances on this. But, again, it was effective, I think.

JA: *Your cityscapes were very modernistic for the time.*

CI: Yeah, that was the whole trade thing. I always wanted to be an architect, and how else could it come out of me? I couldn't afford to go to school to be an architect, so my feelings for art came out in the science fiction and the cityscapes whenever I had a chance. Even if I had a background of forest and trees, you'll notice it was very organized all the time. I liked doing those kinds of backgrounds, too. But I preferred to draw cities.

JA: *When you drew interiors, they looked more roomy than a lot of other artist's interiors.*

CI: Yes, because I'm a fan of the Baja School of Architecture. You know what that is? That was where my base idea of drawing rooms came from. They were very basic with your effects — mostly on the walls. The paintings, the bookcases, and the furniture were simple structures. My own apartment is built that way right now. [*laughs*] There's always space around a couch or at a table or around something when people walked in. I would *design* rooms, I wouldn't just *draw* a room.

JA: *Were you using any reference for this?*

CI: No. They were all my own invention. I was surprised when I heard years later that people paid attention to what I was doing.

JA: *Sometimes you drew backgrounds and cityscapes just for decorative purposes. When would you do a trade-off between decoration and functionality?*

(below) In *Mystery in Space* #72 (Dec. 1961), Adam Strange arrives on Rann 100,000 years in the future, giving Carmine an opportunity to fill the bottom of a page with a futuristic cityscape. But since Adam Strange is still the focus of the story, Carmine has him looming in the foreground, in a detailed suit and with heavy blacks. The city, meanwhile is open and sparsely detailed, leaving it firmly in the background. Inks by Murphy Anderson.

COURTESY OF HERITAGE AUCTIONS (WWW.HA.COM).

ADAM STRANGE ™ AND © DC COMICS.

THERE IS AN INSTANT OF COLDNESS AND UNCONSCIOUSNESS! THEN...

WHERE IN THE WORLD AM I? THESE PEOPLE LOOK LIKE PICTURES I'VE SEEN FORECASTING WHAT MAN WILL EVOLVE INTO -- 100,000 YEARS FROM NOW! IS THAT IT? HAVE I BEEN TELEPORTED ACROSS TIME -- TO NEW YORK OF THE FAR FUTURE?

(above) Yes, Carmine didn't just *draw* rooms, he *designed* them. And here's the proof! This sketch was done in 1961 on the back of an "Adam Strange" page for *Mystery in Space* #72. Carmine uses simple structures and lots of open space in his designs.

COURTESY OF BOB BAILEY.

© CARMINE INFANTINO.

CI: It depended on what was happening in a scene. I never disrespected a storyline. That was very important to me, because the story had to be simple and to the point — always. I got that from watching Alfred Hitchcock movies. That was his main theme. If you've read anything he said about his movies, it's that his storylines were always simple and to the point. You never destroy the storyline. Backgrounds are supposed to be backgrounds. You show them, but you don't make them the most important thing, unless there's a reason to do so. The story dictates that. That's the difference between decoration and function.

JA: *Did you ever look at your work in a mirror?*
CI: No, why would I do that?

JA: *A lot of artists, in order to check their composition, look at their art in a mirror.*
CI: No, I was very confident about what I was doing by this time.

JA: *When you were drawing scenes, say a fight scene or a war scene with lots of noise, did you hear the noises in your head when you drew?*

CI: No, I just let the fantasy take over my head for what I imagined was taking place, period.

JA: *Jack Kirby told me he heard the sound effects in his head when he drew.*
CI: Really? That's amazing. I didn't know that.

JA: *Joe Kubert said he didn't hear them either.*
CI: I'm with Joe.

JA: *Did you ever identify with the characters you drew? For instance, if the Flash was running —*
CI: No, I was not a runner. I played tennis.

JA: *But you never fantasized yourself as being any of the characters?*
CI: No, never.

JA: *Your inking was like your penciling: scratchy, more choppy, rather than a smooth flow. You knew your inks weren't considered commercial, so what led you to ink that way?*
CI: I was comfortable inking that way. I wanted a complete replica of how I penciled. I wanted my inking to be like my penciling, my drawing,

(above) Carmine didn't often get the chance to ink his own work at DC. He was, however, able to ink a dozen ten-page "Elongated Man" back-up stories, including this one from *Detective Comics* #329 (July 1964). Carmine inked primarily with a chiseled-down fountain pen. The only brushwork evident on this page can be seen in Sue Dibny's hair, where it appears Carmine applied a dry-brush technique.

BY THE TIME HIS SENSES CLEAR...

FLASH, THEY GOT AWAY! YOU TOLD US TO STAY AWAY AND GIVE YOU A FREE HAND BUT-- IT DIDN'T WORK OUT!

WHATEVER SUPER-SPEED TRICK I TRY... IS COUNTERED BY ABRA KADABRA'S MAGIC!

HERE'S SOMETHING WE FOUND IN THE HOUSE OF JADE! IT'S ADDRESSED TO YOU!

KADABRA WANTING TO GLOAT OVER ME, NO DOUBT!

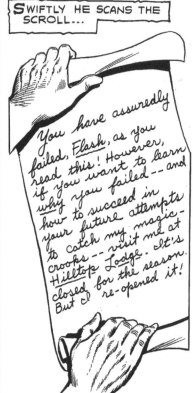

SWIFTLY HE SCANS THE SCROLL...

You have assuredly failed, Flash, as you read this! However, if you want to learn why you failed -- and how to succeed in your future attempts to catch my magic-crooks -- visit me at Hilltop Lodge. It's closed for the season. But I re-opened it!

SECONDS AFTERWARD...

DO I EVER WANT TO VISIT HIM? I CAN HARDLY WAIT! BUT-- KADABRA CERTAINLY IS MIGHTY CONFIDENT! HE'S AS GOOD AS DARING ME TO COME AND CAPTURE HIM! GOT TO BE ON THE ALERT FOR WHATEVER TRICK HE'S PREPARED--

EVEN AS HE ALERTS HIMSELF TO A TRICK, THE FLASH FINDS HIS LEGS SINKING INTO CLINGING, WET CEMENT...

SURE ENOUGH! KADABRA'S TOYING WITH ME, DELIBERATELY MAKING IT DIFFICULT FOR ME TO GET TO HIM! WELL, THE MORE HE TRIES TO KEEP ME AWAY WITH HIS TRICKS-- THE MORE DETERMINED I AM TO GET AT HIM!

CEMENT

6

to reflect my style. I took a fountain pen and chiseled it down. I sandpapered the end of the fountain pen. I wanted a flat, dead line. Then I added little spots of black here or there. It was very strong and different. It was my look. Joe Kubert had his own look, Alex Toth had his own look, and I had my own look. When somebody else inked it, it really wasn't me anymore.

JA: *A lot of pencilers don't fill in the black areas. They'll just put an "X." Did you put Xs in?*
CI: No, I shaded in the black areas with the side of the pencil. I always put the blacks in. I would never leave that to the inker. That's all part of the page design.

JA: *How much brush did you use?*
CI: Very little, just to put the blacks in. I chipped off the end of the brush, just spreading out flat blacks, really. The blacks were pretty solid. I was using a solid mass to get a line, and I thought it worked very nicely. It's pure design. That's why the inkers used to complain — Murphy Anderson and Joe Giella — that they had to fix my drawing. I was very pissed about that. But Murphy, later on, came to understand what I had been doing and has said so.

Murphy kept putting the drawing back into my work. At the beginning, they couldn't figure out what I was doing. Murphy used to complain about inking my work. Joe Giella didn't understand what I was going for. We were on a panel in San Diego a few years back, and Joe said he used to erase my pages down before he inked them. He said he was fixing my drawing. But when he inked — redrew, whatever you want to call it — he enlarged the heads of my figures and made them look like toy dolls. Dan DiDio, who was on that panel, was surprised by this, and said that he didn't think that my work needed redrawing. And it didn't. This always bothered me, because people thought I drew those big

heads on the Flash bodies. The inkers didn't understand what I was doing.

Murphy's inks gave my work a commercial look that the fans liked. But the fans also liked my own inking. Still, I have to admit that, as a team, Murphy and I were popular. We gave DC a good, solid look that turned fans on. Looking back, our work was important to the company.

JA: *But Julie was telling Joe and Murphy to make those changes to your work.*

CI: But, like a lot of artists, I wanted my work to look like *my work.* You're the same way. When you ink somebody, you keep to their style, don't you?

(above) Joe Giella's (seen here with author, Jim Amash in 2008) inked more of Carmine's work than anyone else, including this page from *The Flash* #138 (Aug. 1963).

COURTESY OF TERRY AUSTIN.
ELONGATED MAN, PIED PIPER ™ AND © DC COMICS.

(facing page) Murphy Anderson did as much penciling for DC as he did inking. Here he inked Carmine for *The Flash* #149 (Dec. 1964).

COURTESY OF HERITAGE AUCTIONS (WWW.HA.COM).
FLASH ™ AND © DC COMICS.

(right) Inker Sid Greene favored a bold, heavy line, which, while slick and appealing to the average DC reader of the time, went against what Carmine was trying to accomplish in his pencils.

COURTESY OF HERITAGE AUCTIONS (WWW.HA.COM).

ELONGATED MAN ™ AND © DC COMICS.

(below) Magic in his brush, indeed. There was a very organic quality in Frank Giacoia's inking, and he was widely held to be one of, if not the best inker in the business for many years.

FLASH ™ AND © DC COMICS.

JA: *Always.*

CI: Then you know what I'm getting at. I liked Sy Barry's inks most of the time, but not always. And I wasn't crazy about Sid Greene's inking either. He was heavy-handed on the inks.

JA: *I thought he was trying to imitate Murphy Anderson somewhat.*

CI: He was not as good as Murphy. Murphy knew more about drawing than all of the other inkers. Frank Giacoia was really good. You know why? He never lost the character of my work, and that was important to me. When Murphy got done inking me, it looked like Murphy's work. When Giella inked me, it looked like Giella's work.

JA: *Although later on, when Giacoia didn't care as much, his work got heavy-handed.*

CI: Yeah, I don't think he inked half of the work he had. He had people helping him, like Mike Esposito and Joe Giella. He'd get sloppy, because he didn't care. He'd rather watch movies than ink pages. But when he was on, he had magic in his brush.

JA: *A magician with the brush, but not with his deadlines. Which reminds me of a story I heard about you. You came into Julie's office one day with two pages of a story and you were very tired. Julie asked why, and you said, "I drew four pages last night." Julie said, "But there're only two here." You said, "Yeah. I didn't like the two pages I drew, so I tore them up and did them over." True story?*

CI: True story. I did that often. Many times, I drew a page, didn't like it, and threw it away. I was very meticulous; if I didn't like something, I had to do it over.

JA: *As far as your figure work is concerned, by this time, you quit worrying about anatomical correctness.*

CI: Oh, I didn't want it. I couldn't have cared less about it.

JA: *Why didn't normal body proportions work for you any more?*

CI: Because I couldn't get the flow I wanted. If I wanted all kinds of speed, I'd literally distort the figures. If I got the flow I wanted, I didn't give a crap, because McNulty taught me that if the flow is there, and the design is right, forget the drawing. It doesn't mean anything. Now, not everybody agrees with that, but that's the way I felt.

I was an Impressionist. If creating movement meant drawing broken feet, then I drew broken feet. I drew whatever it took to create movement, at the expense of correct drawing. And it worked for me.

JA: *I kind of think of you almost as much as an Expressionist as an Impressionist, because your lines are Expressionistic. Your ink lines are active, expressive, and dramatic.*
CI: That's what I was going for. I went against the house look.

JA: *Were you, in a sense, rebelling against the Dan Barry-type of DC house style?*
CI: Yes. I could not work that way and I *wouldn't* work that way. But I wasn't being a rebel. I just felt I had to ink my way. Of course, Julie didn't want it. I don't understand that. So I did his things the way he wanted with my penciling, and, when I got a chance to ink, I did it my way. Oh, how Julie hated it. He used to look at those pages, [*imitates Julie growling*] I could see him marking all over it, and I'd sit there and smile at him. [*chuckling*] I could be a bastard sometimes. [*Jim laughs*] Isn't that funny? "How do you like it, Julie?" [*imitates Julie growling again*]

Now, you're laughing at what I was doing. You see, I inked a story for Kanigher, "Tank Trap" [in *Star Spangled War Stories* #21]. I enjoyed that. That was a beaut, I thought. I inked other stuff, like "Pow-Wow Smith" and "Super-Chief." The other editors didn't object to my inking, but Julie did.

JA: *You've got a period here from the mid-'50s to the early '60s where you're really doing a variety of different things, not just* The Flash. *You drew war stories up until 1958, Westerns, "Detective Chimp," and "Adam Strange" came along.*
CI: When I took it over — I'm not trying to pat myself on the back — the sales jumped like crazy.

JA: *Did Adam Strange ever strike you as another version of Captain Comet?*
CI: I didn't think it was that way at all.

JA: *But you did not design the Adam Strange costume.*

(below) It's Adam Strange to the rescue in this commission pencil illustration.

COURTESY OF TERRY AUSTIN.

ADAM STRANGE ™ AND © DC COMICS.

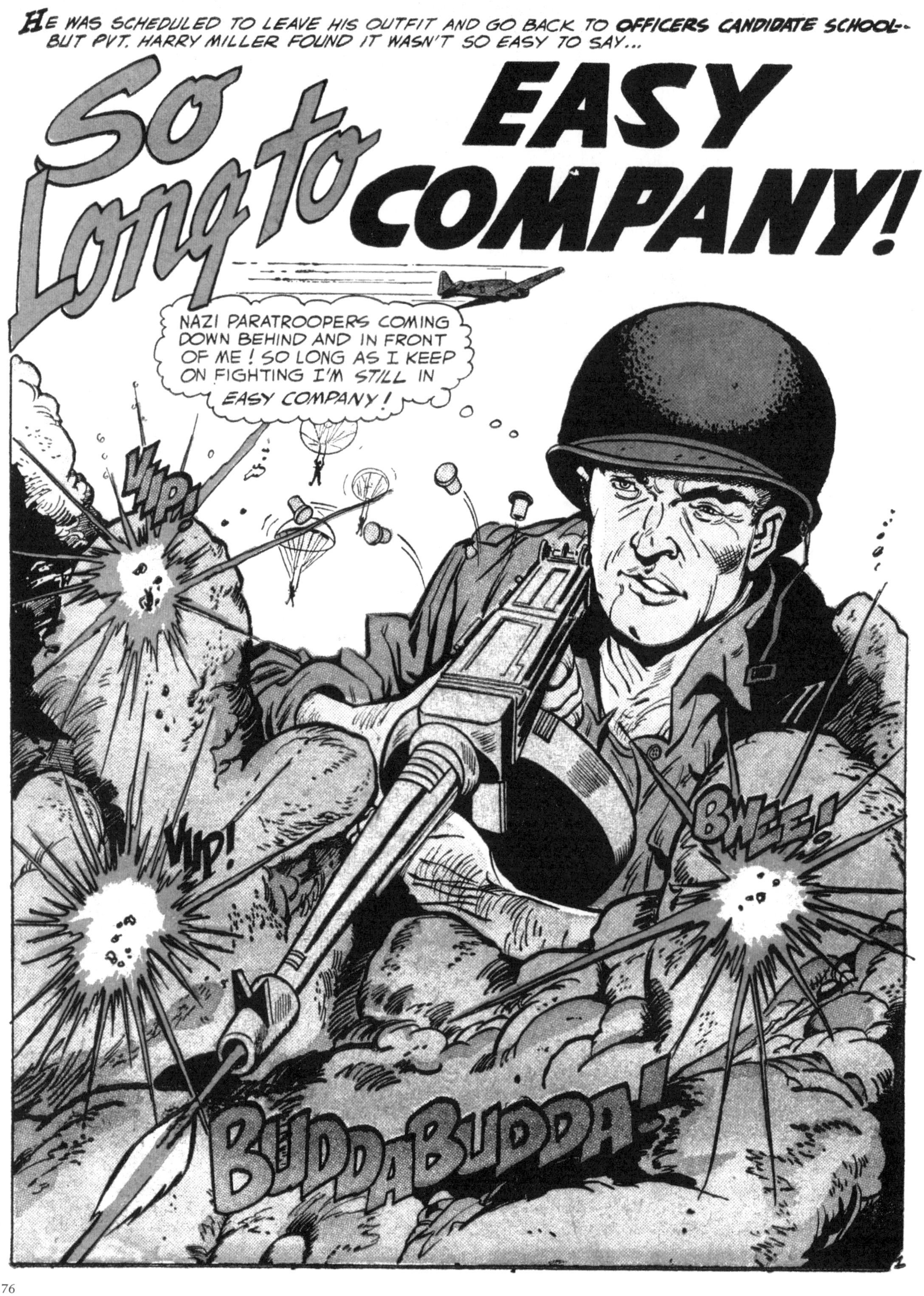
HE WAS SCHEDULED TO LEAVE HIS OUTFIT AND GO BACK TO OFFICERS CANDIDATE SCHOOL--
BUT PVT. HARRY MILLER FOUND IT WASN'T SO EASY TO SAY...
So Long to EASY COMPANY!
NAZI PARATROOPERS COMING DOWN BEHIND AND IN FRONT OF ME! SO LONG AS I KEEP ON FIGHTING I'M STILL IN EASY COMPANY!
VIIP!
VIIP!
BWEE!
BUDDA BUDDA!

(left) One of the odder strips Carmine worked on was "Super-Chief," written by Gardner Fox. This splash panel is from *All-Star Western* #119 (June-July 1961), the final issue of the title.

(right) After penciling their debut in *All-Star Western* #58, Carmine drew nearly half of the "Trigger Twins" features. More often than not he was inked by Joe Giella (or Sy Barry), but he was able to ink several of the strips himself, such as this one from *All-Star Western* #105 (Feb.-Mar. 1959).

(facing page) Carmine may not have enjoyed doing them, but he drew quite a few war stories in the mid- to late '50s. This splash page is from *Star Spangled War Stories* #64 (Dec. 1957), written by Ed Herron and inked by Robert Stuart.

(above) It takes more than clothes to make the man. Though Carmine generally preferred John Broome's writing to Gardner Fox's, in this case the opposite was true. Carmine saw Fox's "Adam Strange" as a much better strip to work on than Broome's "Captain Comet." Shown here are the covers for *Mystery in Space* #83 (May 1963), inked by Murphy Anderson, and *Strange Adventures* #10 (July 1951), inked by Bernard Sachs.

COURTESY OF JOE AND NADIA MANNARINO AND HERITAGE AUCTIONS (WWW.HA.COM).

ADAM STRANGE, CAPTAIN COMET ™ AND © DC COMICS.

CI: No, I did not. It was a bout between Murphy and Gil Kane about who designed that costume. I think Gil did it, but Murphy claims he did. I don't know who the designer was. I was on an overseas tour with the National Cartoonists Society at the time "Adam Strange" was developed. But Julie told Mike Sekowsky, who drew the *Showcase* issues, that "Adam Strange" would be my feature when it got made into a regular series. I made sure of that, because I didn't want to take a character away from anyone. I spoke to Mike, and he said, "I knew from the beginning that ['Adam Strange' would] be your feature when you got back." I didn't like the short sleeves that Gil Kane gave Adam Strange, and Julie said, "Change it if you want."

JA: *Then you didn't see much correlation between Captain Comet and Adam Strange.*
CI: Not really, no. Adam Strange was a different character altogether. It was a little more fun, actually, because the stories were better and

tightly written. He had personality, and Captain Comet did not. Of course, we did have more pages to work with, which helped.

JA: *Why were the "Adam Strange" stories so short in length, usually nine to twelve pages?*
CI: I don't know. Maybe because I was too busy with other projects to draw a whole issue of "Adam Strange" stories? Maybe because Julie liked anthology books?

JA: *By the time you drew "Adam Strange," several years had passed since the "Captain Comet" series. Your whole approach to architecture and design changed in the meantime. When you were designing Rann, where Adam Strange would go visit, what entered your thought process on designing a futuristic city?*
CI: That was it. Rann had to be a futuristic city. It was not Central City, where the Flash lived — it was a whole, different city. I did one splash — I don't know if you even remember it — I had three different layers of city where they lived on Rann. The city was built on layers. Of course, the ground was dead. It was gone. It was very interesting, the premise. The scientists of the period said, "We've got to build an area where it's pollution-free, smoke-free." So I built cities in layers, and they got smaller as they went up, and they floated above the ground, which is clever, I think. Gardner Fox didn't write it that way, by the way. He said, "Make three different walls." I

said, "How are you going to have three different walls on Rann? You can't do that. You're going to go to world, to world, to world?" So on my own, I made them layers of cities. Julie said, "Hey, it looks better." I said, "Good, because I'm not changing it." [*laughter*]

JA: *When you drew backgrounds in Westerns, it seems like you were drawing more panoramas when you drew the prairie than when you drew a city.*
CI: Well, I was influenced by the great Western movies of the time: *Shane* and *High Noon*. And of course, the John Ford movies: *She Wore a Yellow Ribbon*, *Stagecoach*, etc. I pulled away from that a little bit. I started with the Ford stuff, but that was very tightly-meshed, not as airy as George Stevens' *Shane*. Stevens was a little more open as a director. You had the feeling of space in his scenes. You always saw the prairie and the sky. Or the town and the sky. That's what I picked up on. I didn't quite get that with Ford for the most part.

Stevens believed in very strong contrasts. You'd have a long, long shot, then — boom — he'd hit you with a close-up. That's the way he worked, which was clever. Remember the great scene where the villain [Jack Palance] came into the bar in *Shane*, and you know he's a villain? All you see are his black boots standing there. The dog gets up and moves to the other side of the room. That's genius. You knew he was the villain just from that reaction. And the great scene where Elisha Cook, Jr. was shot by Jack Palance. His body went flying backwards a long way. That's movement!

JA: *Your panoramic scenes of deserts, jungles... Monument Valley, which was a favorite location of John Ford — you saved those shots for when you needed them. You didn't just put them in there.*
CI: That's the John Ford idea. I read a lot about him and studied his films like crazy. That was his method. Hit them with lots of long and medium shots, and then stun them with a bold shot.

JA: *More often than not, that's what your vertical panels did. They were your close up shots, as a contrast to your horizontal panoramic views.*
CI: Absolutely, and they worked just as you said. I tried to think that way. One of my favorite movies is *The Third Man*. The English directors really understand staging, and I was always attracted to their movies.

JA: *How often did you watch movies during the '50s and '60s?*

CI: I used to go a couple of times a week. Frank Giacoia and I used to go all the time. We worked so late at night, we'd be dog tired. We'd go to a movie, sometimes fall asleep during the thing. And then we'd have to watch it again. [*laughter*]

JA: *Who picked the movies, you or Frank?*
CI: Both of us together. We'd toss a coin. We'd see a Ford film, or a Hitchcock.

JA: *Since the Westerns were starting to fade out in the late '50s —*
CI: And the romance comics were starting to fade. It's basically *The Flash*, "Adam Strange," "Detective Chimp" — he was a back-up character and then he disappeared.

JA: *Did you think the "Super Chief" series was an attempt to save the Western genre?*
CI: In a way, but [the genre] was dying. Nobody could save it. You could see it was toward the end. Name characters from movie or television Westerns — they were dying, too.

JA: *You also drew some "Space Museum."*
CI: Yeah, those were fill-ins. I enjoyed doing it and got to ink some of the stories, too. Gardner wrote good stories there. Julie didn't wield too much of an editorial hand in those because they were short stories. I think Gardner got screwed that way. Julie squeezed him too hard. He didn't let him get a creative flow going. That's my feeling, anyway.

JA: *The Elongated Man originally appeared in a "Flash" story, but eventually got his own feature. You really liked that character.*
CI: I did. He was fun to do; I liked the stories very much. The readers must have liked him, too, because Julie got fan mail about him. He and his wife Sue were like

(below) The "Super-Chief" back-up feature blended the Western, super-hero, supernatural, and sci-fi genres like no other series. Maybe that's why it only lasted three issues. On the plus side, Carmine was able to pencil and ink all three stories, including this one — featuring a race of giant Native Americans — from *All-Star Western* #118 (Apr.-May 1961).

THEN, LEAPING ONTO THE BIG SNOW-BALL, SUPER-CHIEF RIDES IT DOWN THE MOUNTAINSIDE WITH HIS FEET JUST AS THE GIANT BEGINS THE ASCENT--

YOU HAVE NOWHERE TO RUN, BIG ONE--BECAUSE I CAN STEER THIS SNOW-BALL WITH MY FEET ALMOST AS WELL AS I CAN STEER A CANOE WITH A PADDLE!

(right) Carmine, always one to experiment with layouts, made the most of Elongated Man's abilities by often showing him use his powers in very vertical or very horizontal panels. This panel from *Detective Comics* #350 (Apr. 1966), which Carmine himself inked, stretched fully from the top of the page to the bottom — something rarely done at the time.

ELONGATED MAN ™ AND © DC COMICS.

THEY'RE HEADING FOR THEIR CAR! I CAN'T SIT *THIS ACTION* OUT--

(far right) The wide, horizontal panels that worked so well when drawing the Flash in action, worked just as well with a stretched out Elongated Man. Panel from *The Flash* #112 (Apr.-May 1960). Inks by Joe Giella.

ART COURTESY OF HERITAGE AUCTIONS

ELONGATED MAN, FLASH ™ AND © DC COMICS.

Nick and Nora Charles from the *Thin Man* series. They were a good couple.

JA: *Did Plastic Man enter your thinking here?*
CI: No, isn't that strange? It should have, but it didn't. It must have been in the back of my mind. I loved Jack Cole's work, so it had to be in my mind, maybe instinctively.

JA: *Was there any discussion about Plastic Man when you did "The Elongated Man" with Julie?*
CI: No, he never mentioned him. First of all, the Elongated Man was never meant to be an important character. When he became one, we had to figure out what to do with him. John Broome did that.

JA: *When you started drawing "The Elongated Man," this presented another series of layout challenges for you. How did you adapt to the layouts on "Elongated Man," because you've got a guy that stretches? That's a different visual than a guy who runs.*
CI: That's right. Here's a guy who's like a rubber band, so your panels had to work the same way. Horizontal panels worked well here, but I did it for a different reason than I did on *The Flash*.

JA: *Did it take more time to draw the "Elongated Man" stories, because it required a different kind of thinking for you?*
CI: Yes. Look at the panels I used in the stories. They had to encompass that long stretching — vertically and horizontally. The panel shapes had to reflect that. It was a challenge, but I was ready for it. It was hard work, but fun.

JA: *By 1960, you seemed more secure about the business, because you're doing a lot of features. What changed your feelings?*

BUT JUST BEFORE THE *WORLD'S FASTEST HUMA*

GOT IT!

BUT AS HIS FOOT HITS A LOOSE STONE IN THE RIVER...

OHH! THE WATER'S RIGHT BEHIND ME AND--I'VE TWISTED MY ANKLE! IT'LL CATCH ME-- BANG ME AGAINST THE CLIFF WALL-- BEFORE I CAN RECOVER!

CI: When Irwin Donenfeld came into Julie's office and asked, "Who did those covers?" Julie said, "Carmine." That's how I knew my work was selling. And with Julie giving me all the work I could handle, I knew how he felt, too, even if he wasn't going to tell me. [*laughs*]

JA: *When you originally drew Kid Flash, you gave him a cut-down version of the Barry Allen suit.*
CI: Well, the script called for that, but I eventually created a new costume. I was tired of drawing a miniature Flash. I said, "Julie, it's stupid. We're living in a different period." He says, "What do you mean?" I said, "You can't draw the same costume small. It doesn't work. It doesn't look right. It's too confusing to the readers." So he said, "What do you want to do?" I said, "I'll come in with a [new costume]. I want to try it." He said, "All right, give it a shot," and I did. He liked it.

JA: *What do you remember about your thought process when redesigning the new Kid Flash costume?*

REACH THE ANIMAL...

CI: I had to incorporate the same things as I had on the old suit, but differently. It was just another version of my Flash costume, but with a twist.

JA: *Did you suggest the colors or did someone else do that?*
CI: I suggested reversing the color scheme. But Jack Adler in production did the actual coloring. He was good.

JA: *I think that red works better than blue for super speed, don't you?*
CI: Oh, yes. Absolutely. Then I did the reversal on the Kid Flash, with yellow being the dominant color. He had to look differently than the Flash. Now remember, I could submit the idea, but they didn't have to listen to me. [Artists] didn't have that much influence, but I was lucky they listened to me.

JA: *Did you color-design the villains?*
CI: No, no, I just created them.

JA: *What made you decide to color-design Kid Flash?*
CI: I felt it was very important. And then the villains, I couldn't do it. I had too much work to do. It was more important that I design them. Once they were designed, I said, "Color them any way you want to." At times I did suggest colors to them. I'd put a little notice, "I'd like him blue, I'd like this red, this guy green," but that's about all. Whether they'd listen to me or not was something else.

JA: *Did you have a favorite Flash villain?*
CI: Captain Boomerang. He was a real nut. He was in love with Iris. He loved Barry's girlfriend. [*chuckles*] I used to tell Julie, "Make him a little more involved there, Julie."

JA: *What did you think when Barry Allen married Iris?*

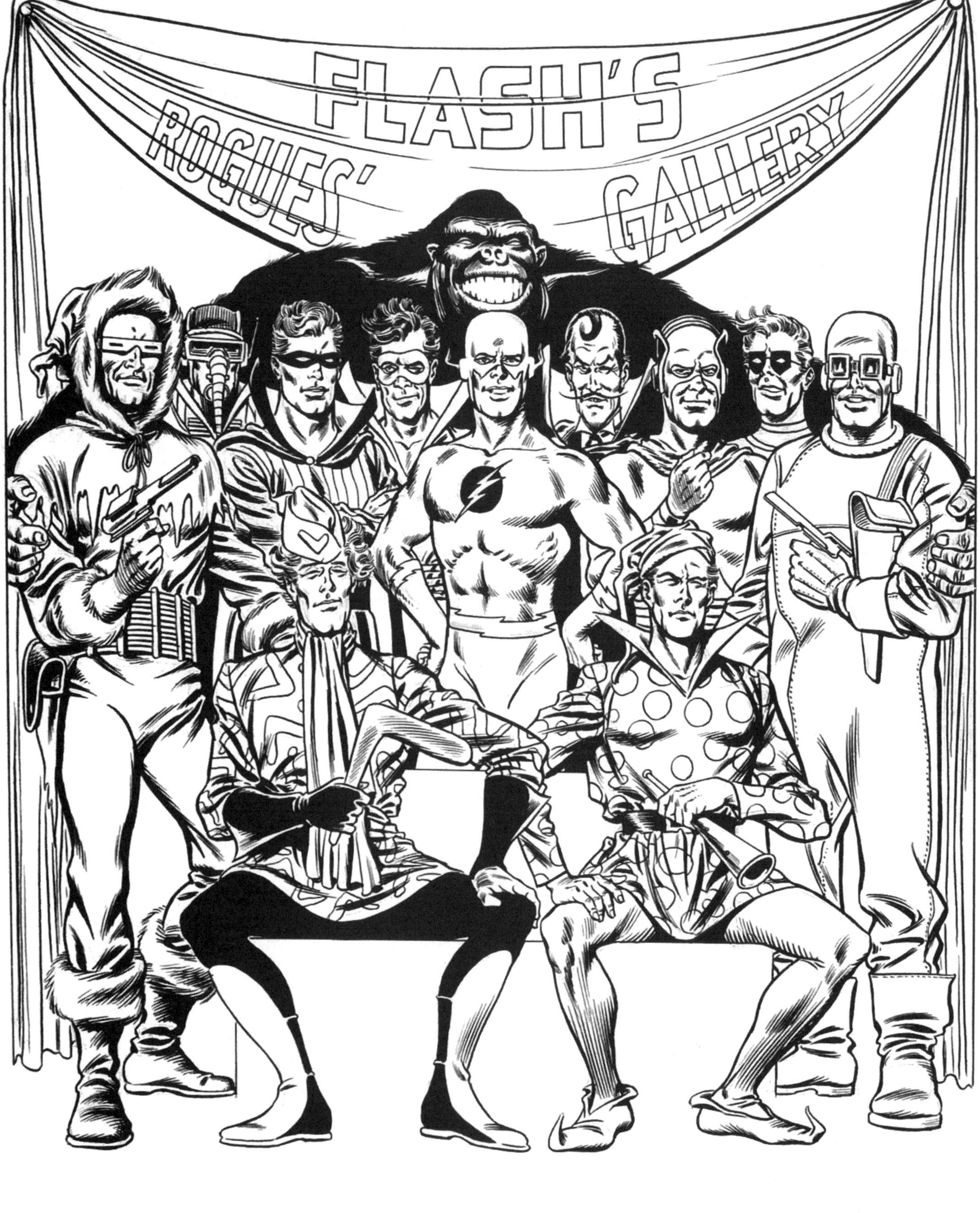
FLASH'S
ROGUES' GALLERY

WITH ALL PRESENT IN ENTHUSIASTIC AGREEMENT, PLANS ARE SWIFTLY LAID...

EACH OF US, IT SEEMS, TOOK CARE TO HIDE A SPARE *SPECIAL WEAPON* -- IN CASE WE WERE CAPTURED! SUPPOSE WE RETRIEVE OUR WEAPONS NOW FROM THEIR SECRET CACHES -- AND MEET BACK HERE IN ONE HOUR TO PLOT THE CAPER!

BRAVELY *THE FLASH* EATS HIS UNAPPETIZING MEAL...

THE CURE IS ALMOST WORSE THAN THE SICKNESS!

They walked different, they acted different, so I gave them different movements, different hand gestures.

What I thought was funny was Broome's idea to have the villains all shop with the same tailor. Julie got the name of the tailor from a fan named Paul Gambaccini, who wrote fan letters to Julie's books.

JA: *What were your feelings when you're drawing the stories, since you designed the characters?*
CI: They were my people. I gave them personalities of my own. Not my personality, but different personalities. Each one had a different personality. I based them on the kinds of people that I had met, though they weren't specifically based on real people.

JA: *Nobody ever drew a more disgusted look on their face, or a better sneer, than you did.*
CI: If they're evil, they've got to be evil, and you've got to go all the way with it. Make them look unhappy or vicious... convince the readers that these are not nice people. Evil was evil, and I had that in mind when I drew these characters.

JA: *Did you feel like you were drawing silent movies?*
CI: In a way, but I was thinking more along the lines of movie serials. I always tried to make things clear and obvious to the reader.

CI: It wasn't a good idea. I think that once the hero marries the sweetheart, you usually kill something in the character. You think of a married guy as a settled-down nobody and super-heroes are not that way. He's a fantasy character. That's my feeling, anyway.

JA: *Do you feel like once you've got a set pattern, that you should stay in the pattern?*
CI: I believe that, because the hero and the heroine should always be at odds. There should be sexual tension all the time, constantly. If you don't believe that, then I'm hanging up this phone. [*uproarious laughter*]

JA: *The posing and animation of your villains were different than the movements of your super-heroes.*
CI: Well, they had to be. They reflected something else. The Flash was sleek and moving. These guys were evil, so you hunched them a little bit, you slowed them down in their movements.

(above) Nothing gives a character more personality on the page than the gestures and facial expressions the artist chooses to give them. In the panel from *The Flash* #155 (Sept. 1965), you can feel the intensity in Mirror Master's eyes as he plots the Flash's demise. And you can almost taste how bad Flash's aged oats must be, in this panel from *The Flash* #146 (Aug. 1964).

FLASH, MIRROR MASTER ™ AND © DC COMICS.

(facing page) This pin-up of the Flash's Rogues' Gallery appeared in *DC 80-Page Giant* #4. All of these nasties were created by John Broome and Carmine.

ART COURTESY OF JOE AND NADIA MANNARINO.

ALL CHARACTERS ™ AND © DC COMICS.

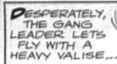

DESPERATELY, THE GANG LEADER LETS FLY WITH A HEAVY VALISE...

I NEVER WENT THERE--ALTHOUGH I WANTED *YOU* TO THINK SO! THAT'S WHY I MADE THAT PHONE CALL --FIGURING YOU'D LISTEN IN AND MAKE FOR YOUR HIDDEN LOOT--!

I KNEW YOU WERE THE GUILTY MAN BECAUSE YOU WERE THE *ONLY* ONE WHO KNEW I WAS COMING, WHO POSSESSED THE OPPORTUNITY AND ABILITY TO GIMMICK UP OUR ROOM SO SUE COULD WORK HER WITCHCRAFT! *KNOWING* IT--AND *PROVING* IT WAS A DIFFERENT MATTER--!

THE HOTEL OWNER GRIPS A WOODEN PANEL--YANKS AND FREES AN INSECT-SPRAY GUN FROM ITS SECRET NICHE...

SO YOU EXPECTED ME TO PANIC-- GATHER TOGETHER MY LOOT--AND MAKE A BREAK FOR IT! NEAT--AND I FELL FOR IT! BUT I'M NEVER CAUGHT SHORT-HANDED--AS THIS SPECIAL GUN I HID HERE FOR EMERGENCIES WILL PROVE!

YOUR STRETCHING POWERS WON'T DO YOU ANY GOOD NOW! YOU CAN'T CAPTURE WHAT YOU CAN'T SEE!

EYES SMARTING--UNABLE TO SEE--THE *DUCTILE DETECTIVE* DOES THE ONLY THING HE CAN! HE FILLS THE ROOM WITH HIMSELF, LEGS AND ARMS EXTENDED EVERY WHICH WAY TO FORM A MAZE THROUGH WHICH GREGORY HUNT CANNOT GO WITHOUT TOUCHING HIM!...

JUST AS SOON AS YOU TOUCH ME IN TRYING TO MAKE A BREAK FOR THE DOOR--I'LL KNOW WHERE YOU ARE AND SURROUND YOU!

CAN'T STAY HERE ALL DAY! I GOT TO TAKE MY CHANCES!

JA: *Your approach to folds becomes more dynamic, and your lines are more sweeping than they were before.*
CI: But I was simplifying my shapes, too. If you look at the inking, it was getting very simple.

JA: *But when you drew people in suits, or the Elongated Man's gloves before you changed the costume —*
CI: A lot of wrinkles all over the place. Yeah, I stopped that, but it was a good contrast to the rest of his costume. Again, it was a design element.

JA: *Why did you change the Elongated Man's costume?*
CI: Because I didn't like the first one I designed. I asked Julie if I could change the costume, and he said I could. The old one had that drab purple color, and purple was never one of my favorite colors. As [an antagonist], which the Elongated Man originally was, the costume was okay. But now that he was a hero and had his own feature series, I thought it was time to brighten up the Elongated Man. We kept him in that old costume too long.

JA: *When you drew the Golden Age Flash in the 1960s, you changed him just a little.*
CI: Yes, because he was older now. He had a little more weight on his body, and I made his hair grey at the temples. If you notice, I also tilted the angle of his helmet, like he had a little more bravado.

JA: *Now let's get to Batman.*
CI: I was working on a job at home when I got a call from Julie. "The boss [Irwin Donenfeld] wants to see us. Come in." I said, "Well, I'll finish this story up. I'll be in next Tuesday." He hung up. Julie calls me back. "No, he wants you in tomorrow." Okay, he wanted me to come in, so I came in about eleven o'clock. We went in and we sat down, and Irwin was very direct. It was very simple: the Batman was dying. "It's crap," he said. "You two guys, either you save it or we drop it. You've got six months to change things." I got hit with a panic feeling. That's a hard thing to have thrown at you. I didn't say anything. Julie didn't say very much either. We just sat there and said we'd get it done, "Okay, that's it, fellas." Simple as that.

JA: *This necessitates several changes. For one, Julie and Jack Schiff exchanged books. You were taken off* Mystery in Space, *because you were put on* Detective. *You traded "Adam Strange" for "Batman."*
CI: I didn't trade anything. They just took me off the book. I had no choice in the matter. I wasn't happy about it.

JA: *You liked "Adam Strange," didn't you?*
CI: Yes. I heard it died under Schiff.

JA: *They put Lee Elias on the strip, and it just wasn't the same. The writing was not that great, either.*

(above) Ralph admires his new costume in this panel from *Detective Comics* #351. The plot of this story actually revolves around his old costume falling into the wrong hands. In the meantime, Carmine had to give up penciling duties on the "Adam Strange" feature when the *Detective Comics* "Batman" feature was assigned to him.

SKETCH COURTESY OF KEIF SIMON.

ADAM STRANGE, ELONGATED MAN ™ AND © DC COMICS.

(facing page) "Wrinkles all over the place," indeed! But it does make for a dynamic look. From *Detective Comics* #348's (Feb. 1966) "Elongated Man" back-up story, inked by Sid Greene.

COURTESY OF JOE AND NADIA MANNARINO.

ELONGATED MAN ™ AND © DC COMICS.

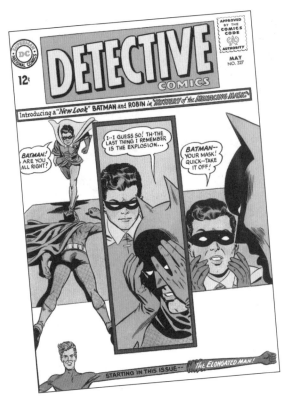

(above) The "New Look" era began with *Detective Comics* #327 (May 1964), and Carmine's cover, inked by Joe Giella, and opening splash page, also inked by Joe Giella, enticed Batman fans with the promise of something new.

BATMAN, ROBIN, ELONGATED MAN ™ AND © DC COMICS.

CI: And Lee was a wonderful artist. I don't know what happened there. He was a good artist.

JA: *What did you think Julie was thinking when he was handed the Batman books?*
CI: I don't know what he was thinking. He didn't say very much in that meeting, so we left the office. The only thing he said to me was, as I told you once, "Carmine, I want you to put a circle around the bat on his chest."

So we went back to Julie's office, and then I said, "Now what do we do?" He said, "What do you want to do with Batman?" I said, "He's very cartoon-like. I just want to bulk him up. He's not the Flash, Julie." He said, "I understand. Do what you want with him, except the add the circle on the chest." I said, "And I want to put the guns back on." Julie said, "No guns."

JA: *Why did you want to do that?*
CI: I thought they looked good on him. It would have been different, but Julie didn't like it.

He didn't want to have problems with the Comics Code.

JA: *However, in one of the very first stories, Batman does hold a gun on the villains. Somebody forgot.*
CI: Somebody forgot. Was it me?

JA: *You drew that one.*
CI: I did? I hope we got away with that. Was that the writer's idea or mine? I can't say now.

JA: *Did Julie want you to do a concept sketch of your version of Batman?*
CI: No, he just said, "Come up with some cover ideas." He said, "Carmine, you know our necks are on the line here." I said, "I know, I know." I said, "Julie, I've got to finish the other job I'm doing." I think it was "Adam Strange." He said, "Well, finish that up, and let's get started on this." When the time came for me to draw our first issue of *Detective*, I drew a three-panel cover. Julie liked it right away.

JA: *What gave you the idea for that?*
CI: I wanted something stark and different. DC had never done it on a Batman book before then.

JA: *You used more vertical panels in "Batman" than you did in* The Flash.
CI: Yes, because Batman was a dark and heavy, brooding kind of character. He needed a very conservative look.

JA: *I thought maybe it was because of the fact that "Batman" doesn't lend itself to horizontal panels as well as* The Flash *or "Elongated Man."*

CI: I think I used some eventually, but not as many, no.

JA: *So that was intentional restraint on your part?*

CI: Definitely. That's why I wasn't comfortable with the character. I really was not that comfortable with him. I never enjoyed doing it, to be honest. But then I started having fun with some of the covers. Gee, some of the wild covers I did! That's where the fun in drawing "Batman" was for me.

JA: *You made Robin slightly older than he had been.*

CI: I did that purposely, because you can't have a teenage kid like that fighting crime. He oughta be at least 15, 16. Twelve-year old kids — that's not Robin. He's got to think like a grown-up. So I purposely did that. Julie understood that. He had to deal with Bob Kane drawing the other stories... well, actually it was Shelly Moldoff who drew them. But Kane tried to keep it a secret. Whenever he had a change to make, Kane said, "I'll bring them in tomorrow."

JA: *Because he wasn't drawing it.*

CI: Of course. Kane hated my covers, by the way. Oh, he hated my drawing. Julie wanted him to try to make his drawing look closer to mine, but Kane or Moldoff couldn't do it. Kane went to Jack Liebowitz and said, "This guy's ruining my character." And Liebowitz was nice. He said, "I don't think it's your character, Bob." [chuckles]

JA: *But Kane did have some ownership.*

CI: He did, but he had none when he re-signed his contract [in 1968]. He was finished. But in the old contract, he had the right to do so many pages. The contract said he got paid for so many pages, and that was my way of getting rid of him eventually, by the way. DC paid him a lot of money to go away, and I got better artists to draw *Batman* once Kane was no longer under contract.

JA: *Did you ever have a personal conversation with Kane about this?*

CI: Did I talk to him? Not too much, no, except that time we sat there in Liebowitz's office. Kane was screaming that we were ruining his character. And Jack looked at me and winked. I knew what

that wink meant. "Don't say a word." I sat there, I didn't say a word.

JA: *How did Julie react to this pressure?*

CI: Julie wasn't in there.

JA: *But I'm sure Kane must have complained to Julie.*

CI: Oh, I'm sure Julie laughed at him. He just ignored him. Then, at one point, I think Julie told him, "You know we're saving your ass." He didn't like Bob Kane.

JA: *Julie told me that Bob Kane was angry that his name was taken off the stories that you drew, because his name was always on the stories, no matter who really drew them.*

CI: Is that true? I didn't even realize his name was taken off. Maybe Julie did that. I had nothing to do with that. That had to be Julie's idea.

(left) Batman co-creator Bob Kane was a much better businessman than most of his peers (including fellow Batman co-creator Bill Finger), and though his contract was changed in 1968, he continued to receive money for the character until his death in 1998.

COURTESY OF *ALTER EGO* MAGAZINE.

(below) With the "Batman" feature, Carmine went back to a more traditional page layout, often going with six vertical panels on a page.

COURTESY OF HERITAGE AUCTIONS (WWW.HA.COM).

BATMAN ™ AND © DC COMICS.

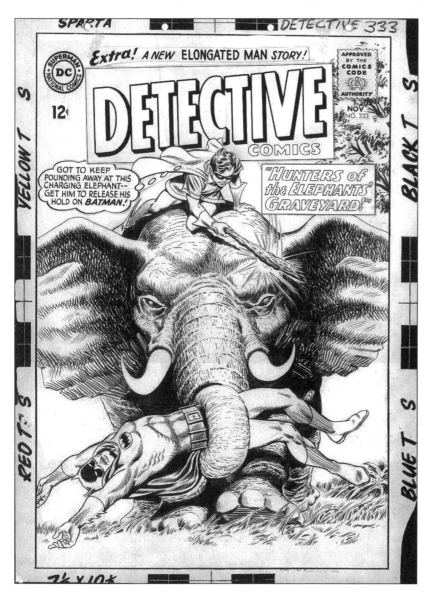

SPARTA   DETECTIVE 333

Extra! A NEW ELONGATED MAN STORY!

SUPERMAN DC NATIONAL COMICS

APPROVED BY THE COMICS CODE AUTHORITY

DETECTIVE COMICS

12¢

NOV. NO. 333

YELLOW T S

RED T S

BLACK T S

BLUE T S

GOT TO KEEP POUNDING AWAY AT THIS CHARGING ELEPHANT-- GET HIM TO RELEASE HIS HOLD ON *BATMAN!*

"HUNTERS of the ELEPHANTS' GRAVEYARD!"

7½ X 10¾

(above) Wild covers, indeed! The Batman and Robin figures in this cover to *Detective Comics* #333 (Nov. 1964) were inked by Murphy Anderson, while the rest of the art was inked by Joe Giella.

COURTESY OF JOE AND NADIA MANNARINO.

BATMAN, ROBIN ™ AND © DC COMICS.

(facing page) Carmine aged up Batman's ward and sidekick, Robin. This page is from *Detective Comics* #367 (Sept. 1967), inked by Sid Greene.

COURTESY OF HERITAGE AUCTIONS (WWW.HA.COM).

BATMAN, ROBIN ™ AND © DC COMICS.

JA: *What was the talk in the office like about the new Batman?*
CI: Nothing, I didn't speak to anybody. I just went home, drew the stories, brought them in. Nobody said anything, no complaints. If there were, I didn't know about it. The only thing we were waiting for was getting the first sales numbers. That, Julie and I were concerned with. And the first numbers, I think when they came in the Batman books were selling about 32%. It was so bad. Batman was losing a lot of money for DC. The first issue, I think, went up about eight, nine points on *Detective* right away, and *Batman* went up, but not as significantly. Julie said to Donenfeld, "You know, Carmine's drawing [*Detective*]. *Detective's* going to go up, but not *Batman*." Donenfeld said, "I know that, but we're stuck with Kane." So he said we'd continue this way, and as long as sales were rising, we were in good shape. So we kept going, and then I asked for more money. [chuckles]

JA: *Did you get a raise?*
CI: Very small, a couple of bucks a page. But then I was already up to the top rate.

JA: *So Irwin Donenfeld and Jack Liebowitz didn't say anything.*
CI: No, nothing. But we would have heard if it didn't sell. Then [television producer William] Dozier saw one of my covers on the newsstand in the airport, I heard, and then he called to make a deal with DC to do the TV show.

JA: *Do you have any idea how Jack Schiff felt about being replaced?*
CI: Very unhappy, very unhappy.

JA: *Did he ever talk to you about it?*
CI: No.

JA: *Obviously, that's the beginning of the end of Jack Schiff at the company. And he leaves about the time you become in charge.*
CI: Yes, before that, I believe.

JA: *I think he left around '67.*
CI: I did not fire him.

JA: *I heard he retired.*
CI: That, he did, but I had nothing to do with that. If you are implying that he was pushed out, well, I just don't know one way or another.

JA: *Do you think he retired because he saw how things were changing?*
CI: He may have, I don't know. I think Jack could have been rehabilitated, I do believe, if I had a chance with him. Of course, I think Jack had lost his confidence altogether there. You know, when they take the main thing away from you that way… it's a tough thing. But I had nothing to do with his retiring or being removed. I liked him, by the way. He was a nice man. I did some work for him.

JA: *Batman certainly suffered by the end of Schiff's tenure.*
CI: The book was dying. You know what he was doing? He was doing bad imitations of Mort Weisinger's *Superman*. Whatever Mort did, Schiff would copy, and that's not a good way to approach it. It was obvious. Mort would have Supergirl and Mxyzptlk, he'd have Batgirl and Bat-Mite, and so on.

JA: *Schiff claimed he was told to do that, but I find that hard to believe.*

IT IS EARLY MORNING IN THE MANSION OF MILLIONAIRE BRUCE WAYNE. THROUGH A SHATTERING WINDOW COMES A RUBY...

KRAASH!

RUBY

IN AN UPSTAIRS BEDROOM, DICK (ROBIN) GRAYSON BELTS HIS DRESSING GOWN AND SHOUTS...

BRUCE!
ALFRED!
WHAT'S WRONG?
WHO BROKE WHAT DOWNSTAIRS?

MOMENTS AFTERWARD, IN THE LIVING ROOM...

ALFRED, LOOK!

THAT'S THE RAJAH RUBY LEFT TO BRUCE BY HIS FATHER!

BUT HOW'D IT GET OUT OF THE WALL SAFE WHERE BRUCE ALWAYS KEEPS IT?

AND--

WHO FLUNG IT THROUGH THE WINDOW, MASTER DICK?

GOOD GOSH!

I WONDER IF THIS IS PART OF THE ROUND-ROBIN DEATHS BATMAN AND I WERE WORKING ON LAST NIGHT?*

SOME UNKNOWN KILLER SENT BRUCE AN "IN-FLAMMABLE" LETTER DIRECTING HIM TO TELL POLICE COMMISSIONER GORDON TO TURN ON THE RADIO...

"HAD HE DONE SO, THE COMMISSIONER WOULD HAVE BEEN DEAD WITHIN AN HOUR! BUT LUCKILY I MANAGED TO RESTORE AND READ THE CHARRED LETTER--AND APPEARED IN TIME TO SAVE THE COMMISSIONER'S LIFE..."

SORRY ABOUT THIS-- COMMISSIONER--

BUT IT'S FOR YOUR OWN GOOD--

I THINK!

KA-RASH

* THE DETAILS OF WHICH WERE RE-VEALED IN LAST MONTH'S ISSUE-- AND SUMMARIZED FORTHWITH...

PG 7-- LAST ISSUE

2

CI: I don't buy that either. That was his own thing. The editors had carte blanche. No, I don't buy that at all. He was copying Mort, this I know.

JA: *Schiff was doing comics for eight-year-olds.*
CI: He probably was. [*laughs*] We went for the teenagers.

JA: *Briefly, you drew the* Batman *newspaper strip in the '60s.*
CI: Yes. I thought it was a badly written strip.

JA: *Did Whit Ellsworth write it from the beginning?*
CI: I don't know who wrote those. I've got to be honest. The strip was confining... only three panels a day. I couldn't do much with it. A newspaper strip is very different than a comic book. I used to want to do a strip, and once I had the chance I couldn't even do them.

JA: *Considering how your work had changed, you were suddenly not suited for a daily strip.*
CI: That's right, although you've seen *Hometown*, which I couldn't sell as a strip. And you saw the style I used there. That was so different, very radical. But the chance never really came for me in strips.

JA: *Did the* Batman *strip pay very well?*
CI: No, I got page rates for what I did. Even when I did the licensing work, I just got a page rate, and you know how they use that stuff all over the place.

JA: *You're talking about that great Batman and Robin on the rooftop drawing.*
CI: I got $30 for that. Could you imagine? And you think they would say, "Here's another $30." No, forget it. They even made a big poster of that image that hung in the office. I got pissed off altogether then. That was Jay Emmett, by the way, Jack Liebowitz's nephew. Emmett owned Licensing Corporation of America. I wasn't particularly fond of Emmett.

JA: *So you're drawing "Batman," and you're still drawing* The Flash. *That's keeping you pretty busy.*
CI: And I wanted to keep drawing "Detective Chimp." That got away from me. That was hard to take.

JA: *You were also drawing "The Elongated Man" up until around '67.*
CI: Then they took that way from me, too. They wanted me to do the advertising, all their promotional art. Irwin Donenfeld was very involved there with me, and I had to draw this and I had to draw that.

JA: *How did your relationship with Donenfeld build? He didn't have a relationship with every artist. Why you?*
CI: I don't know how. He liked my covers, by the way. It was his idea to make me the cover artist. Irwin went in to see Liebowitz and said the books weren't doing well. Stan Lee was kicking the stuffing out of them. Of course, my books were selling: *Detective* and *The Flash*. He said to Liebowitz, "Listen, I want this guy for the cover artist." That was when Stan Lee made me an offer of, I think, $3,000 more than DC was paying. I was making $20,000 a year at DC then. I was going to take Stan's offer.

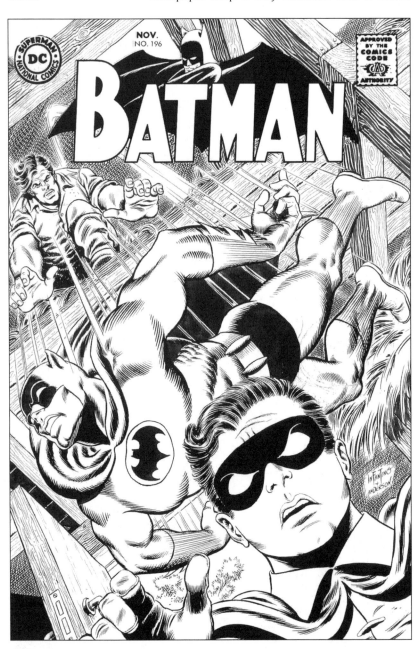

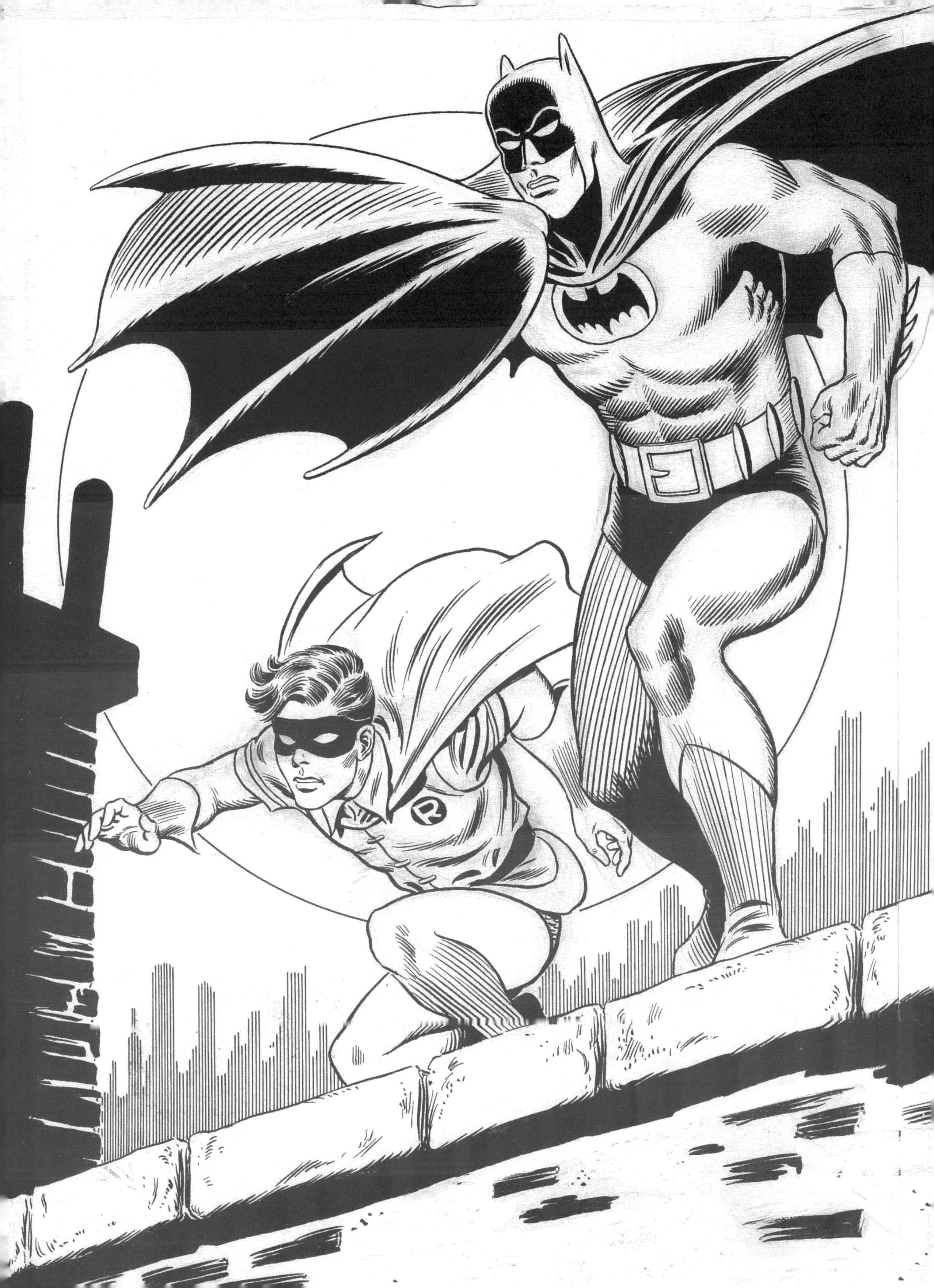

JA: *Who did you tell that you were leaving?*
CI: I told Julie, and he said, "You're going to finish the strip you're doing." I said, "Oh, sure. I'll finish that, but I'm not coming back." He had to come to my house and pick it up. He and Murphy came, I believe. I'm pretty sure they came over and picked up the story. Then I got a call from Liebowitz. He wanted to take me out to lunch with him.

JA: *Do you think Julie told him you were leaving?*
CI: I think it was Irwin. Irwin, I heard, went into him and said, "We're losing Carmine." Irwin was very fond of my work. He told Liebowitz, "I think he's an important cog to our business." This is what I heard he'd said, and apparently, he talked to Jack after talking to me. Then I got a

call from his secretary, "Mr. Liebowitz would like to meet you for lunch." I said "Okay," so I met him at this French restaurant I used to have lunch at, and we just talked in general and on and on about everything and nothing. Then at the end before he paid his check, he said, "You know, Carmine, I like you a lot. But I never thought you were afraid of a challenge." Oh, that hit me between the eyes. I said, "I'll be in tomorrow."

JA: *How did Irwin find out you were leaving?*
CI: Julie told him. It was buzzing all around the whole office. Everybody was upset about that, because I was a mainstay there on the covers and everything. All I was to do was to draw all the covers in the office. I couldn't draw them all, so I laid out the ones I didn't finish.

JA: *This was a staff position, so you were on salary.*
CI: Oh, yes. I had to come in every day.

JA: *How much did they pay you?*
CI: $30,000 a year.

JA: *Before we get any further into that, let's talk about "Deadman." When Arnold Drake pitched "Deadman" to Jack Miller, Miller turned it down. Arnold told me that you were sharing an office with Miller. What led to that?*
CI: I think he had invited me to come up there. I wanted to work in the office for a while, and they gave me space to work.

JA: *This is right before you become cover editor.*
CI: Yeah, I was drawing "Batman" all the while and I even said, "Irwin, I'm sick of working at home. I want to work in the office." He said, "Well, come in and share the office with Miller." So I did.

JA: *Then you were working in the office before you became the cover editor. For how long a period?*
CI: It wasn't very long at all.

JA: *Was anyone else besides Miller in that room, or was it just the two of you?*
CI: No, it was Miller, me, and his girlfriend.

JA: *Barbara Friedlander? She was an assistant editor.*
CI: Yes. It was a small room with them there. I sat in one corner. Irwin gave me that corner, and Jack was not happy with my being there, by the way, because that was his domain. But I didn't care. I did my work.

JA: *Plus, you were interfering with his love life, probably.*

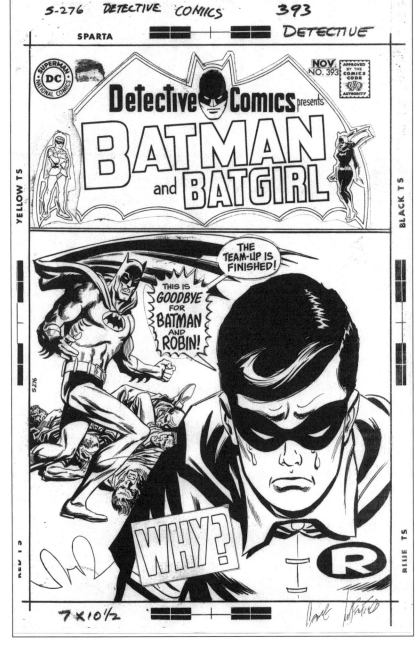

CI: Of course. He was stealing stuff all over the place — artwork and books. That's a different subject, though. I wasn't totally fond of him. He showboated a lot. He was having an affair with his assistant. He used to go have lunch with her all the time, and he'd write these stupid romance stories. He held the department in his hat, you know what I mean? But he ran out of money, because he'd taken her to lunch and dinner, lunch and dinner. He didn't make that kind of a salary, so he had to steal. Oh, you know how they found out? The guy that began the selling comics to

JA: Phil Seuling?
CI: Yes! Phil came to me and said Miller offered him the first couple editions of *Superman* from the office. He said, "Carmine, I've got a problem here." I said, "What did you do?" He said, "I bought them." I said, "You bring them right back. Whatever you paid, I'll give you." I saw the old man [Jack Liebowitz]. "Jack, we've got a

problem," and he went through the roof. "Get that S.O.B. out of here. Get him out of here now." And we had to get rid of him. I had to do it. He knew they'd caught up to him. I discovered later he was dying.

JA: *Tell the story of how "Deadman" was accepted.*
CI: Arnold Drake was pitching it, and Jack Miller didn't like it. No, he didn't say he didn't like it. He said, "We'll never get it through the Comics Code." And I said, "You've got to give it a shot. It's different." Arnold looked at me, and... you know how you put your two fingers together?

JA: *Like the high sign?*
CI: Yeah, and I winked at him. "Pursue it," in other words, and Arnold pushed them on that series. And then he said, "Look, Carmine, you'll draw it for me." You know, I looked at him. What do you say? And Jack looked at me, "You'll do this?" "If Arnold will write it," I said, "I will draw it." That was it.

(above) Boston Brand wasn't exactly the most likable guy under the big top, but this decidedly different hero made a big impact with fans. And though Carmine was only able to draw the first story, he left the series in the hands of the more than able Neal Adams. *Strange Adventures* #205 (Oct. 1967), page 3, panel 4. Written by Arnold Drake and inked by George Roussos.

(above) Carmine's cover for *Strange Adventures* #205. Whether Carmine saw "Deadman" writer Arnold Drake's sketch or not, the final product is a beauty.

DEADMAN ™ AND © DC COMICS.

JA: *Now Arnold had done a basic drawing of the cover —*
CI: He claims that. Hey, I dispute that. If he did, I didn't even look at it. I don't think he did. I didn't bother with anyone else's drawings, you know me. It didn't look like anything he would do. I don't remember seeing the sketch. If he claims he drew one, so be it. He may have suggested something and not pushed it — you know what I'm saying? Because you know what he did? He gave me the cover copy, and that made the cover. He probably said, "Here's the copy I want. What can you draw?" That is what happened.

JA: *What I want is your thought process, because you couldn't use a skull face. How did you get to the face that you used?*
CI: I think Arnold asked me about doing a skull face originally. I said, "No, a skull is not going to

look right. It's got to look somewhat human. Otherwise, you can't relate to it." I wouldn't have been able to do much in the way of facial expressions — or, at least, not the kind I had in mind. I thought of a very tight mask on someone's face, but it couldn't be the typical mask with the black thing around the eye. I wanted the thing to cover the whole head, which is what I did. The key thing was to make him look like a dead man.

JA: *Was there an inspiration for that costume?*
CI: No, I wanted it like the Flash in a way — simple, but different. Deadman had a circus background, so the costume had to be flamboyant, but uncomplicated. Miller hated it. He didn't know if the Code was going to accept it. The book was dead. *Strange Adventures* was dead.

JA: *Miller was just trying to save it at this point.*
CI: That's right. And we did, boy, I'll tell you. The sales jumped on our first issue. But I only drew that first story.

JA: *But until that point, "Deadman" was one of the best things that you had done in comics.*
CI: You felt that? I didn't know that. It was the most *different* thing I did up until that time. That's what it was. I can't say it was the best, now. The inking was not great.

JA: *I think the inking was bad, but some of your panel compositions are different from your previous work.*
CI: It had to be, because this was a different kind of series. This wasn't *The Flash*. It's a different character completely. My *Flash* art was very airy and open. That was very important for *The Flash*; but "Deadman" was dark and brooding, so I had to approach it very differently. Arnold gave me a tight script, and I took this as a challenge. I worked very hard on that story.

JA: *Did he give you stage directions?*
CI: No. That was one thing he didn't do with me. Arnold told me he did it with everybody, but he didn't do it with me. He even said to me, "Carmine, look, Deadman!" [*chuckles*] That's all he kept saying, "Deadman."

JA: *I think you're artistically stretching here.*
CI: If I'd have stayed a cartoonist, I would have stretched even more. I would have gone in so many different directions as an artist. I was going through more directions, different and strange, you know? I was feeling very different again, and when I stopped — I'd describe it like a woman

being pregnant, only I never gave birth to what I wanted.

JA: *Any idea where you might have gone?*

CI: I have no idea, but I know it was changing radically at that point. I could really feel it. I was going to do some wild concepts, and I was getting ready to do them because I got bored easily. It never happened. I probably would have stayed on "Deadman." Who knows?

JA: *In the late '60s, Arnold led the attempt to unionize the freelancers.*

CI: Arnold wanted to unionize the company, and he asked me to join. I said, "Are there any other artists involved?" He said, "No, just the writers." I said, "I don't think I can do that alone." I didn't join.

JA: *Why did you feel that way?*

CI: I felt that if it was a total group, fine. If it wasn't, I was going to be a little, single participant — you know what I'm saying? Maybe they were trying to use me to suck others in, I don't know.

JA: *Well, you were one of the most important pencilers at that company.*

CI: Right, and I had a relationship with management. I was happy with what I was doing, but I did say to them, "If you get the others, I'll come along." They couldn't get the other artists to join.

JA: *Why do you think the artists didn't want to go along? Did they have more to lose?*

CI: I suspect so. Most of those guys were worried about getting work, and they didn't know how DC or Marvel was going to react.

Jack Liebowitz pulled a beauty. When Arnold went to him about starting a union, Jack said, "I'll tell you what I'll do: You get Marvel to go along with it, and I'll join up." [*chuckling*] Meanwhile, Arnold called up Marvel, and they told him the same thing. They played with his head. I like Arnold. Don't misunderstand me, he's a good guy.

JA: *Well, Arnold was looking to get more, and he'd been with DC for a long time. You can't blame him.*

CI: No, I had no problems with him. And then he took off for Europe, and I had problems on my hands when I became part of management: writing, drawing covers, everything all at one time.

JA: *We should say here that you and Arnold were very good friends.*

(left) Boston Brand is shot and falls to his death. The narrow, vertical shape of this panel — it stretched from the top of the page fully to the bottom — intensifies the sense of dizzying height of the fall. *Strange Adventures* #205, page 9, panel 1.

DEADMAN ™ AND © DC COMICS.

(above) A 2009 photo of Batman, Arnold Drake, Carmine, and Joe Giella. Arnold Drake wrote some "Batman" stories before Carmine and Joe Giella came onto the titles, but the first "Deadman" story was one of only a handful of times he and Carmine worked together.

PHOTO BY JIM MURTAUGH. COURTESY OF KEIF SIMON.

(right) Barry Allen was the epitome of calm, cool, and collected. Maybe that's why much of fandom came to think of him as something of a boring character. But wouldn't you want to relax after running around the city at top speed all day?

FLASH ™ AND © DC COMICS.

CI: Oh, absolutely! We were then, and we remained that way.

JA: *How commercial an artist do you think you were?*
CI: I must have been commercial, because my books were selling.

JA: *But did you feel that?*
CI: No, but I was told that. I went by instinct, the whole thing. I felt what I was doing. And then when I made the big change in my work, from an artist to designer, that was a big change. Julie didn't like what was going on in the in-between part, and he was ready to fire me. He said, "I got so mad at the stuff Carmine was drawing, and all of a sudden, bang, he blossomed out." Then he was happy.

Cartoonists know that feeling of working in a room by yourself, usually late at night, no one around to talk to, so you have your fantasies. That's all you have going for you, which you put on paper. I loved working at one, two in the morning. That was my favorite time, because I just felt free at that point. You are the same way — I know how you work. The world was asleep, and I was there by myself, quiet, and everything was flowing out of me. It just wouldn't stop. I would work until three, four in the morning from noon, from one o'clock.

JA: *Usually, artists just don't suddenly change. Weren't you a little bored with* The Flash *by this time?*
CI: Yeah, I was beginning to get very bored. I was trying to get different things going. Anything to make it different. I had done all I

could have as a cartoonist, and I didn't want to be redundant. I saw a lot of other guys toiling along, and their work looked the same year after year after year. I didn't want that to happen to me.

By the way, when Barry Allen wasn't the Flash, he acted very casually. He would sit back casually, he would walk very casually, hands in his pockets... very laid back. It kept him very human when he wasn't being a super-hero. He was almost like two different people, in a way.

JA: *In regard to "Deadman," I'm thinking the change in subject matter might have been part of what re-invigorated you.*
CI: It's very possible. I was looking forward to drawing "Deadman," but I told Jack Miller, "You don't know what the hell you're going to go through to get me to do this, because the boss doesn't want me to." Donenfeld didn't really want me on "Batman" or anything else at this point. He wanted me to do covers and licensing art. I couldn't do anything without his permission, in other words. I had to insist on drawing "Deadman," and Arnold backed me a hundred percent. He wanted me, definitely, to do it.

JA: *I think it's a clear departure for you.*
CI: Yes, that's why I enjoyed it. It was another direction; it was a new beginning. The designs were different, the panels were different, you know what I'm saying? That was definitely done well.

JA: *But the only problem was George Roussos' inking.*
CI: He really messed it up. Everybody in the office said that. Jack Miller picked him. He didn't have any faith in "Deadman." Remember, I was only a penciler at that point. I wasn't even asked if I wanted to ink it. If I was asked, I would have inked it myself.

JA: *Your standing in DC was important by then. Didn't you ever feel that you could say, "I want so-and-so" to ink me?*
CI: I should have said something. I didn't. I just shut my mouth and let them do what they wanted to. I was busy on all kinds of stuff, Jim. Look, I made room for that thing. I was off doing more advertising and all the Batman crap. I didn't even look at my pages [after they were inked] any more.

JA: *But Sid Greene inked you on* The Flash, *and I know you didn't like those inks.*
CI: Right. I just didn't open my mouth, simple as that.

JA: *Were you afraid to?*
CI: No! I was busy. I was so busy, I didn't think about it. No, I assumed they'd put a good inker on ["Deadman"]. I was shocked when I saw it.

JA: *You never saw the books when they were published?*
CI: I saw the finished books, yes, and then they told me George Roussos inked it. Now George was a good inker at one time. I think George had lost interest in comics by that point. I think he crapped that out; that's my feeling. I don't think his inking was sensitive enough.

JA: *Were you seeing the finished product when you were drawing* The Flash?
CI: No, I'd see them when they were done. Julie had the final say there.

JA: *If you said to Julie, "Look, I don't want Sid Greene on this book..."*
CI: He'd say, "Go to hell. I'm the editor." And he was. I didn't fight him on that stuff. He had his favorites. He had plenty of Sid Greenes to take him out to have a pastrami sandwich. It's true. That's why he gave him the work. I know why he did it. So what're you going to do?

JA: *Of course Julie was so dogmatic in his thinking that once he had an idea, he was going to go with it.*
CI: Yeah, he wouldn't deviate. That's why I think Murphy was full of it when he said he created the first "Adam Strange" [for *Showcase*] cover, and Julie rejected it. Julie never rejected a cover in his life. I know that for certain. He would ask you to make little changes, but he never rejected a cover. I still think Gil Kane created the costume.

JA: *About "Animal Man" —*
CI: Oh, yes, I drew those, too, for Murray Boltinoff. I liked working with Murray. He was very nice.

JA: *What was the difference between him and Julie?*
CI: He was warm and soft. He was very pliable. If I said to Murray, "I'd like to —" "Go right ahead," he would say. I'd have to explain it, but he would have said, "Go ahead." He loved everything I did. He used to have Eddie Herron there, who was championing me. Eddie had a lot to do with me becoming what I became. He used to say to me every time I was ever there — like a father — he'd say, "Don't be satisfied. Never, never be satisfied. Move up, move up. Think up. Think up." When I became cover editor, he said to me, "Carmine, up, up, you've got to think 'up.'" He kept pushing me, pushing me, instinctively pushing. He had that quality. He couldn't do it for himself, but he did for me.

JA: *Why do you think he couldn't do it for himself?*

(above) Sid Greene was one of editor Julie Schwartz's favorites and it showed in the amount of work Julie gave him. This page is from *The Flash* #170 (May 1967), with inks, of course, by Sid Greene.

THERE I WAS IN THE WILDERNESS--ATTACKING A TEN-TON ELEPHANT THAT HAD GONE BERSERK! A FOOLHARDY ACTION FOR ANY MAN-- ANY *NORMAL* MAN! BUT YOU SEE, I WAS MORE THAN THAT-- I HAD SUDDENLY FOUND MYSELF GIFTED WITH INCREDIBLE ABILITIES THAT NO MORTAL MAN HAD EVER KNOWN, FOR...

I WAS THE MAN WITH ANIMAL POWERS

WHUMMP

WOW! WHAT A COMBINATION-- A *TIGER* SPRING AND A *GORILLA* SOCK TO CLOBBER THIS BERSERK ELEPHANT!

J-1396

CI: He was an alcoholic, simple as that. He'd come to my house, broke and disheveled. I had to give him whatever cash I had on me so he could eat. He did this a couple of times a month.

JA: *How did you find out that he had cancer?*
CI: I went to see him in the hospital. I was told in the DC office that he was in the Veterans Hospital House, so I went to see him. There were ten guys in a room in that Veterans Hospital, and he was lying there, one foot kind of hanging off of the bed, so I had to push the foot back onto the bed. They didn't take very good care of him. We sat, we talked. He wanted a drink. I said, "I can't bring you a drink. They won't let me." I would have given it, but they wouldn't let me. We just talked for a little while and then, "I'll come back and see you in a couple of days." He died the next day. And that broke my heart. I didn't see him again. I would have loved to. I was very close to him.

JA: *Was Eddie a talkative guy, Quietly*
CI: He was talkative at times. You see, I knew him with his first wife and son. He was talkative, but sometimes when I'd buy him a drink, he'd talk more and more. He'd talk about his whole life. You know, he was the editor-in-chief of *Stars and Stripes* newspaper. He had some famous people working for him. Charlie Knickerbocker and Andy Rooney worked for him; so did a bunch of other people.

JA: *He also was an editor for Fawcett, on "Captain Marvel."*
CI: Right, he did that, too. That's where I first met him, I think, when I went up there one time. He saw me and talked to me and took me in. He showed me Mac Raboy's work; he was very sweet to me. I was a young guy, and he treated me like a king. He was a good soul. His first wife… well, they had problems. He left her, and then he married Betty. Betty was his second wife. Once, she was named the Most Beautiful Hat Check Girl in New York City. And she was. She was gorgeous, absolutely stunning. He had a son with her, and then he started drinking. Betty left him, and he ended up with a woman I didn't like.

I think the first marriage ruined that man. That's what had happened to him. It's too bad. I just thought he was brilliant. I loved his writing;

(above) Buddy Baker, the man with animal powers, debuted in *Strange Adventures* #180 (Sept. 1965), in a tale written by Dave Wood and inked by George Roussos. It wasn't until his third appearance in issue #190 that he got his costume

COURTESY OF HERITAGE AUCTIONS (WWW.HA.COM).
ANIMAL MAN ™ AND © DC COMICS.

(facing page) Meet Buddy Baker — at this point just another strange adventurer.

COURTESY OF BOB BAILEY.
ANIMAL MAN ™ AND © DC COMICS.

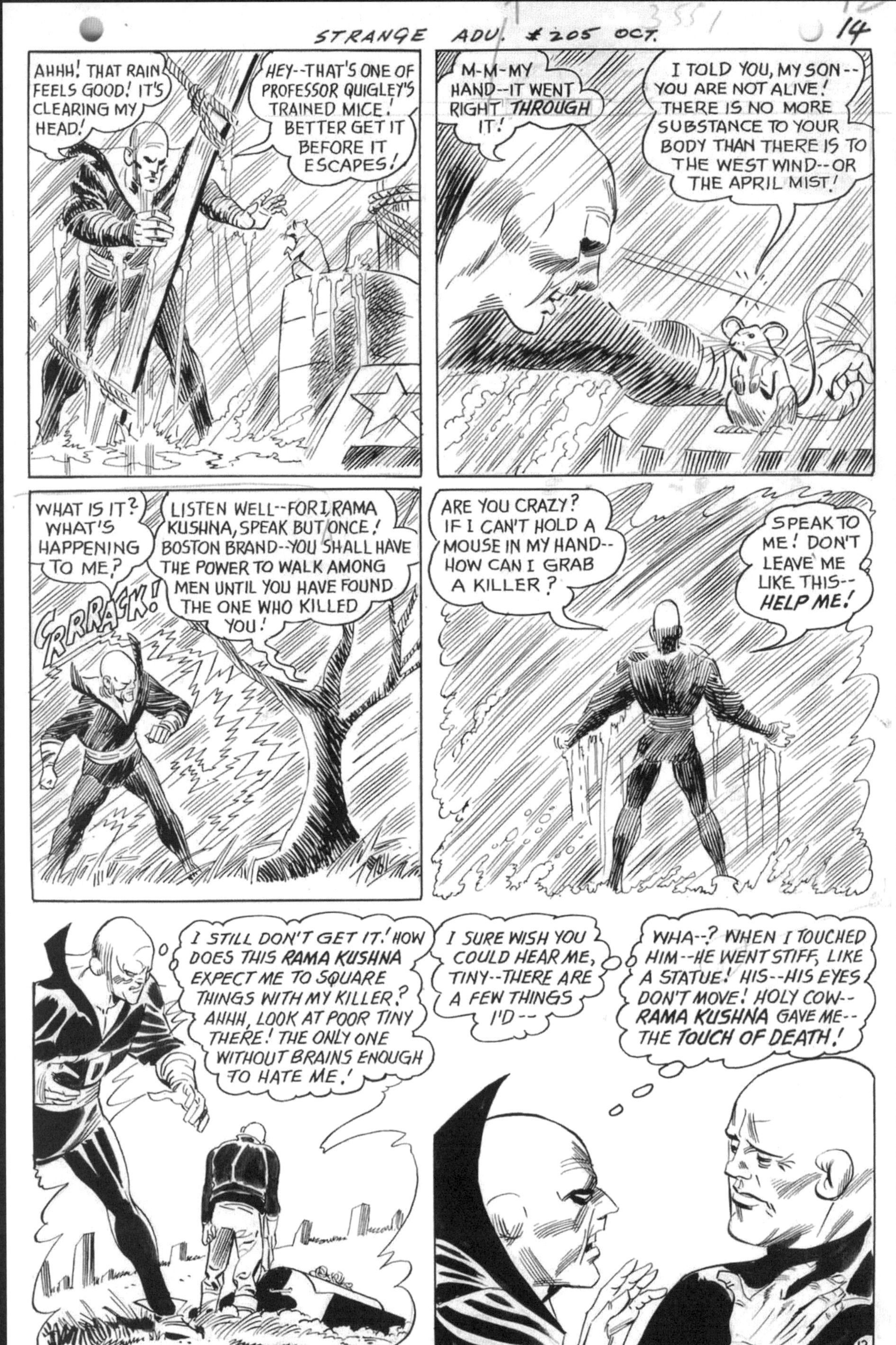
STRANGE ADV. #205 OCT.
14
AHHH! THAT RAIN FEELS GOOD! IT'S CLEARING MY HEAD!
HEY--THAT'S ONE OF PROFESSOR QUIGLEY'S TRAINED MICE! BETTER GET IT BEFORE IT ESCAPES!
M-M-MY HAND--IT WENT RIGHT THROUGH IT!
I TOLD YOU, MY SON--YOU ARE NOT ALIVE! THERE IS NO MORE SUBSTANCE TO YOUR BODY THAN THERE IS TO THE WEST WIND--OR THE APRIL MIST!
WHAT IS IT? WHAT'S HAPPENING TO ME?
LISTEN WELL--FOR I, RAMA KUSHNA, SPEAK BUT ONCE! BOSTON BRAND--YOU SHALL HAVE THE POWER TO WALK AMONG MEN UNTIL YOU HAVE FOUND THE ONE WHO KILLED YOU!
CRRRACK!
ARE YOU CRAZY? IF I CAN'T HOLD A MOUSE IN MY HAND--HOW CAN I GRAB A KILLER?
SPEAK TO ME! DON'T LEAVE ME LIKE THIS--HELP ME!
I STILL DON'T GET IT! HOW DOES THIS RAMA KUSHNA EXPECT ME TO SQUARE THINGS WITH MY KILLER? AHHH, LOOK AT POOR TINY THERE! THE ONLY ONE WITHOUT BRAINS ENOUGH TO HATE ME!
I SURE WISH YOU COULD HEAR ME, TINY--THERE ARE A FEW THINGS I'D--
WHA--? WHEN I TOUCHED HIM--HE WENT STIFF, LIKE A STATUE! HIS--HIS EYES DON'T MOVE! HOLY COW--RAMA KUSHNA GAVE ME--THE TOUCH OF DEATH!
12

anything he wanted me to do in a story, I did it. Any strip he worked on, I did them. I would do them any time, no questions asked. He's the only man I would do that for.

JA: *Dick and Dave Wood — did you know them?*
CI: They were nice guys. They worked for me at DC. They were good writers. Boltinoff, Kashdan, and Schiff used them quite a bit, and when they poured it on, they were good. But the Woods were drunk a lot, so the editors had quite a bit to deal with there. They'd disappear for days. They would hole up in a two-dollar hotel and get loaded for days on end. That's why the quality of their writing was so uneven.

JA: *When you did "Deadman" with Arnold, how well did you know him?*
CI: Not that well. I used to see him in the office all the time. We knew each other, but we weren't friendly. He was friendly with a couple of the editors, with Murray and a couple of others, like George Kashdan. He used to do a lot of writing for George. They had a very close relationship.

JA: *There's a story that when Marvel was gaining on DC in the '60s, Irwin Donenfeld held a meeting of editors and artists, and that Bob Kanigher held up a Marvel comic — I don't know whether Kirby drew it or whether Ditko drew it — and said, "The secret of Marvel's success is bad art."*
CI: If this happened, I wouldn't know about it, because I was not in editorial then.

JA: *But I understand that some freelancers were at the meeting.*
CI: I was not. If I was invited, I would have remembered that. I don't believe that there was such a meeting. I know they had meetings with just the editors, but I don't believe any freelancer was ever invited to any of those meetings.

JA: *We haven't talked about Harry Donenfeld. I know that he was deceased by the time you started moving up.*
CI: I knew very little about him. I'd heard a lot of stories about him, but I don't know what was true and what wasn't. I'd see him walking to the office once in a while, but not that often. He was away most of the time, but he seemed friendly enough.

JA: *I know you know who Herbie Siegel was.*
CI: Herbie was very nice. The story went around that he took the rap for Harry Donenfeld over the pornography stuff — or what was considered such in those days — that they were printing.

When he came out, he was allegedly promised — I use the word "allegedly" because I don't know for sure — "When you come out, I'll take care of you for life." That's what I heard.

[Ed. note: Herbie Siegel was an editor for Merwil Publishing Co., which was owned by Harry Donenfeld and published a line of racy magazines such as Spicy, Pep Stories, and La Paree. In 1934, Pep was found guilty of breaking New York obscenity laws due to one of the pictures in its March issue of that year, and, as publisher of the magazine, Harry Donenfeld faced a jail sentence. Herbie Siegel took responsibility by claiming he edited the magazine and ran the obscene material without Donenfeld"s approval. He served a brief sentence in jail.]

JA: *What did Siegel do at the office?*
CI: He used to roam the halls. He was paid so much a year and did nothing, walked back and forth, back and forth — a very boring life. He wanted to get married one time, by the way. And Harry said, "You marry her and I'll fire you," so he dropped the girl.

JA: *Why didn't Harry want Herbie to get married?*
CI: He wanted his company. He wanted constant company. Herbie was always with him. Harry wanted to get drunk with him and always have someone around to pick him up when he fell down or whatever. He was like his bodyguard, his babysitter, whatever you want to call it, okay? In fact, it was Herbie who found Harry on the floor after he had taken a fall. Herbie put him back into bed, and essentially Harry stayed there until he died.

Harry used to let him go to Florida every year for a couple of weeks, and he used to pay for it. So I'm in the hall with them and saw Herbie was very downcast. I said, "What's wrong, Herbie?" He says, "Irwin won't let me go to Florida." I said, "Well, let me talk to him. I can't promise you anything, because I have no influence." I was not the publisher yet. I told Irwin, "What the hell is the matter with you?

(facing page) Page 12 of *Strange Adventures* #205, as Boston Brand starts to realize he now truly is a dead man. Inks by George Roussos.

COURTESY OF BOB BAILEY. DEADMAN ™ AND © DC COMICS.

(above) The cover of *Pep Stories* vol. 4, #7 (July 1934), illustrated by Earle K. Bergey. Earlier that year the magazine was brought up on obscenity charges. After editor Herbie Siegel took one for the team, as it were, Donenfeld stopped doing business under the name Merwil Publishing Co. and picked up his publications right where they left off, as D.M. Publishing, Inc.

©1934 D.M. PUBLSHING, INC.

What that guy did for your father, no one would ever do for him, and no money in the world can repay him." "Well," he says, "you know what a pain he is." I said, "A pain? Your father would have been in jail." Then he said, "Well, let me think about it."

Finally, he acquiesced, and then I heard he called Herbie in and said, "You're going. When do you want to go?" "Next week." "Okay." So Irwin sends his chauffeur to pick up Herbie. He was supposed to pick him up at nine o'clock in the morning and take him to the airport. So he shows in front of the door. Herbie used to live right down the block from DC on 46th Street. And he's sitting there, waiting and waiting there, and Herbie's not showing up. So he rung the bell — no answer. He goes upstairs, knocks on the door — nothing. The door wasn't locked, so he

walked in. Herbie's sitting on the couch. He had died. Isn't that something? He had his ticket in his hand and just died.

JA: *Do you have any idea how much they paid Herbie Siegel for doing nothing?*
CI: No, it wasn't that much, though. Once in a while, Liebowitz would send him out on errands and other menial jobs.

JA: *How was it that everybody knew about Herbie Siegel? How does a story like that get around? You knew about him before you were ever in Editorial.*
CI: Oh, I'd see Herbie roaming the halls there. I asked somebody, maybe Eddie Herron, "Who is this guy? What does he do here?" Herbie didn't talk to anybody. He had an office next to Liebowitz's. But he sat there some days and slept.

JA: *Why do you think Irwin didn't want to spend the money for Herbie's vacation? Was he just being cheap?*
CI: I don't know, maybe he was getting on his nerves or something. But Herbie took care of the old man when he was sick, too. When the old man was bedridden, he fell out of bed a couple times. Herbie would pick him up and put him back in bed. Maybe he reminded Irwin of the past and he didn't want to be reminded of it. It's very possible.

JA: *Let's talk about your stint as the cover editor.*
CI: That was a challenge, because I was working for Julie and now I'm not working for Julie any more. All the editors were told I was given an office by Liebowitz — the one where the writers used to congregate. Irwin told the editors that I was laying out all the covers. It was quite a challenge, 30, 40 covers a month there. I was not the art director.

It was working out very nicely, and then one day Irwin had a big fight with management, and also Kinney Corporation had taken over the company. Jack Liebowitz sold the company all of a sudden. A couple of nights before, I was working. I see these guys coming in and out, in and out. Then one of them decides, "Carmine, go home. We're busy here." I said, "Okay." I left, and that's when they were working on the final arrangements. But there was a piece in the paper, "Kinney Buys Batman?" Bob Kane had ownership in it, and he came in with his lawyer.

JA: *When DC was sold to Kinney, what was Bob Kane's deal?*
CI: He owned a piece of the character. Then when it appeared in the newspapers that DC was selling to Kinney, Kane went in with his lawyer. He said, "I'll stop the sale," until he settled something. So Liebowitz played hardball, too. He says, "You get a million bucks, $50,000 a year for 20 years. That's it." Kane also had a contract that allowed for him to draw so many pages a month, but, as you know, it was really Shelly Moldoff who drew most of them. When Kane sold his stake in Batman, we were out from under that contract, and I got rid of him. And everybody was happy that Bob Kane was gone.

JA: *And Irv Novick started drawing* Batman.
CI: Right, Novick and Neal Adams, Bob Brown, and Jim Aparo [on *Brave and the Bold*].

JA: *And Frank Robbins. But I understand that Bob Kane still had some kind of percentage deal, even after the sale.*
CI: I never knew what that deal was, but yes, he obviously had something going. But look at poor Bill Finger. He never gave Bill a nickel.

JA: *Did you ever have a discussion with Bill about that?*
CI: Bill was very unhappy about what they did to him. But he also wrote the original Green Lantern... he created a lot of things, from supporting characters to villains and got no thanks for any of it.

JA: *But he was never in a position, or possessed the type of personality to try to do anything about it.*
CI: He couldn't! Bob Kane owned it, and they promised Bill the world. "Oh, we'll take care of

(below) Carmine laid out this cover, penciled and inked by Irv Novick, for *Batman* #210 (Mar. 1969). The published cover (done from the same layout) was drawn by Neal Adams.

COURTESY OF HERITAGE AUCTIONS (WWW.HA.COM).

BATMAN, CATWOMAN ™ AND © DC COMICS.

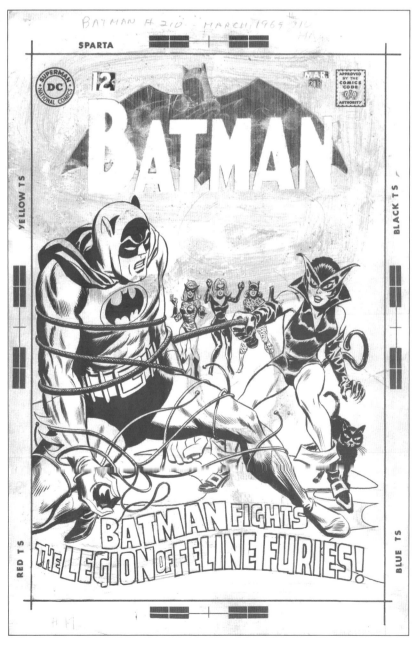

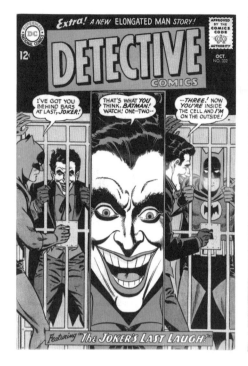  

(above) Carmine only drew the Joker in three issues of *Detective Comics*. From left to right are issues #332 (Oct. 1964), inked by Joe Giella; #341 (July 1965), inked by Joe Giella; and #365 (July 1967), inked by Murphy Anderson.

you." Took care of him! They *took* him. Bill asked to meet in the office a lot. We'd sit and talk, and he'd tell me stories about all the villains he'd created for Batman. He had an ex-wife who gave him a bit of a hard time, and their son caused him grief, too. Bill didn't have the money to pay the alimony, and he'd be in every couple of weeks to see Jack Schiff. He'd say, "Jack, my aunt just died. I need some money." "I thought you told me she died last week." [*chuckling*]

Bill was really a con man in his own way. He always needed money desperately. But he was such a talented guy, that's what bothered me the most. He shouldn't have been in this position. Bill had no self-esteem. He kept a picture of the Joker head from some Coney Island ride in his wallet, and he used to show it to me. That's why I know he created the Joker. You disagree, but that's your fault. [*laughter*] It's okay. I know my version. I don't believe Jerry Robinson created the Joker — Bill Finger did.

JA: *Yes, we disagree on that one, although I can see Finger being a co-creator. Nobody really thought — and I'm talking about the '40s, '50s, '60s period — too much about having ownership of the characters they created, did they?*
CI: No, we were happy to be working. To be working was very important. We never conceived that these things were worth anything. No one did in those days.

JA: *Basically, you had no warning that DC was sold until it was sold.*

CI: I saw it in the paper. Then Irwin had his problems with Liebowitz, I guess, and the board. Here's the story I got, because Irwin told me later that he was going to be on the board of directors. He owned a lot of stock. When they sold the company, they decided he was going to be on the junior board. That was a move designed to get rid of him. Well, they did. He got up and he left. So I went into Jack Liebowitz's office one day and asked, "Jack, who do I answer to now? Who's in charge?" He said, "You are." Pow, that was it. How do you like that one between the eyes? I was stunned. Everybody was stunned.

JA: *With that title also came a raise, I hope.*
CI: No, we never talked about a raise. How about that? I swear I was stupid. I didn't say a word. I was too stunned by the whole thing.

JA: *I think, also, you were really a devoted company man by this point, weren't you?*
CI: Right. Life takes a hold for some strange reasons and takes you where you don't expect to go. Suddenly, I was in charge of the company.

JA: *Why do you think you were chosen? They could have chosen Sol Harrison.*
CI: Oh, Sol was flipping mad. Ooh, was he sore. I know one day Marvel's Martin Goodman was up at DC visiting Jack Liebowitz, because he used to distribute Goodman's books. This was right after I became cover editor. He told Jack that he never saw the place hopping so much the way that it was that day. Somebody

told me that, not Jack. Some guy was in the room with them, one of the distributors, and he said, "Who was the new guy you got?" Liebowitz told him, "I took a chance on Carmine, because he's an artist. We need a fresh look at how we do things." But he never told me that himself. Jack was very strange that way. Straight as an arrow, but he wouldn't compliment you.

JA: *Because he was afraid a compliment might translate into wanting a raise?*
CI: No, I don't think so, because he was very generous with me. He was a fine egg, old-fashioned. He said, "It's your job. Don't bother me. I hired you for it, so do it."

JA: *How good an executive do you think Irwin was?*
CI: I think he was a better publisher than people thought he was. He had some good ideas, but Liebowitz and Howard Chamberlain didn't pay much attention to him, unfortunately.

JA: *Being the son of Harry Donenfeld didn't garner Irwin any respect?*
CI: Here's a story that I heard. One day, Liebowitz was in Irwin's office talking to people about buying the company. He said, "I've got to think about the future, because I'm going to die someday, and the company's got to keep going. I've got to put it in the right hands." So Irwin said, "Well, I'll take over." And allegedly Liebowitz said to somebody, "When I heard

that, I knew I had to sell the place." He didn't have any respect for Irwin at all.

JA: *You replaced Irwin. Why do you think they were unhappy with him?*
CI: They were not unhappy. He quit because they had promised him a bigger job in the Kinney organization [than what they gave him]. It wasn't Time-Warner then, it was Kinney and DC. When the deal was consummated, he did not get the job that he was promised. That's what he told me. He decided to quit, and he opened his boatyard up in Westport, Maine.

JA: *Why do you think he didn't get the job?*
CI: I have no idea. I heard he spoke to Steve Ross. Irwin was supposed to be on the board of directors, then he was told he was on the junior board of directors, and that rubbed him wrong. He said, "That was a nothing job." He refused to accept it and quit. He was a very good friend. We really liked each other.

JA: *What do you think were Irwin Donenfeld's strong points and weak points?*
CI: Well, he used to judge every comic by the cover. He felt that the covers sold the book, and that's true to a degree, but the insides mattered, too. That was the only disagreement we had, but I did agree about the cover part. The cover got the reader to buy the book, but the insides have to get them to buy next issue. If you don't have good stories, you're not going to keep readers.

(below) The men in charge of Independent News in an early 1960s photo. From left to right are: Herb Siegel, Harry Donenfeld, Irwin Donenfeld, Paul Sampliner, Harold Chamberlain, Jack Liebowitz, and Ben Goldberg.

COURTESY OF IRWIN DONENFELD AND *ALTER EGO* MAGAZINE.

JA: *Was it Irwin who had the idea to put the checkerboard headers at the top of the covers?*

CI: No, that was Sol Harrison's idea. It was a bad idea; it didn't look good, it hurt the cover compositions... it was just ugly. It told the readers, "Hey, don't buy this book!" I made sure we got rid of it as soon as I could.

JA: *Do you feel like anybody knew Jack Liebowitz?*

CI: No. I know there are some terrible stories going around about him not offering Siegel and Shuster much money, but that's not true. He had offered them a substantial amount of money. That was during the bad times. But Jerry said, "No." I can understand that, too. Siegel said, "I want my character. I want my character." Liebowitz said, "Let's avoid court. It's going to cost us a lot of money, and nobody's going to be happy." But Jerry insisted, so they went to court, and it cost Siegel and Shuster. They lost. They could have made big money and had security if Jerry had been willing to compromise. His lawyer probably got more money than he did.

JA: *Was this payment supposed to be a one-time payment?*

CI: No, that was a continued contract, continuous for life. So Siegel and Shuster were out of DC. You know, Shuster wasn't that great an artist, but his style had charm.

JA: *There was quite a bit of Roy Crane in that style. [Carmine agrees] Anyway... now that you were in charge, having some doubters must have made you nervous.*

CI: Yes, at the beginning only. But then I fell right into it, Jim. There was no problem at all. The editors, I think, had a problem. I called an editorial meeting and said, "Gentlemen, I'm the new editor-in-chief." There was stunned silence around the table. I said, "Now, if anybody objects, please don't hesitate to talk to Jack Liebowitz. Or if you want to leave, whatever you choose to do at this point, it's okay by me. I'm just as stunned as you are." I told them the truth. I said, "We can probably work together, or we can't. It's up to you."

JA: *Did anyone try to fight you?*

CI: No. In the beginning — when I was the cover editor — Julie was a pain about it. He didn't want to make changes, because he had his own way of working. I went along with him as long as I could, and finally I said to myself, "This is not going to work." I tried working with him at the beginning. I really tried. But we did get to the point where we each just did our jobs.

JA: *Since Julie had been your main boss, was your relationship with Julie cool for a while when you became his boss?*

CI: No, we learned to work together, and I think we worked well together. Change is hard for some people to accept, I understand that. But I still did cover sketches for him and let him choose what he wanted to use. I did that with all the editors, because I wanted them to be comfortable with the covers on their books. My relationship with Julie never changed. I'd tell him, "If you don't like the covers, say so. I'll do another one." Julie was always honest about how he felt, so finding common ground was never a problem.

If there was a problem with any editor, I'd sit down with them to find out what we could do to fix things. And we'd work things out.

(above) Even after Carmine was promoted to editorial director, he still found time to lay out covers for DC's line. Occasionally, he would actually do full pencils, as with this cover for *Action Comics* #396 (Jan. 1971), inked by Murphy Anderson.

JA: *We talked earlier about you being a loner. How does a loner, sitting at home, drawing by himself with no other artists around, go from doing that to working in the DC offices every day?*

CI: I haven't figured that one out myself. It was very difficult at the beginning. All of a sudden, I'm running things, I'm talking to people, I'm just working and pushing. And then I'm learning about the office politics. Who liked each other, who disliked whom. Jack Adler had some resentment toward Sol Harrison, because Sol often took credit for things Jack did. And when Nick Cardy asked for a raise, Irwin Donenfeld said, "Well, I was thinking about clearing out some of the dead wood around here." Both he and Sol complained about Nick Cardy's drawings. They claimed that Nick didn't put enough fish in *Aquaman*. I mean, come on. When I took over, Nick just walked in and he

(above and left) In this 1972 photo, Carmine goes over a cover — which he probably laid out — with its artist, Nick Cardy, and editor, Julie Schwartz. In case you can't make it out, the cover in question is *Superman* #254 (July 1972), penciled and inked by Cardy.

(below) Moving Neal Adams from *The Adventures of Jerry Lewis* to *The Brave & the Bold* may have been the easiest decision Carmine ever made. Carmine, was no stranger to DC's humor titles, either. He drew the cover and an interior story for *The Adventures of Bob Hope* #103 (written by Arnold Drake), as well as this cover of *The Fox and the Crow* #104.

COURTESY OF BOB BAILEY.

BATMAN, ROBIN, STANLEY & HIS MONSTER ™ AND © DC COMICS.

said, "I'm quitting." "Quitting? Why are you quitting? I just got here, Nicky." He said, "Well, this guy is bugging me." And I said, "Nobody'll bug you any more. Listen, give me a chance, will you please?" He said, "All right, I'll stay a while," and he did.

JA: *Personality-wise, you described yourself as a loner. Would you say that you were a shy person?*
CI: Yes, more than you'll believe.

JA: *But you had to overcome that shyness to some extent to be an editorial director, to be a publisher.*
CI: Well, those were eight to ten, sometimes twelve, 13 hours a day, I had to deal with people. But after that, I was myself with no one else to play to.

JA: *How did you learn to deal with people? Was that hard for you?*
CI: At the beginning, it was very difficult, because you get pushed full. Like Neal Adams was always pushing and pushing and pushing, and I had to push him back. Who else? Mort Weisinger. He tried to give me a hard time, and I nailed him to the cross. Then I realized that I had to play the game. Some people you've got to pat on the head, others you've got to kick in the behind. Just as simple as that.

JA: *That must have been tough to learn at first.*
CI: Yeah, because these were old friends, and all of a sudden I couldn't deal with them as friends any more. So the friendships I had were cut off completely, and it became very tough. Joe Kubert and I were very tight. I couldn't be friendly with him any more, at least not in the way I had before.

JA: *Did you feel from some of these people maybe a certain resentment because now you're the boss?*
CI: I suspected it in some of them.

JA: *But on the other hand, you also made Joe Kubert an editor, which was a smart move.*
CI: Yes, it was. I thought he was good in that the job. The same with Joe Orlando. I didn't let one thing interfere with another. If I felt they had special qualities, I would push them further. I

took Neal Adams off the *Jerry Lewis* books he was doing, and I put him on *The Brave and the Bold*, though he denies that was my idea. He claims he walked in to Murray and asked for the book, but Murray wouldn't make a move without asking me, neither would Julie.

JA: *Murray was a rather timid man, wasn't he?*
CI: But a wonderful editor. I think he was one of my best editors. I don't think he got enough credit.

JA: *Why was he insecure?*
CI: I heard that when he came back from the Army he wanted to go to Hollywood and be a writer out there, but his mother said "No." Now, he was in one of those old, tough, Jewish families, and he said, "Momma led the pack. She told you what to do." So he didn't go, but he resented it all his life. He ended up doing comics, but I remember sometimes he used to yell at his mother on the phone, and it's like he never forgave her. But I loved him. He was a wonderful man, a great editor.

JA: *What did your parents think about your promotion?*
CI: They were very proud of me. My father was very quiet. He never said a word to me, good, bad, or indifferent, but I think he respected it. My mother didn't want me to do it. She said, "You're doing so well as a cartoonist. They love all your work. Why do you want to change for? Why do you want to take a chance?" I said, "Mom, I've got to do it."

JA: *So you had to be a success, not only for yourself.*
CI: I didn't want the success. I didn't think of it as success, but I knew I had to do something new. I had to change. I felt that drawing comics would eventually lead to a dead end. I saw that happen to others. I just felt that it was time to move on, once the opportunity came.

JA: *What's the first thing you did once you were management?*
CI: I knew the purse was too tight, editorial-wise. Writers had control over there. That had to change, so I had to hire new people. I needed to bring artists into editorial. I brought Joe Orlando in. I got Dick Giordano from Charlton. I insisted that he bring his best people with him.

JA: *Pat Boyette, Jim Aparo, Steve Skeates. Steve Ditko was already at DC.*
CI: Yes, all of them and Denny O'Neil, too. I knew Denny was not a good plotter, but he was

(above) Carmine hands out assignments to his "staff." Carmine's cover art (pencils and inks) for *The Amazing World of DC Comics #8.*

ALL CHARACTERS ™ AND © DC COMICS.

good on dialogue. He was like having a Stan Lee in my pocket, so that was part of the deal, and he worked out for us. Dick came over, and I fired George Kashdan. He was the weakest editor we had. George was a nice man, highly intelligent, but his books were not good for the most part. I honestly think he wasn't cut out to be an editor, because he lacked vision. We were coming into a new age, and I needed editors who had vision. George's books were as passive as his personality. It was nothing personal because I liked George — everybody did, especially Arnold Drake — but I had no choice but to let him go. I had to strengthen the line [of books we were publishing].

JA: *Barbara Friedlander left then, too. Did you fire her, too?*
CI: She left on her own accord, actually, and then she came back. She wanted to work for us again, "Would you let me work here?" I said, "If any editor wants to hire you, please don't hesitate." Nobody wanted her, and she left.

I started making changes in the editors. Originally, Kanigher was very "iffy" on me, and he started having emotional problems. He was hanging around the office, pacing back and forth; he would roam up and down the halls, doing nothing. It was really sad to see. I couldn't handle this any more. His books weren't being done; they were laying there, limp. So I called him in. I said, "Bob, I've got to send you home until you get well. I'm sorry." He said, "I understand," and I got Joe Kubert to take his place.

JA: *Julie Schwartz told me that one day, Kanigher called the office. He said, "I'm in the subway, and I can't get out. I need someone to come and get me."*

CI: I've heard that story. It may be true. Kanigher was very sick.

JA: *Do you know what triggered his breakdown?*

CI: No, no one knew that. He kept writing for Kubert.

JA: *He kept all his writing jobs except for* Wonder Woman, *which you took him off of.*

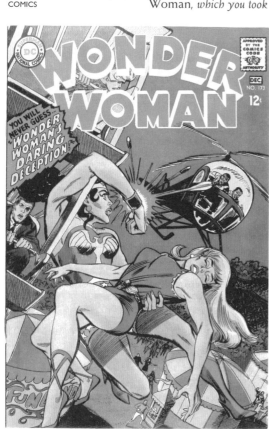

(below) The cover of *Wonder Woman* #173 (Nov.-Dec. 1967) was laid out by Carmine and penciled and inked by Irv Novick.

COURTESY OF HERITAGE AUCTIONS (WWW.HA.COM).

WONDER WOMAN ™ AND © DC COMICS

CI: I used Denny O'Neil for the dialogue on that one. Denny claims he created the new direction [for *Wonder Woman*]. He did not. I had Mike Sekowsky and him in my office and I plotted the stories right there, and my secretary typed up the plots. She died, the poor woman. She was the first secretary I had. She had been Donenfeld's secretary.

JA: *Did you discuss these editorial changes with Liebowitz first?*

CI: No, he didn't bother me. There were a couple of times he'd call me in to discuss what was and wasn't selling. But he wouldn't talk about the overseas numbers. He was very cute that way. I liked him. We got along well. Then Kinney Corporation took over, and they dumped him. Howard Chamberlain was part of Independent News. He and the guys from Kinney, they talked, they threw him out.

JA: *Jay Emmett was still running Licensing Corporation of America [LCA], right?*

CI: Yes, but they were all plotting against him, including Jay Emmett. He started with Harold Chamberlain and some other guy.

JA: *Paul Sampliner?*

CI: No, they got rid of him first. He was old. He went on vacation — this is an awful thing — they took all his furniture and pushed it against the bathroom wall. When he came back, there was no place to sit. He was told, "Go home. It's over." That was awful. Sampliner was a very gentle, quiet man. He deserved better treatment.

Anyway, Paul Wendell was the guy I was thinking of. He was the accountant for Liebowitz and the whole company. Nice man.

JA: *Not Bernie Kashdan?*

CI: Bernie just worked for DC. He was the business manager and the head of accounting. And he was George Kashdan's brother.

JA: *How much authority did you have over Licensing Corp? Any?*

CI: No, they were a whole, separate company. If they wanted to use any of our characters, they had to ask me. Like one time, some company wanted to use Superman and they offered $50,000 a year, and the guy from Licensing came down with it. He took the credit for it, that guy. but he had to get my approval.

I went out on the road to talk to the distributors. I couldn't believe what I was seeing. They were selling Marvel's books, promoting them like crazy. I said, "What's the matter with you guys? Why aren't you pushing *our* books? Why push the competition's?" They never gave me a good answer. They didn't care whose books they put on the stands. I was at one store near the DC offices, watching these jerks promoting Marvel over us — and they were working for us! Marvel got better slots on the newsstands, which made no sense to me. I said, "You're supposed to push DC *first.* It's *our* company." Well, nobody listened to me.

I wanted Independent News to drop Marvel, and eventually they did. But I think that was Martin Goodman's doing more than anything else. Independent News was charging DC 12% for handling our books, and charging Marvel 10%. I tried everything I could to get the same deal, but Independent News would not budge.

Harold Chamberlain was a good distributor, and he had great contacts across the country. I didn't deal that much with Hal, though, except for discussing sales. He brought the numbers in and let me make a judgment on what books to keep or cancel.

DC, Independent News, and Licensing Corp were separate entities, but were all part of the same family. Sometimes the other parts of the

family did things that I felt were detrimental to the DC side, but there was little I could do to change the corporate structure that was in place. DC was actually low man on the totem pole. I know it seems strange, but that's how business was conducted there.

I learned the art of negotiation from Jack Liebowitz. He always told me, "Think big. You don't think small when you're in business. Never accept a first offer." Here's an example of what I'm talking about. One of the people who worked for LCA — I can't remember his name — came to my office with two advertising men. They wanted to license Superman and Clark Kent for a hair cream campaign at $50,000 for three years. I said, "No, I want $50,000 a year." The Licensing Corp guy said the ad men wouldn't accept my offer. I said, "Well, that's the deal." He talked to the two ad men, and came back to me and said, "They accept."

The producers of the first *Rocky* movie wanted to license Plastic Man for a feature film. The Warner executives made me turn it down, because they felt it would be competition for the *Doc Savage* film that was in production. I could never understand their thinking. We owned Plastic Man and not Doc Savage. And there's no comparison between the two characters, so how those executives could have the idea that one would conflict with another is beyond my understanding. Again, we got screwed because of the shortsighted thinking of the big boys.

You know, it's funny how some people claim I didn't know how to run a business, but when you are only a part of a larger structure, some things are beyond your control. Not everybody understands that. They think that when you have the title of "boss," that it means you are in charge of everything. That's not true. It wasn't true at DC or virtually any other major corporation that you hear about. But nobody cares about the details of how things work. They just criticize and point fingers without knowing the facts. And if you look at the history of DC, you'll see other instances by other regimes where it looked like they didn't know what they were doing, either.

JA: *When you met with Sampliner or Chamberlain, would they give you recommendations on canceling a book?*

(above) Carmine drew these 1967 *Plastic Man* covers — both of which were inked by Mike Esposito — once again showing his flair for humor. DC Comics had bought the character (along with many others, such as the then-popular Blackhawks) from Quality Comics in 1956, when Quality closed shop.

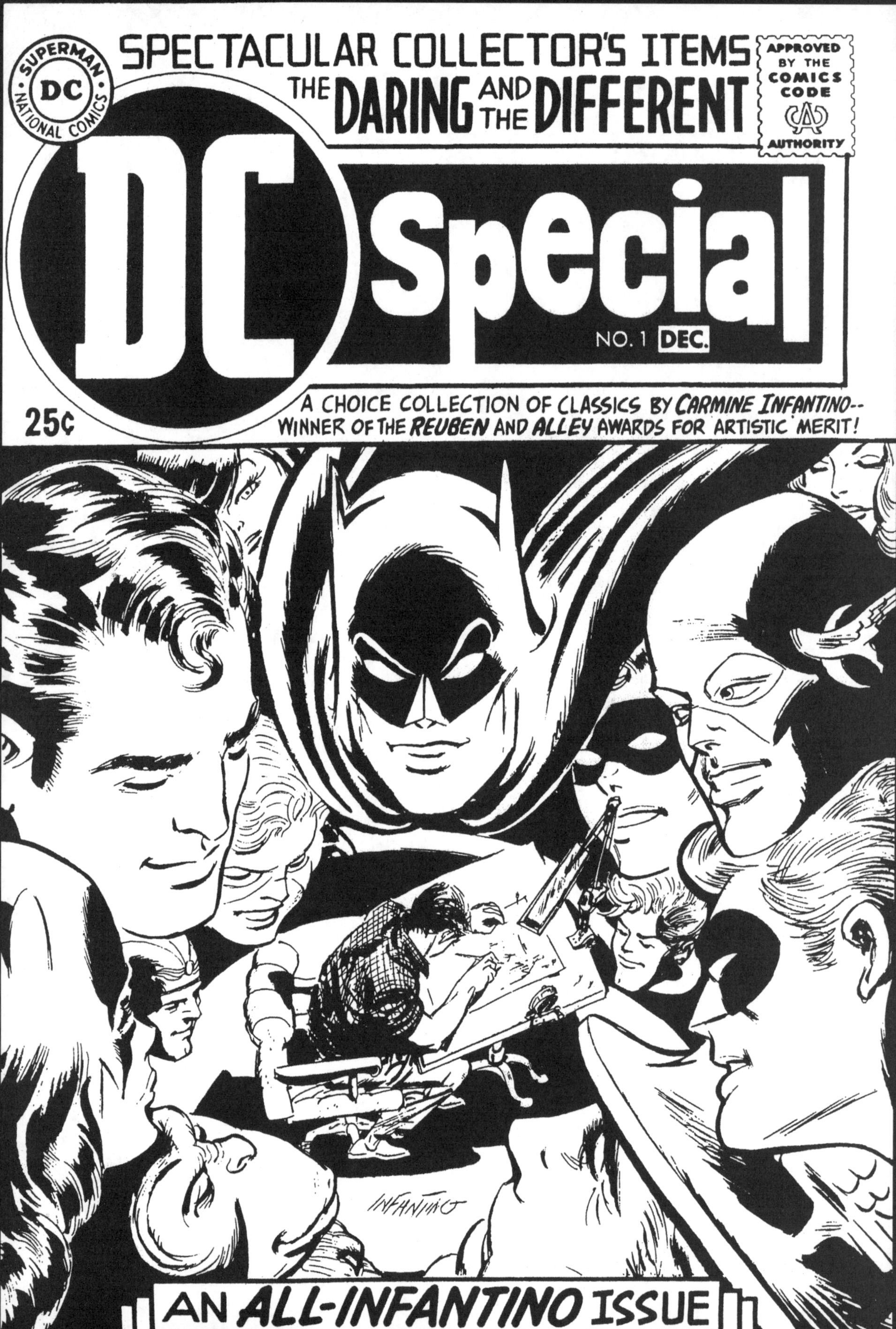
SUPERMAN
DC
NATIONAL COMICS
SPECTACULAR COLLECTOR'S ITEMS
THE DARING AND THE DIFFERENT
APPROVED BY THE COMICS CODE AUTHORITY
DC Special
NO. 1 DEC.
25¢
A CHOICE COLLECTION OF CLASSICS BY CARMINE INFANTINO--
WINNER OF THE REUBEN AND ALLEY AWARDS FOR ARTISTIC MERIT!
INFANTINO
AN ALL-INFANTINO ISSUE

CI: No, and it would be very tough to get them to move the print run numbers up. Now, of course, a print run, once you went past that line, you lost money if you didn't sell so many copies. If you sold below 50%, you were in trouble. Above 50%, you were okay, and I had to estimate what I thought each book would sell. I was pretty good at that. It was working pretty good.

JA: *The relationship between Liebowitz and Sampliner —*
CI: Excellent! Yes, they were like brothers. They were very close.

JA: *On the business end, Sampliner was his partner. Did he have a percentage of DC?*
CI: I don't know, but his company was Independent News, and Jack had DC Comics. I think they married the two together, that's what happened.

JA: *Then Sampliner probably didn't own any of DC, but they were partners because he owned Independent News.*
CI: That's pretty much it.

JA: *Did you deal with [former DC editorial director] Whitney Ellsworth much?*
CI: He was a nice man. He had emphysema, though, and had a hard time. I used to go out to California on business and have lunch with him. He was in charge of the TV and film business out there. He had to report to me on the films. We'd go over things, but, actually, I didn't do that much with him. I think it was more a formality to have lunch and talk. It was a business thing, but I respected him.

JA: *You had a few guys like Gil Kane, whom you had known for many years. How did people like Gil look at you once you're in this position of power?*
CI: I'm sure he didn't like it. He'd come in with Julie when they would do covers. He was giving Julie a lot of problems. He didn't do his work on time, which was a big "no-no" with Julie. Finally, Julie came to me and said, "I can't take this guy any more. Get rid of him." I said, "Well, tell him he's fired. What do you want from me?" He said, "You do it." So I called him in and said, "We can't use you any more." He said, "Okay, I understand." He went to Marvel, and that was the end of it. But Julie didn't want him, period.

You know, Julie told Gardner Fox that I wouldn't give him a raise, and it wasn't true. He never came in and asked me. I asked Julie, "Why did Gardner leave?" Julie didn't want to use him any more, so he used my name to do it. He

could be pretty cold-blooded, you know.

Julie was friends with Mort Weisinger. He was not close with Jack Schiff, I don't think. Or with Murray Boltinoff or George Kashdan. Julie didn't really socialize with the other editors. He was all business in the office. You knew him after he retired, so you got to see a different side of Julie than those who worked in the offices. He was a very private man.

JA: *When you decided to change the look of things, you did that for the company. You weren't saying, "I want to put my own stamp on these books."*
CI: No, I worked for the company. I changed the face of the office, which was very sterile in those days. New artists were afraid to come in there. They couldn't even get in, because nobody wanted to talk to them. The editors had their own people, and that was the end of it, period. I opened the doors and got the fresh air in.

JA: *Why do you think they didn't want new blood in?*
CI: I don't know. Maybe they were just backwards in their thinking, or maybe to protect their behinds? I don't know what it was.

JA: *Maybe they were afraid of change.*
CI: That's very possible, probably that more than anything else. But change had to come or we were going to get killed. We couldn't stay still. I had a room designated just for the artists and writers. No editors or I could go in there. Freelancers could go there, bitch, complain... you know a lot of us never had the chance to do that before.

(above) Early '70s photo of Carmine.
COURTESY OF *ALTER EGO* MAGAZINE.

(facing page) Towards the end of 1968, DC launched a quarterly reprint series called *DC Special*. Each issue had a theme, and the theme of the debut issue was none other than Carmine Infantino. Only one other artist, Joe Kubert, was honored in this way. Carmine, of course, penciled and inked the cover, which depicted himself hunched over his drawing board while the characters he helped make famous look on approvingly.
ALL CHARACTERS ™ AND © DC COMICS.

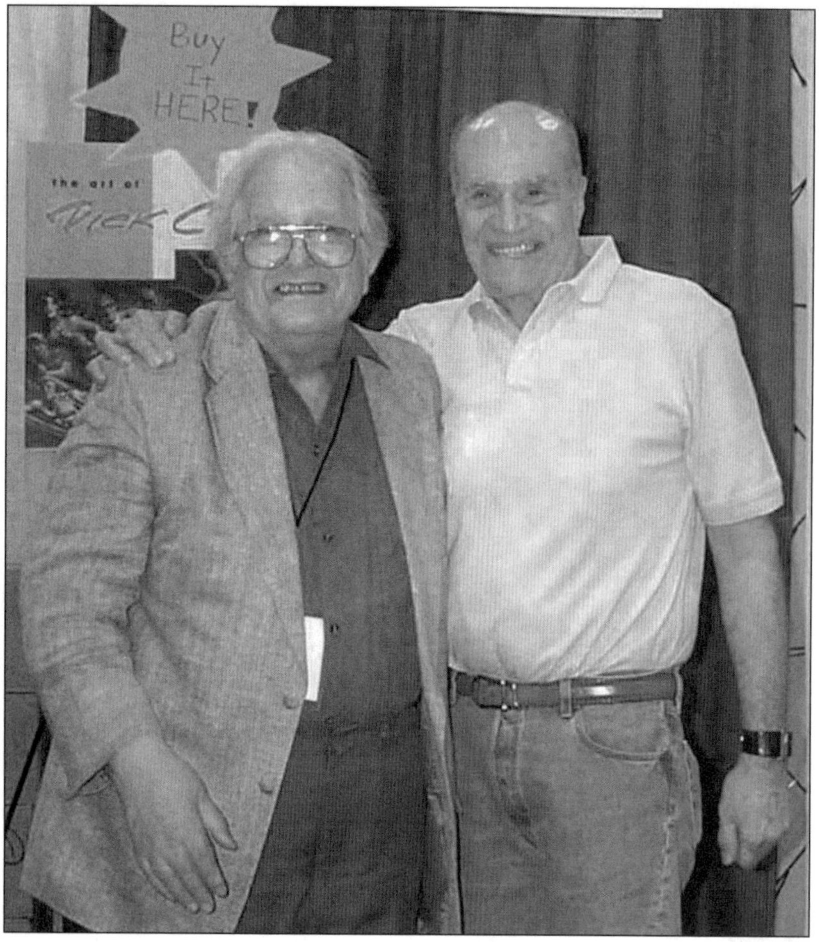
Buy It HERE!
the art of

(above) Carmine and Nick Cardy at the 2000 Heroes Con in Charlotte, N.C.

COURTESY OF BOB BAILEY.

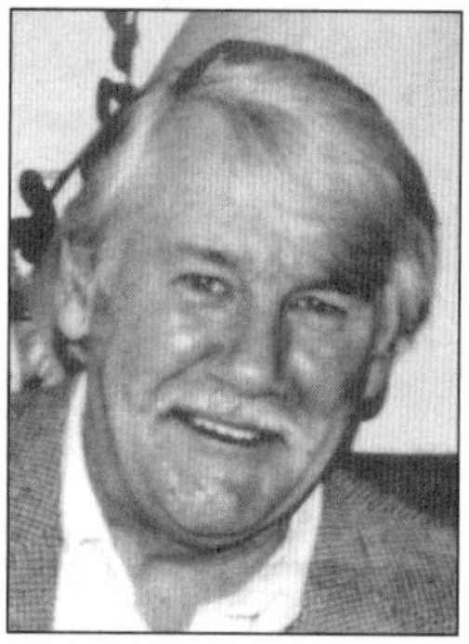

(right) 1987 photo of Alex Toth.

And I'll tell you, it was good for them to get everything out of their system whenever they wanted to. It also got very creative for them. People heard about it, they wanted to work for me. So we started getting a lot of good people coming in, like Bernie Wrightson and Mike Kaluta. Those guys were terrific! Irv Novick used to come in once in a while... all the guys but Jack Kirby, who lived in California. My favorite was Nick Cardy. He was a genius, I think. I think he and Kirby were in a class by themselves.

JA: *You wouldn't put Alex Toth in that category?*
CI: Oh, yes. Alex was there, too. But you know what? The difference was that Jack and Nick's work was commercial. I don't think Alex's work was commercial. Of course, he was a terrific artist, but not commercial. Those three guys had no peers. That's my personal opinion.

JA: *How close of a relationship, as far as you could tell, did Liebowitz and Marvel's Martin Goodman have?*
CI: I can't be certain, but I heard they used to play golf every weekend, or every once in a while. But there was contact there, I know that. How much? Of course, Independent News was distributing Marvel's comics. Liebowitz limited Goodman to 18 titles at the most, and then Martin kept sticking a couple more in all the time, putting more and more in constantly. There was a story going around that we did not sell their books. That wasn't true at all, because the salesmen made their money based on how many books they promoted. So that was not true at all.

JA: *But Marvel's sales continually went upward.*
CI: They passed DC in sales. That's why I got the job.

JA: *So even when Marvel started selling books more and more by, say, 1964 or '65, you don't think there was ever an attempt from DC to limit Marvel's newsstand presence.*
CI: No, it would have been very difficult to pull that off, because the distributors controlled the newsstands and wanted to make as much money as they could.

JA: *When Marvel went up to twelve cents, DC went up to twelve cents. When one company went up to 15 cents, the other did, too. Was there collusion between the two companies?*
CI: I think so, in their own way. At one point, both companies went to a quarter, and Martin Goodman pulled a fast one. He immediately reduced the price of his comics to 20 cents, and he made a fortune. He outsold us like crazy. He even threw a party across the street from DC to celebrate it.

JA: *Who made the decision to go from 15 cents to a quarter and do thicker books?*
CI: That was the Independent News guy, Harold Chamberlain. He and Liebowitz were involved with that. I had nothing to do with that. When Marvel went down to 20 cents, I thought we should have gone back down to 20 cents immediately. I said, "It's not going to work. We're going to get creamed." Chamberlain said, "I know more than you do about this. We're staying at a quarter. Our readers are loyal." Well, bull! The fans went for the cheaper books. You can't blame them.

JA: *Well, as a kid, I got my favorite DCs at a quarter apiece.*
CI: But I'll bet you limited them, didn't you?

JA: *Yes, I did. If it was a matter of only having one dollar, you can only get four DC books, but you could get five Marvel books.*

CI: You see what I mean? There was the rub. Marvel made a lot of money with that. Marvel used the same printer we did. They knew exactly what was going on with us months ahead of time. We knew what they were doing, too.

JA: *Do you think the distributors got together and fixed prices? Because both companies always raised their prices at the same time.*
CI: The printer [Sparta] was involved, too. Their guy would come and visit us, he'd go visit Marvel, saying things like, "You did this, they did that."

JA: *Once you were president and publisher, did you ever have any dealings with Martin Goodman?*
CI: I met him a few times, but Jack Liebowitz was the one who dealt with him. Goodman seemed like a small, likable guy, but was a tough businessman.

JA: *How much power did Liebowitz have by the time you left? He was on the board of directors at Warner Brothers.*
CI: That was a nothing job. He was pushed aside. They had a meeting — Chamberlain and Mark Iglesias were there — and they were talking about all this. They told me what they were planning, and I said, "I don't want to be a part of this." But then they got rid of me later.

JA: *What was their problem with Liebowitz? Was it a matter of power?*
CI: They didn't want him around making decisions. They wanted Iglesias. They sent him down to corporate. Iglesias wanted the job and had his nephew Herrera there with him — a real killer, this Herrera guy. He was dropping people like rocks. Then they wanted to put in a time clock. I said, "What, are you kidding? These are professional people." I had a big fight about it. Finally, I talked them out of it. What a mess that would have become.

The Kinney guys fired a lot of people. They said there were too many people in the production room, so they started cutting back like crazy. They had been undertakers, everything worked that way for them. [*Ed. note: Kinney Corporation, among other things, owned some funeral parlors.*] I had a lot of trouble with them upstairs. My boss, William Sarnoff, called me up one day and said, "We've got to get rid of some bodies." So I stared at him, I said, "I know one body you can get rid of and never miss." [*chuckling*] He gave me a dirty look. Sarnoff was a dud as far as I was concerned.

I was not close to the guys upstairs. They had their own morals up there. They were very different morals. They didn't care about people, only about money.

JA: *Do you feel like they looked down at you?*
CI: Yes! Absolutely. They didn't like comic books, they didn't care anything about the characters... didn't even try to understand what they were about. DC was just something they owned that could make money for them. We were nothing to them... more an annoyance than an asset. In fact, they had windows open at 75 Rock, downstairs. They said, "Why don't you put some of your books down there for advertisement?" I got some books and toys and games in there. One of the higher-ups, Steve Ross came

(below) Nick Cardy is mainly known for the many, many covers he drew for DC Comics in the late '60s and early '70s and for his fantastic work on the *Aquaman* series. Carmine didn't deal with Aquaman very much, but he did pencil this cover for *The Brave and the Bold* #73 (Aug.-Sept. 1967), which was inked by Chuck Cuidera.

COURTESY OF HERITAGE AUCTIONS (WWW.HA.COM).

Superman DC National Comics
The Brave and the Bold presents
Approved by the Comics Code Authority
Sept. No. 73 12¢
Aquaman and the Atom
Hail, Galg the Destroyer!

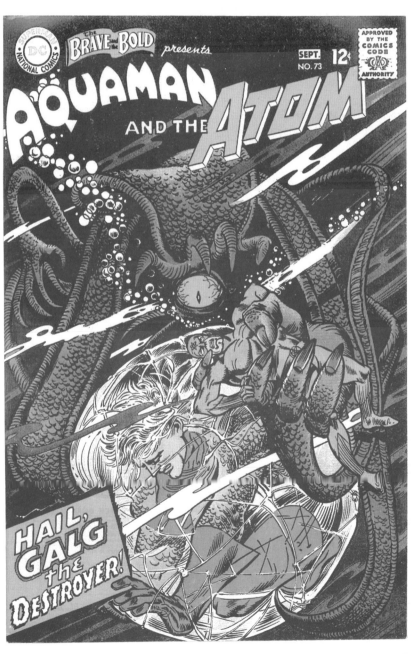

(above) Early 1970s photo of Carmine with Jack Kirby. Early on in his career, Carmine worked for the Simon & Kirby shop. In 1970, Carmine brought Jack Kirby to work for him at DC Comics. (He would later bring in Joe Simon, as well.) Artists moved from company to company as a matter of course, and in fact Kirby had worked for DC many years earlier, but times were changing. Marvel Comics had risen steadily to the top over the last several years, and a great deal of their success was due to the creative work of Jack Kirby. The fact that he was leaving Marvel to work for their biggest (and, by that time, practically their only) rival was big news indeed. But that's not to say there wasn't resistance at DC.

by one day along with Jay Emmett, and Ross said, "Get that crap out of my windows!" He was screaming and yelling. And there's Steve Ross walking around with a Superman emblem pinned to his lapel. [*Jim laughs*]

JA: *Your job sounds like a lonely one.*
CI: It really was, because I grew up with many of these guys. I was one of them, and now I couldn't be social with them, because sociability meant other things, and you can't do that. A number of them tried to get raises, figuring I'd give them because I had been in their number. I said, "This is business. I can't do this just because we know each other." I know it made some people mad at me. I had to separate the business from the personal for myself and for the good of the company. I did have friends outside of comics, and in some ways felt more at ease with them. I knew there wouldn't be any conflicts with them. Of course, I was so busy that my social life wasn't as full as it could have been. I was married to my job. I was dedicated. And I felt that I had succeeded, but sometimes success comes at a price. It was a price I was willing to pay, because I loved my job.

JA: *Let's talk about Jack Kirby. Getting him from Marvel was a real feather in your cap.*
CI: I thought it was a very important signing. Jack was always one of my favorites, and I wanted to get him back to DC. There were many people who didn't want him with us, primarily because of the bad feelings left over from the lawsuit with Jack Schiff. [*Ed. note: The lawsuit was over finder's fee payments for the Sky Masters newspaper strip deal that Schiff set up for Jack*

Kirby and Dick and Dave Wood, the strip's writers.] I had to smooth over a number of fences first, but I did.

JA: *Did you know about the rift between Kirby and Schiff at the time?*
CI: No. I found out about it when I wanted to hire Kirby away from Marvel. I don't recall hearing about the problem when it happened. I wasn't around the offices enough to pick up on those kinds of stories. This stuff wasn't up for common discussion. Julie never would have talked to me about it. We were just worried about making a living. We didn't worry about this other nonsense.

JA: *Who gave you the most problem over hiring Kirby?*
CI: Upstairs and Independent News — and Schiff's friends who were still there; they were all complaining. The art department didn't want Kirby; nobody liked him, only because they defended Schiff.

JA: *But Sol Harrison didn't like Kirby's art, either.*
CI: I don't think he did. Sol had his likes and dislikes. Anyway, Jack had a great idea with *New Gods* and the other books, but they just didn't sell well enough to continue.

JA: *Why do you think that was?*
CI: Partly it was because of Jack's dialogue. He had good ideas, but he couldn't write good dialogue. It made the stories harder to read, and if it's harder to read, then the fans can't relate to the characters.

JA: *I always thought part of the problem was that, besides Jimmy Olsen, the books were bi-monthly. I think if Jack had done, say,* New Gods *and* Mr. Miracle *as monthlies and maybe no* Forever People, *they would have done better. It's hard to keep track of continuing and interlapping stories when the books take two months in between issues to come out.*
CI: Maybe... I don't know. It's possible, but Jack had a very loyal following, and he wanted to prove that he was the main creator of the Marvel comics, which he was. He had all these ideas that he wanted to use, and I let him do what he wanted, until sales figures came in and we had to talk. I was heartbroken over this. I loved Jack, loved his work, but I had to put the company's best interests ahead of my personal feelings. It just didn't work out. I caught a lot of flack for canceling those books, but I did what I had to do.

JA: *Do you think the price increase from 15 cents to a quarter hurt sales, too?*

CI: Maybe. But maybe those characters weren't as strong as his Marvel characters, and the readers just weren't as interested because of it. And you know I caught a bit of flack from some fans because I had the Superman and Jimmy Olsen faces changed.

JA: *Why did you do that?*

CI: Because we had to maintain the look of the Superman characters. We had licensing agreements all over the world, and they wanted — expected — a consistent look to the characters. It's the same thing with Mickey Mouse. You don't change the look no matter who the artist is. Mickey Mouse has to look like Mickey Mouse. Same thing with Superman. I know you disagree with me.

JA: *Well, I understand your reasoning from a licensing standpoint, but it was terrible for the comic books. As a reader, I found it very disconcerting to see Jack Kirby/Vinnie Colletta faces talking to Murphy Anderson re-dos. It disrupted the story flow, because I would stop reading to see who was drawing what.*

CI: But you weren't the typical reader. You were serious about the art, much more so than most fans. I think the fans want to see a consistent look to the characters. I don't think it bothered most of the readers. They were more interested in the characters than they were the art. You were too sensitive to it.

JA: *Well, would you have liked it if they had done that to your work?*

CI: I wouldn't have said a word about it. I would have understood the reason why. And I'm not saying the fans don't care about the art. I'm just saying they want their characters to look the way they're supposed to. Jack just didn't draw a very good Superman, or at least keep him on model. And we had to keep him on model. I discussed this with Jack, and he agreed.

I got Jack to do other books. He was a great idea man, maybe the best ever in comics. I

(below) Carmine felt that Superman, due to licensing interests, needed to maintain a consistent look, no matter who was drawing him. When Jack Kirby's Superman heads went a bit too far from model, Al Plastino was called in to correct them. Later, such as in this panel from *Superman's Pal, Jimmy Olsen* #145 (Jan. 1972), Murphy Anderson was tasked with the job.

(above) A 2009 photo of Carmine with Al Plastino.

PHOTO BY KEIF SIMON.

(right) Carmine himself wasn't above being corrected on a Superman drawing. According to Curt Swan, he was asked to make changes to Carmine's Superman figure in this cover for *Action Comics* #401 (Jan. 1972), which was then inked by Murphy Anderson.

COURTESY OF HERITAGE AUCTIONS (WWW.HA.COM).

SUPERMAN ™ AND © DC COMICS.

the stuff back, they'd let it lay in the warehouse, and you had to help sway these guys. Half of the guys out in the field didn't know Marvel's books from mine. One guy told me, "Boy, your books are selling. *Spider-Man* is doing well."

JA: *I want to ask you about Al Plastino. Did you know him?*
CI: A very talented man, a very nice guy, but I didn't get to know him. He worked at home. He used to be a great imitator of other styles.

JA: *He drew the* Ferd'nand *newspaper strip, and he penciled for Mort Weisinger. When Plastino started on* Superman, *he followed the Wayne Boring model. And by the mid- to late '60s, he followed the Curt Swan model.*
CI: Yeah, I was not a fan of Boring's work. His stuff was very flat-looking to me.

JA: *Plastino was the guy you first picked to retouch the Kirby faces on the Superman characters. Why him?*
CI: Because he drew Superman. Then he quit, and I got Murphy to do it.

JA: *At one point in the '70s — and I think you were still in charge at DC at the time — Stan Lee decided he wanted to try an underground comic book. It never occurred to you to ever go in that direction, did it?*
CI: No, because I felt that was a whole other audience, which wasn't that big at the time.

suggested he do a version of *Planet of the Apes*, which became *Kamandi*. Jack did *The Demon*... he did a number of things. *Kamandi* was the best-selling series he did, but the best-selling book was *The Sandman* he did with Joe Simon. That had big sales. I think Jack did his best work when he worked with Joe or with Stan Lee. He needed someone to help with the dialogue. I wanted to keep Jack and Joe together on *The Sandman*, but Jack didn't want to work with Joe Simon — or anyone else — anymore. He wanted to do everything himself, and I could not get him to change his mind. And then he went back to Marvel and had the same problems there.

There was this story out about the sales of Jack Kirby's books, that I had two sets of books. Do you remember that story? Well, none of that was true. What would happen was before a book would go on sale, I would sit with somebody from Independent News and we would set up a number, let's say 50%. I would get paid on that number. Three months later, those numbers started coming in, and it didn't mean anything. Then we got figures at six months. At the end of nine months, when we had final sales figures, my accountant, their accountant, and I got together. Either I owed them money or they owed me money, and we'd settle up. That's how it worked.

JA: *Why did it take so long to get accurate sales figures?*
CI: Because the books would come trailing in at the last moment. Distributors, again, they'd get

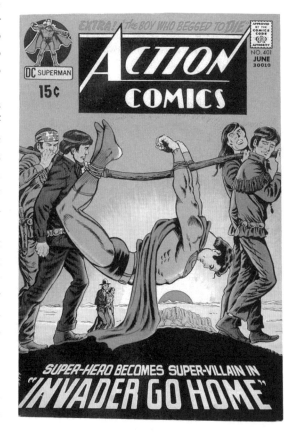

JA: *Marvel started doing lots of black-and-white magazines in the '70s, but except for Jack Kirby's* In the Days of the Mob *and* Spirit World, *you didn't do that. Why?*

CI: Those books didn't make much money, and Marvel was trying to get themselves extra shelf space with their black-and-whites, but the distributors weren't buying them. They were throwing them right back at Marvel, so they didn't make much money with those.

JA: *Well, Marvel's* Conan *books sold well. Anyway, on the two Kirby magazines you tried, I understand the distribution on those was terrible, that they were hardly distributed.*

CI: Well, they got out to a degree. As I said, that space was already taken up by other magazines. We couldn't crack through to these guys with that stuff.

JA: *Do you think that the guys working for Independent News didn't really want to deal with that?*

CI: No, no. These guys… that's their job. The salesmen didn't care. It's the distributor who controlled the situation. I had a guy, he was a friend of Paul Sampliner. This guy used to take our comics and give them away at schools. Then they'd send them back saying, "no sales, no sales," and the schools had playgrounds named after him. And the distributor was no help. When I went out there one time, I yelled like mad at him. So he gave me a couple of months of reprieve and then he went back to the old habits.

JA: *The old days, when books were returned, they would just rip the cover off and return the cover.*

CI: No, not the whole cover, just the top of the cover.

JA: *But later, it was the whole cover. I know that because by the mid-'70s, I used to help a guy on a magazine distribution truck, so I remember that from my childhood.*

CI: They used to take whatever was left and put them in bags and sell them, too.

JA: *Was there anything you could have done about that? Because that's obviously fraud.*

CI: No, these guys had so much power, you couldn't fool with them. If you ever tried, they would cut you off altogether. I went to visit one guy in California, and he said, "I never sell that garbage you guys are putting out anyway." I had to shut up. I kept my mouth shut. They gave us very limited areas of distribution.

JA: *I know that in the '40s, and at least into the '50s, DC actually had road men for distributors, and Irwin Donenfeld was on the road a lot. Did you have very many road men?*

CI: Yes, I went out with them a number of times, but they were not DC's men. They worked for Independent News. What we had was a rep, but he wasn't that helpful. He just went out and drank with these guys. He really didn't do us that much good. The guys in the back room were the guys you had to get in with. You had to entertain them, because they were the key guys. They'd be back there pushing the books or not pushing the books.

JA: *You were president and publisher. Did you have any sway over Independent News?*

CI: No, none. They were totally independent.

JA: *In your opinion, did Independent News care more about the magazines than the comic books?*

(above) Another of Carmine's Superman covers, this one for *Superman* #248 (Feb. 1972), inked by Murphy Anderson.

COURTESY OF HERITAGE AUCTIONS (WWW.HA.COM).

SUPERMAN ™ AND © DC COMICS.

(above and facing page) In 1972, DC launched a series of tabloid-sized books, mostly reprinting older, classic material. But in late 1975 the unthinkable happened. DC and Marvel joined forces to produce the first crossover event featuring characters from two different comic book publishers with *Superman Vs. the Amazing Spider-Man*. DC spearheaded the project, which was to be the first of four such joint books (DC and Marvel would alternate the actual publishing duties). As such, who else should have designed the cover than Carmine? The chosen sketch (facing page) gave the two companies' heroes equal status.

CI: They didn't care about the comics at all. They had *Playboy*, *Mad* magazine, all kinds of magazines. We were not their top priority.

JA: *If you had been publisher at the time the direct market took off — ?*
CI: It had started before I left DC, but it was very small at the time. Phil Seuling was the first one to buy from us for the direct market. We got a lot of heat from the distributors on that. They didn't like the idea. They wanted us to knock it off. I said, "The hell I will." At the beginning, they ignored the direct market because it was too small. It was a couple of thousand here, a couple of thousand there, and they couldn't care less. But as it started to grow, they got very angry about it.

JA: *Did you have any idea that the direct market would explode the way it did? Because DC and Marvel both practically dumped the newsstand and concentrated on the direct market.*
CI: No, I was gone by that time.

JA: *But would you have done it?*
CI: No, I would not have, because don't forget the distributors sold a lot of books. If they put out 20,000 books, it's a good sale now. In those days, on *Superman*, if we put out 900,000 and we got 65% sales, it was a bad sale. You've got to

have all the outlets you can get.

JA: *Even though DC and Marvel haven't totally abandoned the newsstand sales, newsstand sales are just a fraction of sales today.*
CI: I don't know what to tell you, because there are so many big chains involved. I mean, how do you not get them, like the K-Marts? They're important. Archie Comics has stayed with them, and they've done very well because of it. They have good numbers there.

JA: *Do you think that abandoning newsstands to the extent that the companies did — ?*
CI: I think that was stupid. We tried a lot of different formats and sizes. A hundred pages for 50 cents — that's a great deal! And no ads! They sold well.

JA: *Eventually, DC started putting ads in them. Then you published the tabloid-sized dollar comics.*
CI: That was my idea. We had trouble with those. They sold, but not the way I wanted them to sell. What happened was that outlets like 7-11 wanted special racks and special bookcases and all the other crap to go along with it. They were a big factor for us, the 7-11s, but it got to a point where we couldn't make money on them anymore. I was sorry about that, because I liked those books.

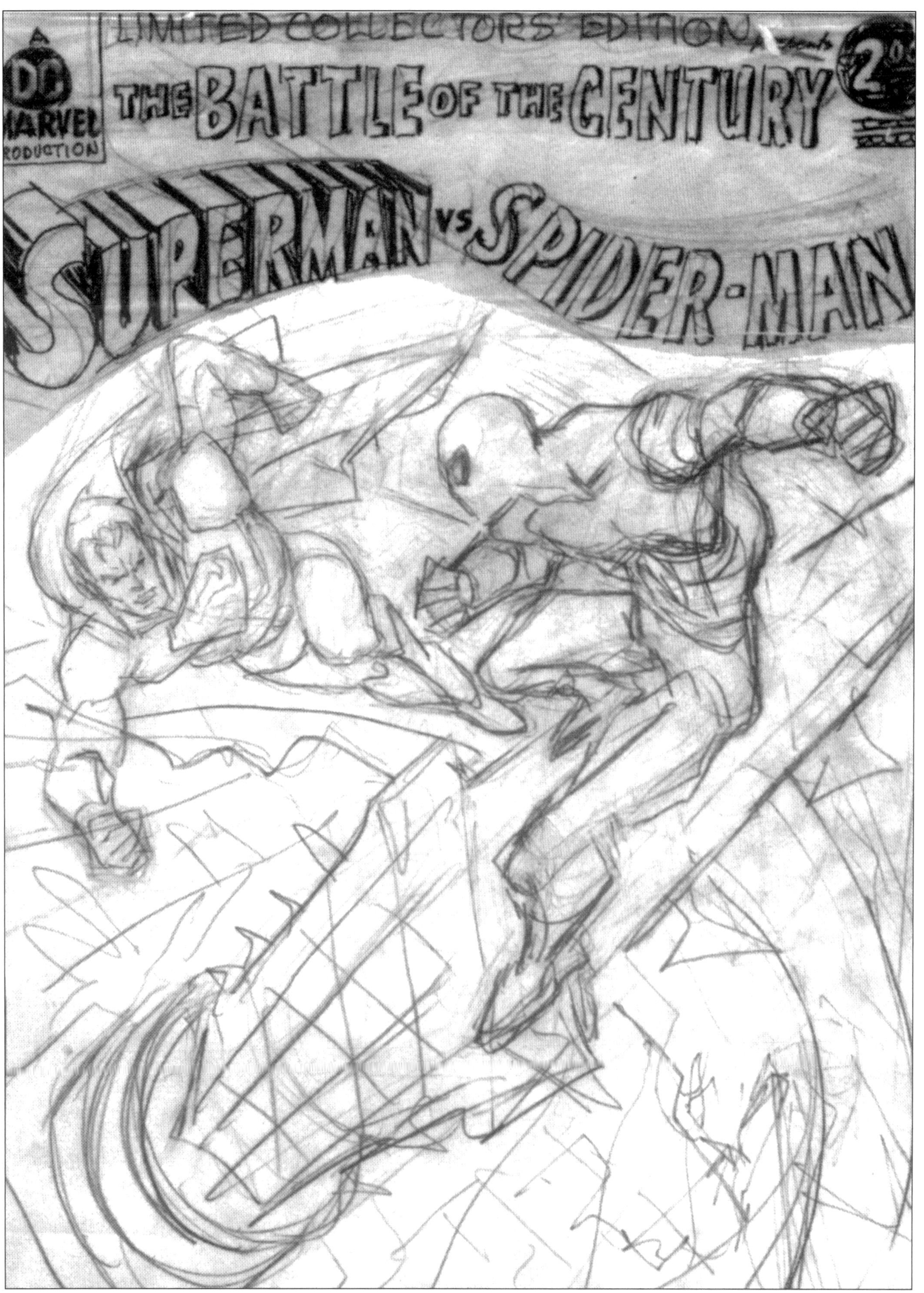
LIMITED COLLECTORS' EDITION
DC MARVEL PRODUCTION
THE BATTLE OF THE CENTURY
SUPERMAN VS SPIDER-MAN

JA: *I did, too. I also think the content in some of them was not as strong as it could have been.*
CI: You're right.

JA: *Were there any other formats that you had thought about trying?*
CI: Before I left, I was going to create a super-sized book about *King Kong*. And I was going to get Bernie Wrightson to draw it, double the big size we had. That thing would have been sensational all those years ago, but it would have been a big gamble. I was willing to try it.

We never even considered trade paperbacks. They were too small, I think [to properly reproduce super-hero comics]. But there were paperbacks out later on from Marvel. And Archie had their digests. You had to watch out. You see, comic books had their own racks, and paperbacks had their racks, and they could never overlap each other. It was all about distribution, as I keep saying.

JA: *Charlton Comics was still around — a lesser publisher on the fringes. Did you guys even pay attention to them?*

CI: I used to read their books. That's why I got Giordano and his best people to come over. Especially Jim Aparo, who I always had my eye on. But we never worried about them. Around 1972, '73, they wanted to get our business away from World Color Press in Sparta and print our books. We said no.

JA: *When DC started publishing Captain Marvel, what exactly was the arrangement? Did you pay a licensing fee?*
CI: Getting Captain Marvel was my idea, and we paid Fawcett a licensing fee, but we didn't do well with that character. Eventually, DC bought all of the Fawcett characters. You know what? I think I shouldn't have given Captain Marvel to Julie Schwartz. C.C. Beck wanted to do it all by himself, but he never came to me and said, "Carmine, I want to package the book." If he had talked to me, I probably would have let him do it. Captain Marvel was supposed to be humorous, and Julie never had much humor in his books. There was a charm to Captain Marvel that Julie's writers couldn't capture.

(below) C.C. Beck's promotional ad art for DC's new *Shazam!* series. Beck had been Fawcett's Chief Artist (his official title) for all their "Captain Marvel" material up until their settlement with DC, not long after which they ceased operations. Beck was very opinionated and his opinion of the stories he was given to draw for DC's revival of the good Captain wasn't very high. His last work for the series ran in issue #9.

COURTESY OF HERITAGE AUCTIONS (WWW.HA.COM).

BILLY BATSON, CAPTAIN MARVEL ™ AND © DC COMICS.

JA: *I thought the reprints of the old stories in the back were better than the new stories.*

CI: Yeah, that was the point. I used to complain to Julie. "Julie, for Christ's sake, are you reading the old stories?" "No, I don't want to bother looking at that." He was very dogmatic at times. So I blame myself for giving it to him and not giving it to C.C. Beck.

JA: *Do you think that the fact you brought back Captain Marvel the way he looked back in the '40s and the '50s, and Julie hadn't changed him in the way like he did others, i.e., Batman, was a mistake?*

CI: No, I didn't want to change him. It was a terrific costume.

JA: *No, I don't mean the costume. I'm talking about the drawing style and the tone of the stories.*

CI: Oh, no. I loved Beck's style. That was the beauty of the revival. Beck was very upset that he didn't get the editorship, the writing, the whole works.

Marvel tried to sue us over this. They said, "You've got our title. You're not allowed to use our title." That's why the book was called *Shazam!* We couldn't use the name "Captain Marvel" on the cover.

JA: *You had "The Original Captain Marvel" below the* Shazam! *logo, and then it became "The World's Mightiest Mortal" on the covers.*

CI: We couldn't use the word "Marvel" on the cover. When I laid out those covers for Beck... you remember the dollar-sized one that had Billy Batson and Captain Marvel on the cover? I laid that one out on cardboard at the airport. To me, the real charm of Captain Marvel was Beck's drawing style. All the very young kids loved Captain Marvel, but I guess the parents didn't buy enough of them. It didn't sell that well.

JA: *When you licensed Captain Marvel, did you license Bulletman and the other Fawcett characters?*

CI: They threw everything in the pot. I don't think we used them much at all. I was heartbroken that Captain Marvel didn't sell. I really thought it would do great things.

JA: *I'm a big C.C. Beck fan, but I thought the new stories were very silly.*

CI: They were. They screwed up that book. Beck should have handled that whole thing himself. But you know, I blame him, too. He should have contacted me. My door was always open. He should have said to me, "I want to do the whole thing." He never did, never did! Then I heard he went out to conventions and complained that he never got more to do. That's unfair. Why didn't he say something to me? I didn't want to give it to Julie, but I had no one else to give it to.

JA: *Why couldn't you have given it to Murray Boltinoff?*

CI: Murray was busy. He was booked solid. Julie had a little time open for that one. In retrospect, I don't think I would have given it to Murray anyway. That's not his kind of book, and it really wasn't Julie's kind of book, either. That's where I screwed up.

JA: *Was* Shazam! *more of an attempt to court younger readers than Superman?*

CI: Absolutely. I was a big fan of that character. I preferred him

to Superman, frankly. He had charm. Him, Mary Marvel, Dr. Sivana and his gorgeous daughter — that was funny stuff. And then my buddy, Eddie Herron, was the editor and bought a lot of that stuff. If Eddie Herron had been alive, I'd have given him the book to do. All the key guys from the old days were retired, or, in the case of Kurt Schaffenberger, busy.

JA: *When you dealt with Fawcett to get the rights, why didn't you buy them outright? Fawcett couldn't publish them, because they had lost the lawsuit over Captain Marvel.*

CI: I don't know. At the beginning, I figured, just let me get the rights. But later on DC bought them. I think it was a good buy, because they would have made good TV shows.

JA: *It would have, and as you well know, it became a TV show, because your name was on it. But you didn't really merchandize the character much.*

CI: That was because we had that problem with Marvel Comics. This is funny: they wanted me to give them the character to publish. I said, "No way I'll do that." [*Jim laughs*]

(above) From 1973 to 1975, DC expanded many of its titles to 100 pages, filling most of those pages with reprint material. *Shazam!* was one of those titles, and many fans found the old Fawcett stories much more enjoyable than the new stories that were being produced. *Shazam!* #8 (Dec. 1973) featured a C.C. Beck cover, and other than a few activity pages was made up entirely of reprints.

JA: *Backing up to Mort Weisinger, he retired....*

CI: He'd been threatening to do that for years. Every time he did, Liebowitz would give him more money to stay. Finally, I decided enough was enough, and I told Mort, "Well, okay, we'll miss you. Bye." Then two weeks later, he came back in. He said, "You know what? I changed my mind. I like what's going on here now. I'd like to start again." I said, "It's too late, Mort. It's over. You're finished." You know, Mort had gone crazy with Superman. He had made him too powerful, and it was boring. I thought the original version was the best, especially the fact that he couldn't fly too much. He was more of a vigilante than anything else in those days. Julie was afraid of [going in that direction], though. He was afraid of doing it, but I pushed him a little bit in that direction, just a touch. But we needed to make Superman more relevant to the times, and there's no way Mort could have done that.

JA: *I've heard that Mort was upset that you were put in charge because he saw himself as the most important editor at the company.*

CI: That could very well be. He was real close to Liebowitz. They both lived in Great Neck, and they'd drive in to work together every day. Mort was a strange customer. Nobody could deal with him. Mort was not the kind of guy many people could deal with. But he did very well financially. He sure did a lot of writing. He claimed it was his work, anyway... I don't know.

JA: *Did you have problems with Mort when you designed his covers?*

CI: No. He wrote stories around them the same way Julie did.

JA: *Around 1976, there was an article about him in* Parade *magazine. He wrote that he spent years going to the psychiatrist because he didn't feel like he could measure up to the Superman character.*

CI: That's just full of crap. That's all.

JA: *But he didn't like himself.*

CI: No, I don't think he did. He had this Ouija board in his office at one time, but we laughed at him. He threw it away after that. He was not a good-looking man, you know. He was very unattractive, actually, and he used to laugh all the time. That made me nervous. He was brutal to some of the writers who worked for him. He was a detriment, because he used to give me a hard time when I was there. He used to go in Jack Liebowitz's office all the time and yell and scream and cry whenever he was unhappy. Jack used to tell me, "Leave him alone, leave him alone." So I let him go his own way, but I didn't like it and I didn't say anything to him. Mort was all business.

JA: *Boltinoff was all business, too, wasn't he?*

CI: But there's a difference between being all business and being nasty. Murray was not nasty. Weisinger used to take ideas from one writer and give them to another, acting like he was supplying the writers with his own ideas. He had power and he liked to use — abuse — it.

JA: *One of Mort's — and Murray's — writers was Leo Dorfman.*

CI: He was terrific. He was very quiet, unassuming. He looked like an insurance salesman. He

and Murray Boltinoff would sit and plot for hours at a time. I think he enjoyed writing for Murray more so than for Mort Weisinger. Mort was hard on Leo.

JA: *When Mort Weisinger retired, Murray Boltinoff became the editor of* Action, *and Julie became the editor of* Superman.
CI: I split those books up purposely. I wanted different thinking on both books to see which one sold better. And you know what? Murray's did. Murray's stories were tighter, fuller, and Murray was a terrific editor, you know. Julie worked by formula, Murray did not. That's not putting Julie down. It's just the way he worked.

I wanted different thinking on each book, but let me clarify that. The basic original concepts were still the same. There were little modifications each editor made on their own. That's what I wanted.

JA: *Then Julie made Clark Kent become a TV newsman.*
CI: Right, that was our idea. I sat down with Murray and Julie, and I said, "How can we update Superman? What can we do with him to make him more in tune with the times?" Television had become so big by that time, and there was a change in the country in regard to how people got their news, so I figured, "Why not do it?" So instead of being a newspaper reporter, we had him on the TV and on radio.

JA: *You didn't have to go to any higher-ups for that change?*
CI: [laughs] I was the higher up, as it was my decision.

JA: *When the first Superman movie was being made, they decided to keep Clark Kent as a newspaper reporter. Was that because you felt that the general audience knew him that way?*
CI: That's how they knew him. Mario Puzo [the screenwriter] hit me on that one. He said, "What do I do with this?" I said, "You better stay with

YOU'LL BELIEVE A MAN CAN FLY.

THE ADVENTURE CONTINUES
The three outlaws from Krypton descend to Earth to confront the Man of Steel, in a cosmic battle for world supremacy.

the original concept." He said, "I think that's the best idea, too."

You know, I did a lot of work on that movie, which was actually two movies, since they shot both of them at the same time. Puzo had some very strange ideas in his original script. He wanted to have the Pope assassinated and he wanted Lois Lane and Superman having sex. I blew my top over that. Puzo had no real idea of what Superman was all about. I went upstairs to my boss, Bill Sarnoff, and he told me that he loved the script. I said I wanted no part of this, and he said, "Well, if you think it's bad, then go out and fix it," which I did. I spent seven days in The Beverly Hills Hotel Bungalow working with Puzo and the Salkinds [who produced the movies] on the story that eventually became *Superman I* and *II*.

JA: *For a year or so, Archie Goodwin worked for you, editing* Detective Comics *and a couple of war books.*
CI: Oh, he was a great editor and a terrific writer. I loved Archie. Everybody did. He was soft-spoken and he knew his business. But there was something about him I never could understand. Archie would go work somewhere and then, for some reason, he'd become unhappy and leave. I was so happy to get him when he left Warren [Publications] and was sorry to see him leave us. I never understood why he was unhappy at DC.

(above) One-sheet posters for *Superman: The Movie* and *Superman II.* The first two Superman movies met with great success. Maybe the producers should have had Carmine go over the scripts for the third and fourth movies, too.

JA: *For a little while, you had Dorothy Woolfolk editing romance comics.*

CI: Yeah, that was a bomb. She was awful. She was always late. She did a lot of talking, but no work. After a point, I had to get rid of her. Sol Harrison brought her in. He said, "She's a great writer, a great editor," a great this, great that. I tried her, and every couple of months, no books, no books, no books. She wasn't doing anything. I said, "This is not for you. Out! Goodbye."

JA: *You replaced her with Joe Simon on the romance books.*

CI: And those died, too. If Joe couldn't save them — since he started the romance books — then nobody could. We tried to make them for the young readers, and that didn't work.

JA: *Then you tried a book that was very interesting:* The Haunted Mansion [of Forbidden Love], *combining the love stories and the gothic genre.*

CI: That had good initial sales, but didn't last. What was interesting was that the word "weird" in a title always sold for some reason. I don't know why, but it did.

JA: *If an editor had an idea for a series, I assume the first thing he did was to come to you, and then you would either approve it or reject it.*

CI: Yes.

JA: *Were there any rejections that you regret?*

CI: Not that I can think of.

JA: *How often would you reject an idea?*

CI: It wasn't that often. New concepts were presented at staff meetings. I would listen to them, I'd get input from around the table, and then make a decision.

JA: *Obviously all the editors were there. Was that the main time you dealt with the editors?*

CI: Yes. If I had some problems with some books, I'd call the editor in and discuss it with them personally. At one point, Julie was editing all of the Superman titles. They were not doing well, but he was very dogmatic and wouldn't change. He wouldn't bend at all. I reached the point where I was going to get Roy Thomas to take over those books. I talked to Roy, but then I was let go, and that was the end of that.

JA: *What would you have done with Julie?*

CI: I would have put him back on science fiction. He was probably more comfortable there anyway.

JA: *But science fiction never really sold in comics. Why do you think that is?*

CI: I don't know… "Adam Strange" sold pretty well.

JA: *Yes, but do you think that maybe because most science-fiction books were anthologies and didn't have reoccurring characters much of the time it hurt sales?*

CI: I have no idea. But "Adam Strange" sold. I know that very well. And our mystery books sold well, and when Joe Orlando was the editor, there were no regular features in those books.

JA: Hawkman *was never a big seller either, at least the Silver Age revival wasn't.*

CI: No, that died. Hawkman was a cumbersome character with those wings on his back. How's he going to fight with those things?

(below) Carmine thought Hawkman was a bit cumbersome. Luckily for him, he didn't have to draw the winged hero very often, but there was this cover for *The Brave and the Bold #70* (Feb.-Mar. 1967) inked by Joe Giella.

COURTESY OF HERITAGE AUCTIONS (WWW.HA.COM).

BATMAN, HAWKMAN ™ AND © DC COMICS.

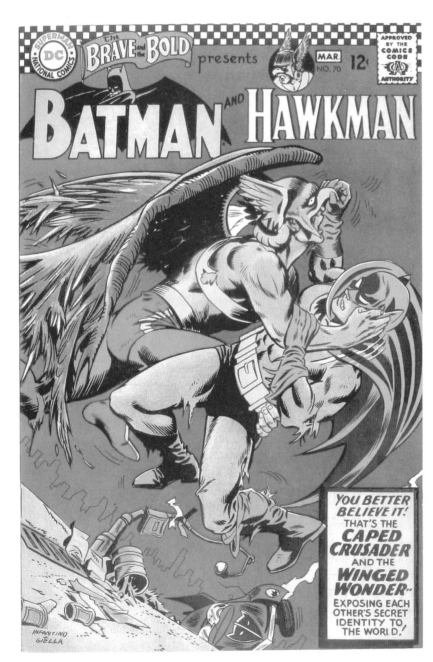

JA: *How did Adam Strange fly with a jet pack on his back without burning his backside?*
CI: [*chuckles*] Well, if you'll notice, I always angled the jet pack so that didn't happen. I mean, he had to sit down sometime! [*laughter*]

JA: The Atom *was not a big seller, either.*
CI: No, it wasn't. It was a silly idea. That was like "Doll Man." You remember "Doll Man"? There's only so much you can do with the Atom. Julie tried and tried, but the book just didn't gather much interest.

JA: *What was the best part of being a publisher?*
CI: I kept my money. [*laughter*] I traveled a lot. I went all over the world because of the job: Europe, the Philippines, California, all over the world. That part was fun.

JA: *In regard to Shelly Mayer, my understanding is that he got a lifetime pension from DC.*
CI: Yes, that he got. I made sure of that. Shelly was a very important man in the company once, and he deserved everything DC could give him.

JA: *Did he have any kind of editorial presence during your tenure?*
CI: No, but he would comment on things. We spoke a lot. But he wasn't well then, and he couldn't travel. By the way, I think we dropped *Sugar and Spike* at one point, and I paid him a salary anyway. Oh, that's the other thing they

fought me on. Not paying Shelly? Oh, forget it. He's getting paid.

JA: *He also did* Sugar and Spike *stories for the overseas market.*
CI: And I had him writing other stuff for me, too. He wrote *Bible Stories* for Joe Kubert, he wrote mystery stories for Joe Orlando. We all made sure Shelly had work. He wrote the first "Bat Lash" story, and I wasn't thrilled with it. So I called him up and said, "Shelly, I've got to re-do this thing." He didn't object.

JA: *What didn't you like about Shelly's story?*
CI: There was no punch to it. It was just a very basic, simple story, but I didn't blame him as much as I blamed Joe Orlando for not getting on the thing, because he was the editor. I said, "Joe, what's the matter with you? There are things missing here." Nick Cardy had already drawn it, so we had to replot and re-dialogue. So I injected the part about Bat Lash leaving town every time. He was a womanizer... little things like that. And then, of course, the thing about his sister in the nunnery. I added all of that.

I plotted the stories with Joe Orlando; then he turned the plots over to Sergio Aragonés, who wrote the scripts; and then Denny O'Neil wrote the dialogue. I loved working on those plots with Joe Orlando. I suddenly realized I loved the writing more than anything else.

(above) A series of panels from page two of the first "Human Target" story, which appeared in *Action Comics* #419 (Dec. 1972). Written by Len Wein, with inks by Dick Giordano, this story was one of the rare instances of Carmine doing interior pencils during his time as publisher.

JA: *Why didn't you do more writing?*

CI: Well, I couldn't, because I had to get involved with the distribution end. I did continue to lay out the covers.

JA: *What did Bill Gaines do at DC?*

CI: Management appointed Bill to help me run DC. He came by once a week to check sales and cost numbers. That was about the extent of it. Bill really wasn't that involved with editorial. I mean, we'd talk about things over lunch, but he didn't interfere with what was going on. After I left, Bill told me that everyone there ignored him, so he gave up trying to help.

JA: *I know you were very busy during this time, but did you ever draw anything just for the fun of it?*

CI: No way. I never had time to breathe, let alone do a personal project. I didn't even take a vacation the entire ten years I was in management.

JA: *You drew that one great "Human Target" story in* Action Comics *#419. That was the one Len Wein insisted you draw.*

CI: I enjoyed that. Len really pushed me to draw it. I drew it late at night and didn't even voucher for it. I didn't think it proper. They made a TV show out of it.

JA: *Yes. It didn't last long and it was bad. But they are trying it again.*

CI: I thought it was pretty decent. I appreciated that they even named a dog after me. I'm very grateful that they gave both Len and me creator credits for the character. That means a lot to me, and I'm sure Len is happy about it, too.

JA: *You were so busy in your job that you didn't have much time for socializing with friends. Did that include Frank Giacoia?*

CI: One day, I was going to go out to meet Frank for a drink. He used to visit DC every once in a while. He said, "I'm going to be with John Verpoorten downstairs when we meet you." I said, "That's nice." He says, "Offer John a job as production manager." I said, "I already have one." He said, "Just do me a favor. Ask him anyway." I said, "Frank, I don't need him." "Please, do me this favor." I said, "Okay." So we got down to the bar, I said, "John, it'd be nice to have you work for me." "Yeah, thank you. I'll think about it, okay?" That was it. Then I got a letter from Martin Goodman, "Carmine, I agree with you. John is a terrific production man, but he's going to work for me and nobody else, period." I didn't know what he was talking about. Then I remembered the conversation. They set me up, and I was unhappy about that. Frank and he were friends, I guess.

JA: *But you and Frank had been friends. Why would he do that to you?*
CI: You tell me. I don't know. I called him and said, "What's the matter with you? What are you doing?" He said, "Well, you know, I tried to do him a favor to get more money for him." That's why he pulled it, to get John more money. Unbelievable. Later on, he was angry with me because I didn't make him an art director at DC. He sort of was one at Marvel, and he was fired because he didn't do any work. He acted like he was a happy person, but underneath he was a very unhappy man. He thought he deserved more than he got, but he was glib and talked a good game. Gil Kane was the same way.

JA: *So was Vinnie Colletta.*
CI: [*laughs*] He was in my office one night. I was working late, and he says, "Carmine, goombah, I've got a question to ask you." "Yeah?" He said, "They're making the *Godfather* movie. So who do you think would be best for the *Godfather* part?" I said, "I don't know," and named a couple of actors. "No, I mean in this room." [*laughter*] "Get out of here."

Another time he said, "I know Stan [Lee], I know you well. I can carry stories back and forth to you guys, whatever you want." I said, "Get out of here. I don't do that kind of thing." He tried to make himself something he wasn't: important.

JA: *Some people have said that he was going to Marvel, telling them what was going on at DC. Did you ever hear that or believe it?*
CI: No. Well, I knew that he used to go over to Marvel a lot, but I don't know what he was doing there.

JA: *I've heard stories that right before DC first released Jack Kirby's Fourth World books — and you guys were still trying to keep secret at this particular point what Jack was going to be doing — that Vinnie, who was inking the* books, *had gone over to Marvel, and told them what the books were going to be.*
CI: Well, maybe. I wouldn't know about it at all. It could very well be. Kirby did not like his inking, by the way, and he didn't want him on his books anymore, so I had to take them away from him. Oh, he was angry.

JA: *I know that Kirby felt that Vinnie was a Marvel spy.*
CI: He said that? He could well have been doing that, trying to help himself. That sort of thing probably did happen more than once.

There was one artist who was always rummaging through drawers after everybody left at night, so we set him up one time. I made up a fake memo that said, "Private to Editors, from Publisher. DC is going to raise its prices. We are going to put out 500-page books for a dollar."

[*chuckling*] We put it in the drawer. The next thing I knew, Stan Lee was talking to people about us doing a 500-page book for a dollar.

JA: *Since we're sort of talking about Kirby again, I want to ask you about* Kamandi. *I've heard that, at one point, DC had gotten Hanna-Barbera or perhaps another animation company interested in doing a* Kamandi *cartoon series.*
CI: Not that I remember.

JA: *If you had a book that was, say, an average seller and was fairly new, if Licensing Corp said they couldn't merchandise it, would that have any effect on the life of a book?*
CI: No, they had no influence there. None. Not on any of the publications, nothing.

JA: *DC did not own* Wonder Woman, *the William Moulton Marston estate did. The story I heard was that because of the licensing agreement, DC had to publish a* Wonder Woman *comic in order to maintain the rights. They had to keep the book on the stands.*
CI: I never heard of that, no. It was a good seller, though, for a while.

JA: *It was? I heard that* Wonder Woman *was kept around because DC made more money in licensing than they did on the comic book.*
CI: Well, that part could be true. I don't remember having a rule that we had to keep publishing it. We wouldn't have dropped it anyway. I guess the

licensing carried that character. It was doing well with the licensing, I know that.

Gloria Steinem loved that character. She came in and talked to me about it. I always wondered what she thought about all of the bondage in the book.

Which reminds me — Marston's widow sent me his notes. I couldn't use them, because they were so sexual in nature. You'd go, "Holy Christ, you'd have the Comics Code around your neck." The notes were full of sexual symbolism. He had her legs wrapped around a cannon all the time, licking lollipops very suggestively. Oh, how the censors would have loved that!

JA: *In the '70s, you licensed* Tor *from Joe Kubert.*
CI: Yes. I'd written some of those for him once. He tried a daily strip, you know. I wrote a couple weeks of those for him. Unfortunately, none of the syndicates were interested.

JA: *And you licensed* Black Magic *from Joe Simon.*
CI: An overseas office company wanted that book.

JA: Black Magic *was a reprint book with new covers. Why didn't you use new stories?*
CI: The people overseas wanted the old stuff. They were Simon and Kirby fans. Carroll Reinstrom, a wonderful and honest man, was in charge of the overseas department. He took all the reprint material and sold it around the world.

He and Liebowitz had a special arrangement. I think he did it on his own. Jack told me one time that Reinstrom went out on his own money to Europe and sold this stuff. It was never sold before; he built our foreign sales. When Liebowitz left DC, he gave Reinstrom a contract that gave him carte blanche to do whatever he wanted, so we never touched him.

I used to meet him twice a year, and we'd go over what was selling overseas, what wasn't selling, and what areas he was most concerned with and in what countries. He used to take me to lunch just before Christmas every year. That was his big thing, and I tried to get out of it a few times. Not that he wasn't a nice fellow. He was a wonderful man, but he insisted on it. That was the thing we had to do. He said to me, "I'm more comfortable doing that," because he used to do it with Liebowitz, then he did it with me. And that was very sweet. I appreciated that.

JA: *During your time as publisher, was there much material done for the overseas that did not see print in this country? Were you doing very much new material?*
CI: No, everything overseas was coming from our operation, but here was the problem: *Bat Lash* was a big winner overseas. It was mediocre here, and I couldn't continue it because the sales here influenced the whole thing. It broke my heart, and it broke the hearts of the guys in Europe. They wrote to me a number of times. They wanted more. I said I couldn't do it.

JA: *When you went back to 20-cent comics, you started putting out some more reprint books:* Doom Patrol, Legion of Super-Heroes, Metal Men, *etc.*
CI: What happened was Marvel was going to flood the stands. The moment we hit 20 cents, they were going to try to push us off the stands. They went up from 30 to about 50 titles a month. I had to start matching them book-for-book. We lost money doing that, but so did Marvel. It was a tough time — and it wasn't the first time Marvel did this — and as you know, my decision was not a popular one.

I knew what Marvel was trying to do, and this is what caused me to be removed from DC. In early 1976, I went upstairs for the big year-end meeting to discuss the previous year, and Jay Emmett said, "You lost a million dollars." I said, "Right, and Marvel lost two million." I told them what I did. Well, they said, "We don't buy that theory." I said "Well, it was a theory Donenfeld used many years ago." Emmett said, "Well, that was then, this is now. I don't buy it."

They became unhappy with me, so I was out!

I'd like to make a point on a couple of things. I gave the artists reprint money. I created that, and I gave them their artwork back. And I put it in print at the time. I don't remember what year that was, but those policies were started by me.

JA: *Was there anybody who still supported you once you were out of DC?*
CI: Murray Boltinoff called me and said, "I miss you. You did a wonderful job." Who else called me? Somebody else, I forget who. But I know Murray did. Bill Gaines was very tight with me, and he was very upset by what happened. He wouldn't go back there anymore. "I have no use for this crowd at all," and he walked out. What I accomplished, I'm happy about. I had a number of new ideas. I was going to bring in new people, new packages, and new ideas. I took them all with me and didn't leave anything, period, and I'm happy about that.

CHAPTER 6

Back to the Drawing Board

(facing page) During the time Carmine worked for Warren, he had a slew of great artists ink his work, among them Walt Simonson, as shown with this page from *Creepy #85* (Jan. 1977).

COURTESY OF HERITAGE AUCTIONS (WWW.HA.COM).

©1977 NEW COMIC COMPANY LLC.

(below) This panel comes from a story in *Vampirella #62* (Aug. 1977) inked by Dick Giordano, who Carmine had brought to DC as an editor and artist from Charlton in 1968.

COURTESY OF HERITAGE AUCTIONS (WWW.HA.COM).

©1977 DFI.VAMPIRELLA ™ AND © DFI.

JA: *Was it hard for you to transition back to being an artist?*
CI: Very. I went to work for Warren at first, and then I went over to Marvel, and that's where I got the tough stuff to do. I drew *Star Wars, Spider-Woman, Nova, Ghost Rider, The Human Fly...* I did a lot of stuff over there.

JA: *Was it harder for you physically or emotionally to going back to being just an artist?*
CI: Both.

JA: *In equal portions?*
CI: Yes. I had a studio in the city. Some advertising people I knew had a studio, and I rented a working space from them.

JA: *Did not working alone at that period help you?*
CI: It was okay. I didn't care one way or another. I got my own room, and they wanted me to do some advertising art, which I did. The ad money was even better than cartooning.

JA: *When you quit drawing to become a publisher, you sold Joe Kubert your drawing board and your files.*
CI: That's true. Joe kept everything, so I bought another board.

JA: *And you had to work up your own morgue files again.*
CI: Yes, I had to do that myself. [*laughs*] By the way, I spoke to Joe recently, and he said, "I've still got the board." I said, "You cheap bastard." [*laughter*]

JA: *This was an interesting time, because when you came back you were still terrific. The layoff didn't ruin you like it might have.*

CI: I was okay, I guess. But don't forget, I was still drawing. I was laying out covers all the time — rough drawings, but still....

JA: *Once you became a freelancer again, did you try to reconnect with any of your old friends?*
CI: No. I kept away from everybody in the business. I withdrew completely. I felt lost. It hurt so deeply to lose that job, I just can't tell you.

JA: *It must have been hard to tell your mother about it.*
CI: It was. I didn't want to tell her. That was one of the hardest things I ever did.

At some point, Jim Warren contacted me and asked me to work for him. I didn't want to do it. He said, "Come on, work in the office. I'll give you plenty of work." So I did some stories for him, and he had some terrific people inking my stories: John Severin, Bernie Wrightson, Walt Simonson... I enjoyed working for Warren. The stories were more intense than the kind I had done before, and I liked the challenge. I had free rein to draw any way I wanted, which to me meant I could concentrate on design and story-telling. And it was interesting to see the kind of inks I got on my stories. They were all good, but Bernie Wrightson's were my favorite. He really knocked himself out on my work.

JA: *Once you were no longer publisher, did you ever think again of being in an executive position?*
CI: No, enough was enough. I began working for Hanna-Barbera out in California, and Barbera wanted me to think about moving out there and becoming an assistant, because I had done some

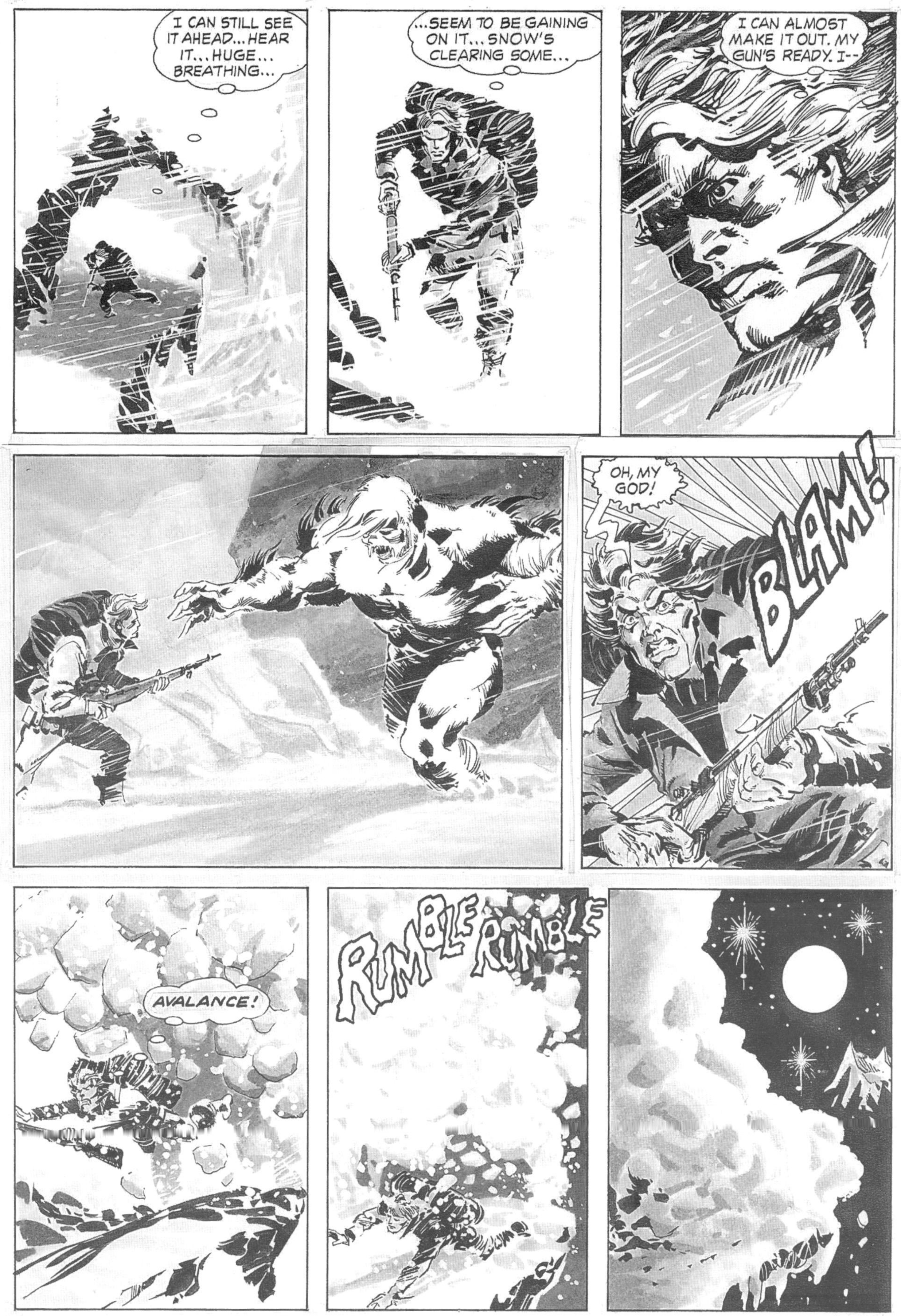
I CAN STILL SEE IT AHEAD...HEAR IT...HUGE... BREATHING...
...SEEM TO BE GAINING ON IT...SNOW'S CLEARING SOME...
I CAN ALMOST MAKE IT OUT. MY GUN'S READY. I--
OH, MY GOD!
BLAM!
AVALANCE!
RUMBLE RUMBLE
16

character creations for him. I couldn't do it. I had to come back East and take care of my mother, who got very sick. I had nurses around the clock, but I took care of her until she died. It took quite a toll on me. I was working and trying to take care of her at the same time. It was a rough time. And then I did a lot of work for Marvel.

JA: *Did you like drawing* Spider-Woman?
CI: I got a kick out of it. I remember the editor said to me, "You know, you changed the look of the character. It's not what we gave you." "Yeah, I think I remember." [*laughs*]

JA: *The way you drew that series was a little darker than you had done before. Was that a conscious thing?*
CI: Oh, yeah. Spider-Woman had to be drawn as mysterious, but she still had to be very feminine. That was important. The stories were interesting, and like with *Star Wars*, I had some good inkers, like Terry Austin, Steve Leialoha, and Klaus Janson. Overall, I'd say I had superior inkers at Marvel than I did at DC. They were quality inkers, some of the best inkers I ever had working on my stuff. Marvel put their best guys on my work. Not one of them was a hack. I can't say the same for DC.

JA: *Did you feel that the Marvel inkers were more illustrative? Craig Russell inked you on one short story [in* Marvel Fanfare *#8], and it was beautiful.*
CI: No, I think they respected my penciling more than the DC inkers. And most of them knew what they were doing.

JA: *Did you like drawing* The Human Fly *and* Nova?
CI: No, I thought they were dumb. The stories were nothing special. *Nova* bored me to tears. *Star Wars* was my best stuff. George Lucas loved my *Star Wars* work. I was told he requested me. It was a good series to be associated with. And Terry Austin gave me great inks.

JA: *How much research material were you given for* Star Wars?
CI: Some. The stories were good, the characters were good... it was beyond "Adam Strange," and I felt good about what I was doing. I guess that's what I'm best known for at Marvel.

Archie Goodwin wrote those and he said, "Just go see the film." He sent me some movie stills, and because I hadn't seen the first one,

CONTINUED AFTER NEXT PAGE

(above and next page) *Marvel Fanfare* was an artistic showcase. The series featured the best talent Marvel had to offer, presented in a high-end format. Carmine penciled this Dr. Strange story in issue #8, written by Peter Gillis and inked by the incomparable P. Craig Russell.

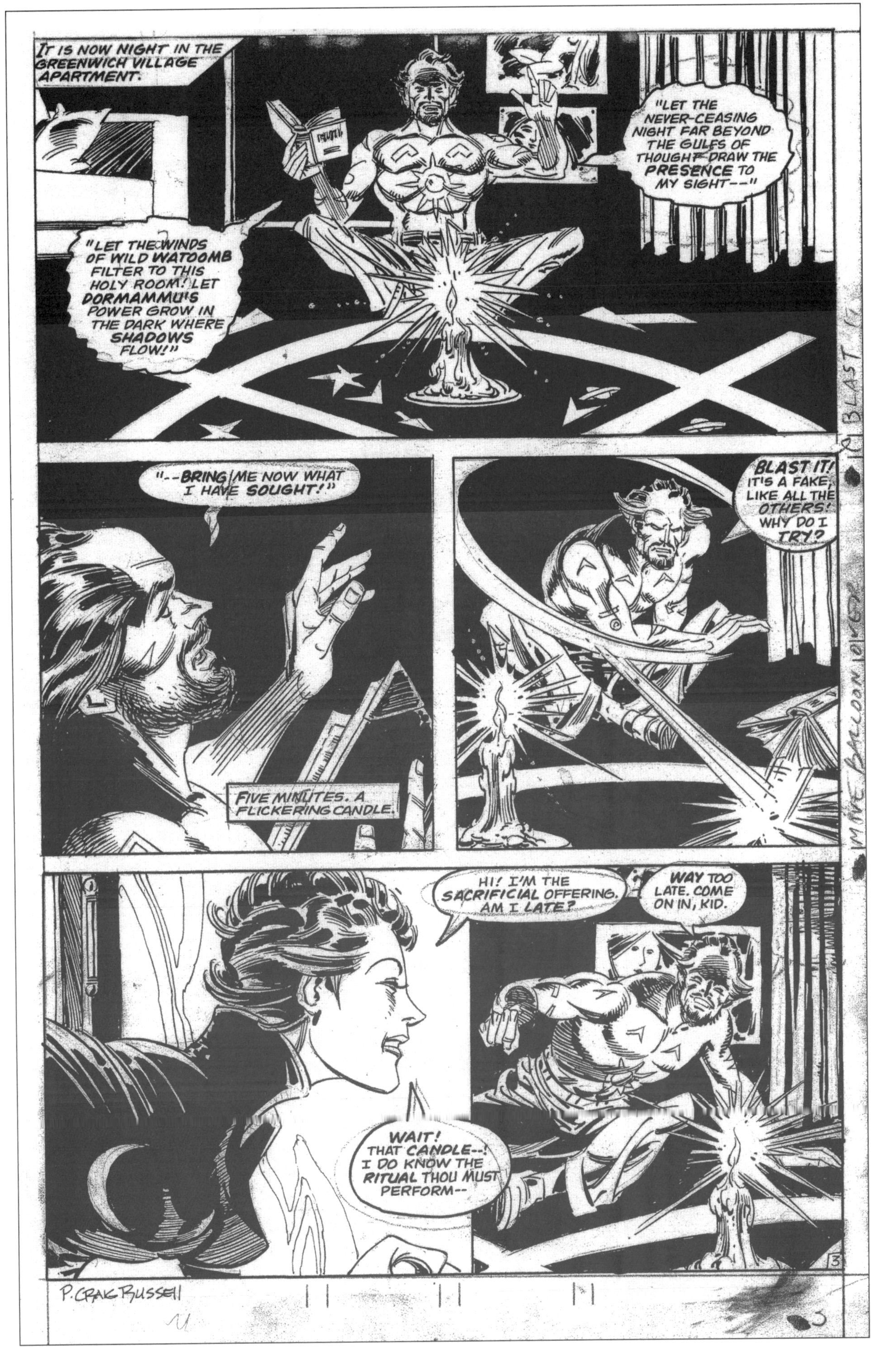
IT IS NOW NIGHT IN THE GREENWICH VILLAGE APARTMENT.
"LET THE NEVER-CEASING NIGHT FAR BEYOND THE GULFS OF THOUGHT DRAW THE PRESENCE TO MY SIGHT--"
"LET THE WINDS OF WILD WATOOMB FILTER TO THIS HOLY ROOM! LET DORMAMMU'S POWER GROW IN THE DARK WHERE SHADOWS FLOW!"
"--BRING ME NOW WHAT I HAVE SOUGHT!"
FIVE MINUTES. A FLICKERING CANDLE.
BLAST IT! IT'S A FAKE, LIKE ALL THE OTHERS! WHY DO I TRY?
HI! I'M THE SACRIFICIAL OFFERING. AM I LATE?
WAY TOO LATE. COME ON IN, KID.
WAIT! THAT CANDLE--! I DO KNOW THE RITUAL THOU MUST PERFORM--
P. CRAIG RUSSELL

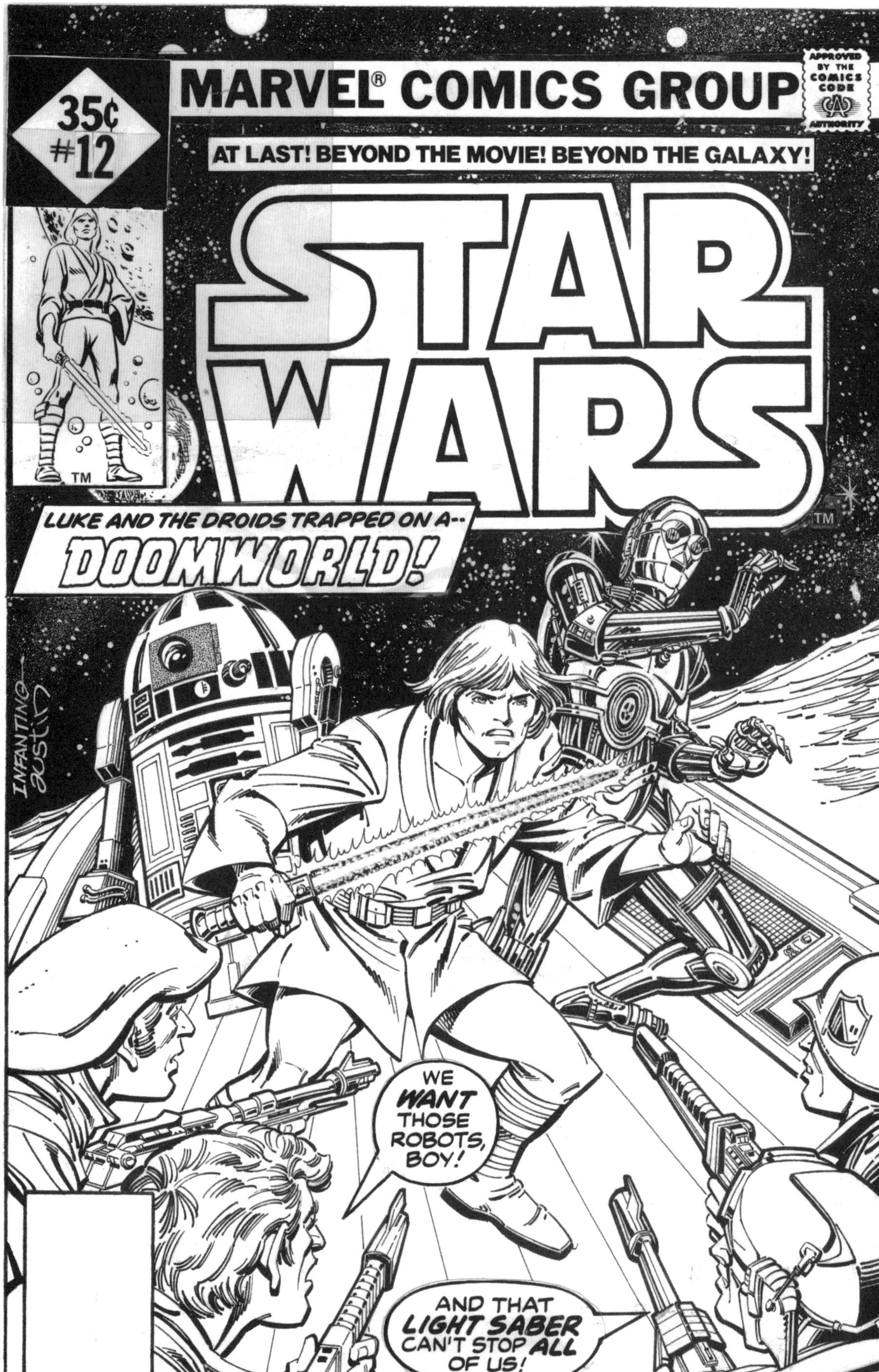
MARVEL® COMICS GROUP
APPROVED BY THE COMICS CODE AUTHORITY
35¢
#12
AT LAST! BEYOND THE MOVIE! BEYOND THE GALAXY!
STAR WARS
TM
TM
LUKE AND THE DROIDS TRAPPED ON A--
DOOMWORLD!
INFANTINO
AUSTIN
WE WANT THOSE ROBOTS, BOY!
AND THAT LIGHT SABER CAN'T STOP ALL OF US!

he said, "Carmine, I think you should go see it." So I went and I picked up on it right away. Then you could see how I developed the characters. Lucas liked the stuff I did very much.

JA: *You had drawn a lot of science fiction stories....*
CI: Yes, but this was more difficult, because you've got these characters that had to be on model to some extent. Those two robots, the ships, and stuff like that, this was difficult at the beginning, and then I swung into my own look. Eventually, it wore me down.

Hey, you know Dark Horse reprinted those stories and didn't give me any reprint money. When I complained, they sent a check for $200. A measly $200! I sent the check back with a note that said, "Here. I think you need this more than I do." [*laughs*] I felt disrespected.

JA: *How detailed were Archie's scripts?*
CI: He drew them. He drew little cartoon figures.

JA: *And he wrote dialogue on the page?*
CI: Yeah, right on the page itself.

JA: *You also drew a Ms. Marvel story [issue #19]. Why only one?*
CI: I have no idea. Look, it was work, and I just didn't question it. I wanted to keep busy, so whether it was "Conan" [*Savage Sword #34*], or *Captain America* [issue #245, breakdowns only], or whatever... I did it. "Conan" was all right. Again, I was just doing pages and never had a chance to get into "Conan" as I could have.

JA: *You also did a couple of Marvel Team-Up issues. One of them [issue #97] starred the Hulk and Spider-Woman. Do you think you did that because you were drawing the Spider-Woman comic?*
CI: Maybe. Probably. I don't remember now. Those issues don't stick out in my mind as anything special.

JA: *You also did a few issues of Iron Man, Daredevil, Ghost Rider, and the Avengers. Any of this ring a bell in your memory bank?*
CI: *Daredevil*, I vaguely recall. I liked the costume.

JA: *You would. It's red, like the Flash's. [laughter]*
CI: I like that color.

(left and facing page) The opening splash panel of *Star Wars* #11 (May 1978), featuring the Millenium Falcon, and the cover of *Star Wars* #12 (June 1978), featuring Luke Skywalker and his two droids. While Carmine was allowed to stray away somewhat from the films with the human characters, the ships and droids and such had to remain on model. Inker Terry Austin ended up doing most of the detail work, something which he excelled at.

COURTESY OF HERITAGE AUCTIONS (WWW.HA.COM) AND JOE AND NADIA MANNARINO.

STAR WARS AND ALL RELATED CHARACTERS ™ AND © LUCASFILM LTD.

(below) Bruce Banner changes into the Hulk in this panel from *Marvel Team-Up* #105 (May 1981) inked by Mike Esposito.

COURTESY OF WWW.ANTHONYSNYDER.COM.

HULK ™ AND © MARVEL CHARACTERS, INC.

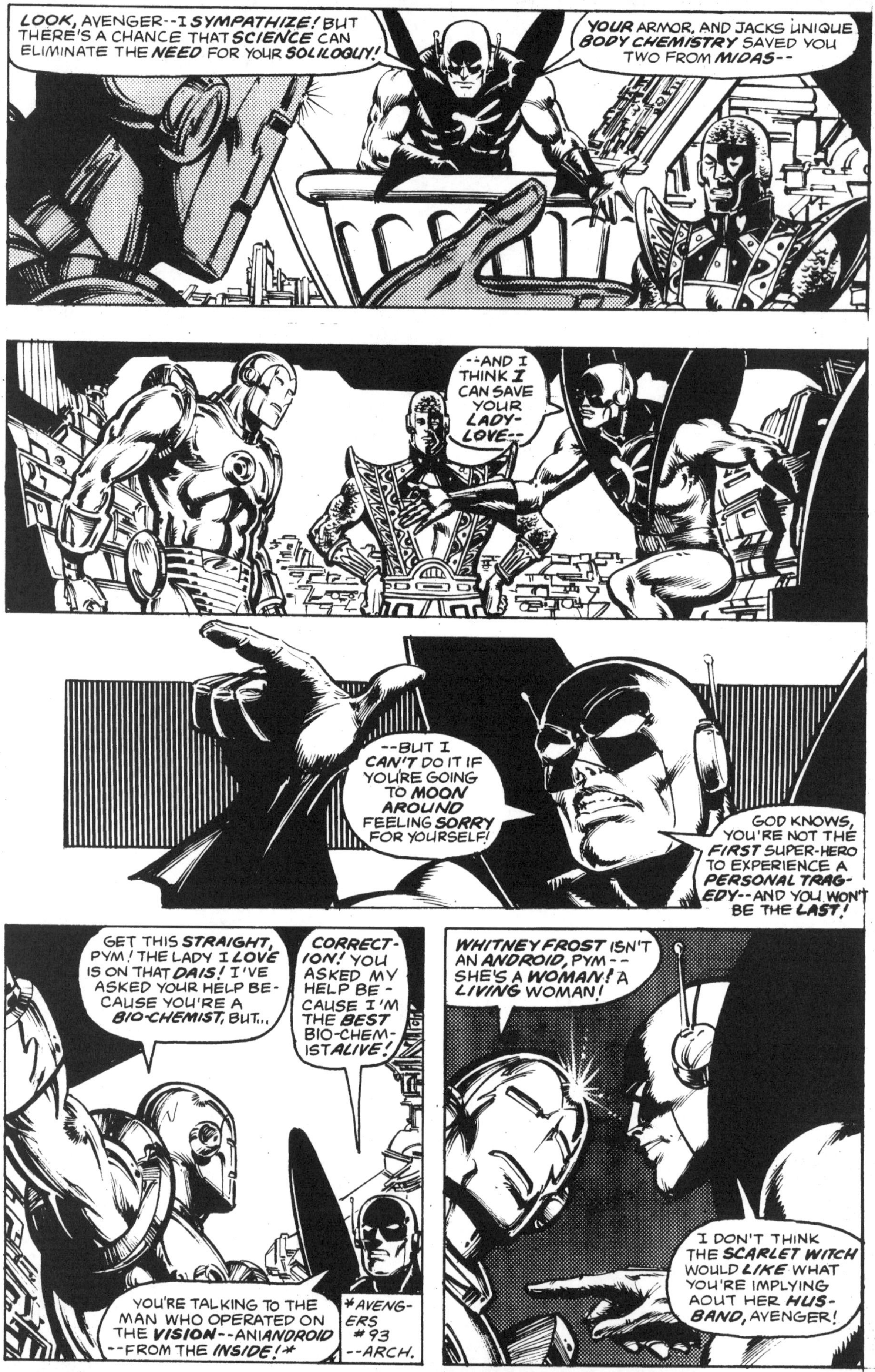
LOOK, AVENGER--I SYMPATHIZE! BUT THERE'S A CHANCE THAT SCIENCE CAN ELIMINATE THE NEED FOR YOUR SOLILOQUY!
YOUR ARMOR, AND JACKS UNIQUE BODY CHEMISTRY SAVED YOU TWO FROM MIDAS--
--AND I THINK I CAN SAVE YOUR LADY-LOVE--
--BUT I CAN'T DO IT IF YOU'RE GOING TO MOON AROUND FEELING SORRY FOR YOURSELF!
GOD KNOWS, YOU'RE NOT THE FIRST SUPER-HERO TO EXPERIENCE A PERSONAL TRAGEDY--AND YOU WON'T BE THE LAST!
GET THIS STRAIGHT, PYM! THE LADY I LOVE IS ON THAT DAIS! I'VE ASKED YOUR HELP BECAUSE YOU'RE A BIO-CHEMIST, BUT...
CORRECTION! YOU ASKED MY HELP BECAUSE I'M THE BEST BIO-CHEMIST ALIVE!
YOU'RE TALKING TO THE MAN WHO OPERATED ON THE VISION--ANIANDROID--FROM THE INSIDE!*
*AVENGERS #93 --ARCH.
WHITNEY FROST ISN'T AN ANDROID, PYM--SHE'S A WOMAN! A LIVING WOMAN!
I DON'T THINK THE SCARLET WITCH WOULD LIKE WHAT YOU'RE IMPLYING AOUT HER HUSBAND, AVENGER!

JA: *I expect a guy named Carmine would.*
CI: Oh, shut up! [*uproarious laughter*]

JA: *The Ghost Rider rode a motorcycle.*
CI: That I remember. He had a flaming skull head. That's the only thing I liked about him. I wasn't crazy about that character otherwise.

JA: *You didn't draw super-team books often, so did you enjoy drawing* The Avengers?
CI: No. Those kinds of books are a drag.

JA: *How did you get along with Jim Shooter?*
CI: No problems there. Jim had great respect for me. He knew his job.

JA: *When you worked for Archie comics in the 1980s, you drew* The Comet. *It was supposed to be a six-issue mini-series, but only the first two issues saw print. You were inked by Alex Niño, and Bill DuBay wrote it.*
CI: I really enjoyed Bill's writing. He wrote some stories for me at Warren, I believe. A good writer.

JA: *But you don't remember anything about that?*
CI: There's a lot I don't recall, Jimmy. I think office politics killed the *Comet* book. [Richard] Goldwater was mad because I got the originals back. I offered to sell them to him, and he said I'd never work for him again. I didn't care. In fact, I stayed as far away from the companies as I could. I didn't go into the offices, I didn't have long conversations. I kept everything on a business level. That's the way I wanted it.

JA: *Terry Austin told me he saw you in Shooter's office once, at Marvel. You guys were discussing* Star Wars.
CI: I don't remember that, but if Terry does, then I must have been there. Believe me, I didn't make a habit of that.

JA: *And then you went back to DC in the mid-1980s.*

(facing page) A page from *Iron Man #108* (Mar. 1978), written by Bill Mantlo and inked by Bob Wiacek.

COURTESY OF BOB WIACEK.

IRON MAN, JACK OF HEARTS, YEL-LOWJACKET ™ AND © MARVEL CHARACTERS, INC.

(left) Though he didn't enjoy drawing team books, Carmine drew four issues of *The Avengers*, including #203 (Jan. 1981), with inks by Dan Green.

COURTESY OF HERITAGE AUCTIONS (WWW.HA.COM).

AVENGERS, BEAST, WONDERMAN ™ AND © MARVEL CHARACTERS, INC.

CI: I got a call from Joe Orlando, asking if I would I consider coming back and working for him in Special Projects? I said if the money was good, I would. The money was very good, so I did.

One thing that upset me was that Joe wanted kickbacks. He did some things that made me very unhappy while I was working with him. It really hurt me. I gave Joe his break as an editor all those years ago, and he pulled a stunt like that!

JA: *In the 1980s, you returned to* The Flash. *How did it feel to draw that character again after all those years?*
CI: I felt like everything fell back in place again, like I had never stopped drawing him.

(below) Marvel must have liked Carmine's take on Ghost Rider, because they had him draw the avenging hero in three different titles: *Ghost Rider* (#43-44, and 50), *What If...?* (#17), and *The Human Fly* (#2), a panel from which is shown here, inked by Dan Green.

COURTESY OF FOUNDATION'S EDGE.

GHOST RIDER ™ AND © MARVEL CHARACTERS, INC.

THE SURFACE OF THE LAKE *IGNITED* WHEN I EMERGED!

THERE WAS *OIL* ON THE WATERS--TO DOOM ANY SURVIVORS TO *FIERY DEATH!*

THE MORTAL WHO DID THIS WILL *ANSWER*...TO THE *GHOST RIDER!*

JA: *When you originally drew the Flash, you drew him as a slim man. When you returned to the feature in the 1980s, you beefed him up.*

CI: I gave the Flash a slim build because he was a runner. Runners are usually slim and trim, not very muscular. That was the point I emphasized. I did make him stockier in the 1980s. I hadn't drawn the character for a long time, and I had seen what other artists had done with him, so I tried to draw him as he had been developed.

JA: *I've noticed that when you've drawn the Flash in your retirement years for commissions, you've kept the bulkier look.*

CI: Yes, because that's the way he has ended up looking, so that's the way I draw him now. But he should be a little thinner.

JA: *When you first drew Barry Allen, how old did you imagine him to be?*

CI: He was about 22 to 25 years old. I wanted him to be boyish looking; that was important. I gave him a bow tie, which was his trademark, and a sports jacket. I gave him a crewcut because guys coming out of college then wore crewcuts. I didn't base his features on any particular person, though.

JA: *How old did you imagine the Elongated Man and Adam Strange to be?*

CI: The Elongated Man was about 30 years old. His wife Sue was a little younger. I'd say Adam Strange was about 30 years old.

JA: *When you drew super-heroes, did you usually consider them to be in their 20s or maybe 30 at the oldest?*

CI: Not in their 30s... almost always in their 20s. The human figure is basically at its physical peak between 20 and 30, so that's why I drew heroes at that age.

JA: *But Superman always looked a little older.*

CI: Yeah, for some reason, he was always bulky. Superman was always 35, or at least he looked it. That was my impression of him. Remember when I did the layouts for the origin story for that tabloid and Curt Swan penciled it? Curt always drew him a little older than the other super-heroes. I guess most of us did.

JA: *Whose idea was it for you to come back to The Flash?*

CI: Dick Giordano.

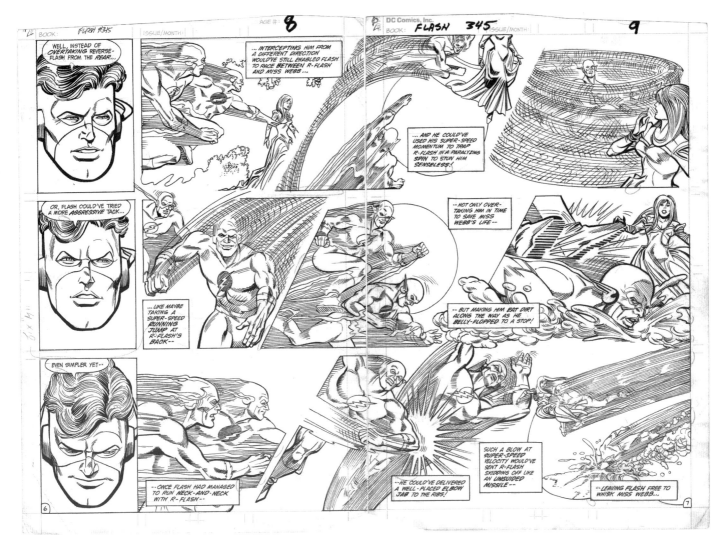

JA: *You came aboard with issue #296, and you drew it up to issue #350. So you had a nice run there.*
CI: Yeah, and they sold well, I heard. The book was floundering, and DC thought I would make a difference. I think I did. I was happy to draw *The Flash* at first. Cary Bates was still [writing] the book. He wasn't as good as John Broome — nobody was — but we did some nice stuff for a while.

JA: *When they started this "Trial of the Flash" series, it drug on forever and ever and ever.*
CI: It sure did. They were sucking it dry. It killed the book. The readers were bored and so was I. Ernie Colón was the editor, so I guess it was his idea, but Dick Giordano hated the Flash and wanted him dead. He wanted to kill it, period. That was his thing.

JA: *You don't think that was a company decision, rather than just Dick's idea?*
CI: No, he *was* the company then. He made the decision, and his decision killed the Flash, period. I really objected, but, as I said, it wasn't my decision any more.

JA: *Cary Bates took over as the editor when Colón left.*
CI: He lost interest, too. We were told the series was ending. Bates was killing time until they could kill the Flash. As far as I'm concerned, Dick Giordano killed the Flash. It's on his head.

JA: *In the* Crisis on Infinite Earths *series, Barry Allen dies and is replaced by Wally West. You're the co-creator of the Barry Allen Flash. How did having your character killed off affect you?*
CI: How would you feel?

JA: *I sure wouldn't like it.*
CI: Well, there's your answer. [*laughter*]

JA: *Did you like the inking on the series?*
CI: There was that one guy [Dennis Jensen] who did a good job. I wasn't overly crazy about the others. I was also drawing *Supergirl* for Julie. Bob Oksner inked those stories. He inked them beautifully.

JA: *Was there any difference between working with Julie this time around?*

(above) Kid Flash plays detective as The Flash's trial drags on. This two-page spread is from *The Flash* #345, written by Cary Bates and inked by Frank McLaughlin.

COURTESY OF HERITAGE AUCTIONS (WWW.HA.COM).

FLASH, REVERSE FLASH ™ AND © DC COMICS.

(above) Before the launch of *The Daring New Adventures of Supergirl* (which became simply *Supergirl* with issue #13) series, the creative team of Paul Kupperberg, Carmine Infantino, and Bob Oksner put together a "Supergirl" back-up story in *Superman* #404 to get the ball rolling.

CI: No, it was like being back in the old days. No problem whatsoever. It was unusual, you know. He made no demands on me, nothing like that. In fact, I never went up to the office again. That was part of my deal. I said I would never go back and I never did.

JA: *Did Julie ever try to get you to?*
CI: No, the vice president, Terri Cunningham — she's very sweet — Terri invited me to have lunch a number of times, so I said, "Save it for when we get to the conventions, Terri. I'd love to have lunch with you." I love her, and I love her secretary — both lovely, lovely ladies. I deal with them a lot. To this day, I respect them highly, both ladies.

JA: *How did you feel about doing* Supergirl?
CI: It was okay. I didn't care one way or another. I really felt that way. I couldn't have cared less at that point about comics, Supergirl, Flash, Batman, anything at that point. I lost interest completely, but I had to do it properly. It was a job you've got to do. I did some good work on there, though.

JA: *But was your attitude predicated, in part, because you were just burned out from doing them, or did the death of the Flash have anything to do with that?*
CI: No, I got over that quickly. The Flash was their problem, not mine. They brought the kid [Wally West] back as the Flash. I didn't care for that.

JA: *Why do you think you were chosen to do* Supergirl?
CI: I don't know. Julie called me up, "Would you like to do it?" I said, "I don't mind, Julie." I was doing the stuff with Joe Orlando at the same time, too. I was making good money then. I got a good page rate, too. I insisted on it, and I got it.

JA: *Did you have any contact with the people who were writing the stories?*
CI: No.

BRAVE AND THE BOLD #190 Sept. 20

THAT NIGHT...

I HAVEN'T HAD A CHANCE TO THANK YOU *MYSELF*, BATMAN, FOR ALL YOU'VE DONE!

THANK *YOU*, ALANNA! I ONLY WISH ALL MY MURDER CASES ENDED THIS HAPPILY!

HOW ABOUT THANKING *ME*, HONEY?

JEALOUS, ADAM? ALL RIGHT, HERE'S...

OH! THE ZETA-BEAM IS WEARING OFF... THEY'RE BEING DRAWN BACK TO *EARTH*!

PLEASE, ADAM... RETURN TO ME SOON...!

THANKS TO THE BATMAN, I'LL BE *BACK*, ALANNA... I PROMISE!

END

(above) The final page of *The Brave and the Bold* #190, featuring Carmine's old pal, Adam Strange. Inks by Sal Trapani.

COURTESY OF NICK KATRADIS.

ADAM STRANGE, BATMAN ™ AND © DC COMICS.

(facing page and following two pages) As these pencil pages will show, Carmine was on top of his game when drawing the 22-page back-up story in the oversized *Detective Comics* #500.

COURTESY OF BOB BAILEY.

BATMAN, DEADMAN ™ AND ©2010 DC COMICS.

JA: *So when you drew* The Flash *in the '80s, you had no contact with Cary Bates.*
CI: None. The editors used to send the scripts over. I'd finish the artwork, they'd send somebody to pick it up. It was back-and-forth a little, the script and artwork. Same thing with Marvel, as I told you.

JA: *In the '80s, you ended up doing some Batman again. You did a few* Brave and the Bold *stories.*
CI: Yeah, it wasn't fun doing those things. I had no feeling for that whatsoever. I think it was obvious, too.

JA: *There was one Batman story you drew for* Detective Comics *#500, where Batman is dead and he sees his parents. It was an effective way to draw it: dreamy and bordering on surrealistic.*

CI: Really? I don't remember that, James. I probably felt that thing if I did it the way you're suggesting.

JA: *Okay, when you say you didn't care anymore, did this just become a craft, just a job?*
CI: That's all it was. It was just a job, nothing more. I had no interest whatsoever.

JA: *What took the heart out of you, Carmine?*
CI: I guess being at DC, doing all the work over the years, being treated how I was treated — that would take the heart out of anybody.

JA: *Maybe so, but there were many times your page layouts were bolder. I'd see stories were you broke out of the standard tier format.*
CI: I'm sure there were times I was experimenting, just to keep myself interested. I don't think it happened as often as you think it did, but maybe I'm wrong. I'd have to see what you're talking about. I'm not sure how conscious I was of doing that.

JA: *Didn't you feel freer to lay out the panel arrangements on a page than you had in your earlier days?*
CI: [*pauses*] I don't know. I didn't have any restrictions, I know that. I did what interested me. And if I was doing it any differently, nobody said anything to me about it. Everything I did was accepted. I think they felt, at least for a while, that I was important to the company, so I was left alone. And I wouldn't have done it any other way.

JA: *You drew a four-issue* Danger Trail *mini-series in 1993. Len Wein wrote it.*
CI: He was a good writer. I really don't remember the story, though.

JA: *Frank McLaughlin inked you.*
CI: Yeah, he's wonderful. I love his inking, then and now.

JA: *Did it make it any difference because, in* Danger Trail, *no one's wearing costumes? They're all wearing regular clothes.*
CI: I enjoyed that more. I prefer that to super-heroes. I prefer that type of character, isn't that crazy? Super-heroes are all too fantasy-oriented. These characters were realistic, and I enjoyed that.

JA: *There was also a DC series,* Secret Origins, *for which you drew some stories:* The Flash, Gorilla Grodd, Space Museum, *and* Adam Strange.

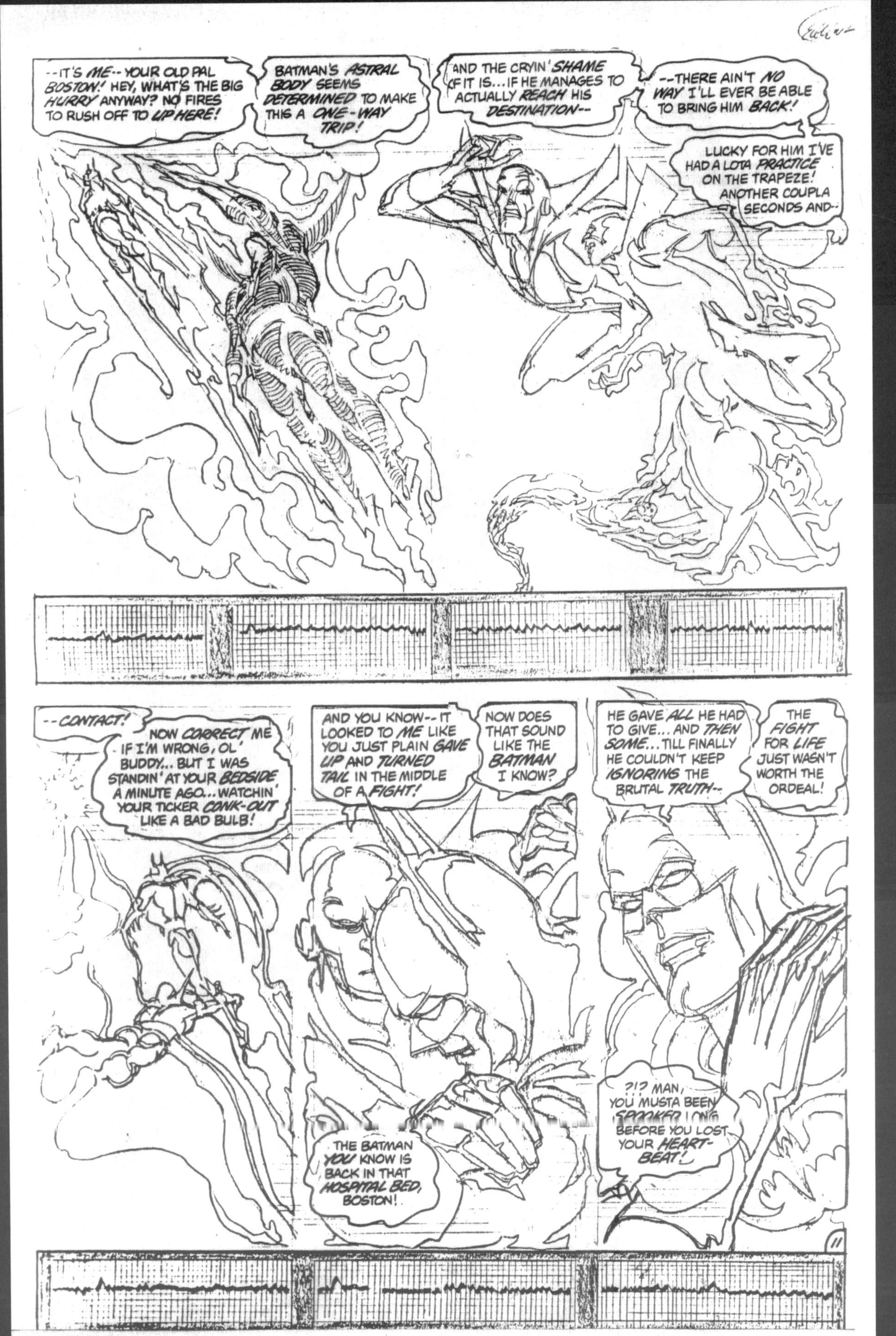
--IT'S ME-- YOUR OLD PAL BOSTON! HEY, WHAT'S THE BIG HURRY ANYWAY? NO FIRES TO RUSH OFF TO UP HERE!
BATMAN'S ASTRAL BODY SEEMS DETERMINED TO MAKE THIS A ONE-WAY TRIP!
AND THE CRYIN' SHAME OF IT IS... IF HE MANAGES TO ACTUALLY REACH HIS DESTINATION--
--THERE AIN'T NO WAY I'LL EVER BE ABLE TO BRING HIM BACK!
LUCKY FOR HIM I'VE HAD A LOTA PRACTICE ON THE TRAPEZE! ANOTHER COUPLA SECONDS AND--
--CONTACT!
NOW CORRECT ME IF I'M WRONG, OL' BUDDY... BUT I WAS STANDIN' AT YOUR BEDSIDE A MINUTE AGO... WATCHIN' YOUR TICKER CONK-OUT LIKE A BAD BULB!
AND YOU KNOW-- IT LOOKED TO ME LIKE YOU JUST PLAIN GAVE UP AND TURNED TAIL IN THE MIDDLE OF A FIGHT!
NOW DOES THAT SOUND LIKE THE BATMAN I KNOW?
THE BATMAN YOU KNOW IS BACK IN THAT HOSPITAL BED, BOSTON!
HE GAVE ALL HE HAD TO GIVE... AND THEN SOME... TILL FINALLY HE COULDN'T KEEP IGNORING THE BRUTAL TRUTH--
THE FIGHT FOR LIFE JUST WASN'T WORTH THE ORDEAL!
?!? MAN, YOU MUSTA BEEN SPOOKED LONG BEFORE YOU LOST YOUR HEART-BEAT!
11

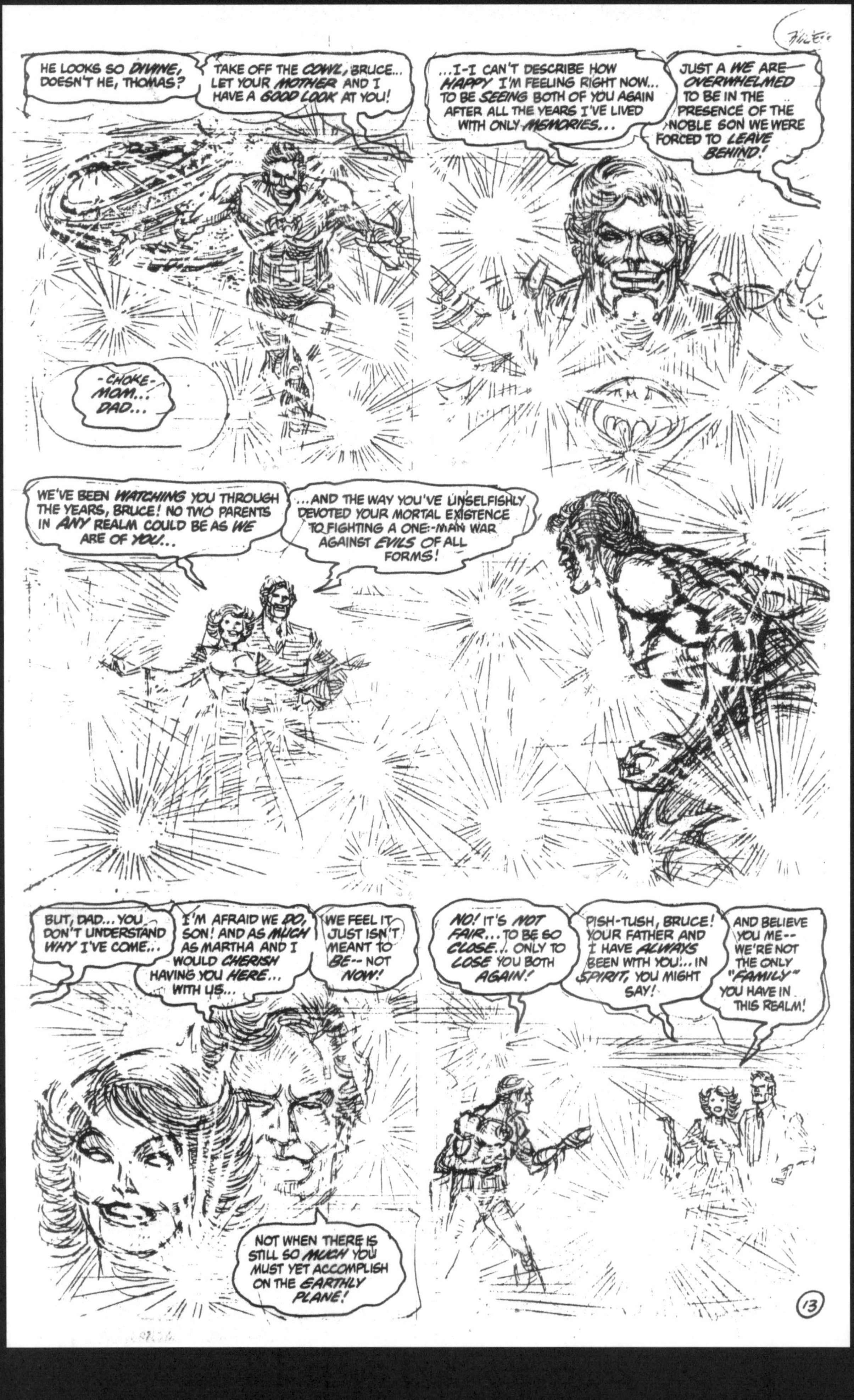
HE LOOKS SO DIVINE, DOESN'T HE, THOMAS?
TAKE OFF THE COWL, BRUCE... LET YOUR MOTHER AND I HAVE A GOOD LOOK AT YOU!
-CHOKE- MOM... DAD...
...I-I CAN'T DESCRIBE HOW HAPPY I'M FEELING RIGHT NOW... TO BE SEEING BOTH OF YOU AGAIN AFTER ALL THE YEARS I'VE LIVED WITH ONLY MEMORIES...
JUST A WE ARE OVERWHELMED TO BE IN THE PRESENCE OF THE NOBLE SON WE WERE FORCED TO LEAVE BEHIND!
WE'VE BEEN WATCHING YOU THROUGH THE YEARS, BRUCE! NO TWO PARENTS IN ANY REALM COULD BE AS WE ARE OF YOU...
...AND THE WAY YOU'VE UNSELFISHLY DEVOTED YOUR MORTAL EXISTENCE TO FIGHTING A ONE-MAN WAR AGAINST EVILS OF ALL FORMS!
BUT, DAD... YOU DON'T UNDERSTAND WHY I'VE COME...
I'M AFRAID WE DO, SON! AND AS MUCH AS MARTHA AND I WOULD CHERISH HAVING YOU HERE... WITH US...
WE FEEL IT JUST ISN'T MEANT TO BE-- NOT NOW!
NOT WHEN THERE IS STILL SO MUCH YOU MUST YET ACCOMPLISH ON THE EARTHLY PLANE!
NO! IT'S NOT FAIR... TO BE SO CLOSE... ONLY TO LOSE YOU BOTH AGAIN!
PISH-TUSH, BRUCE! YOUR FATHER AND I HAVE ALWAYS BEEN WITH YOU!... IN SPIRIT, YOU MIGHT SAY!
AND BELIEVE YOU ME-- WE'RE NOT THE ONLY "FAMILY" YOU HAVE IN THIS REALM!
13

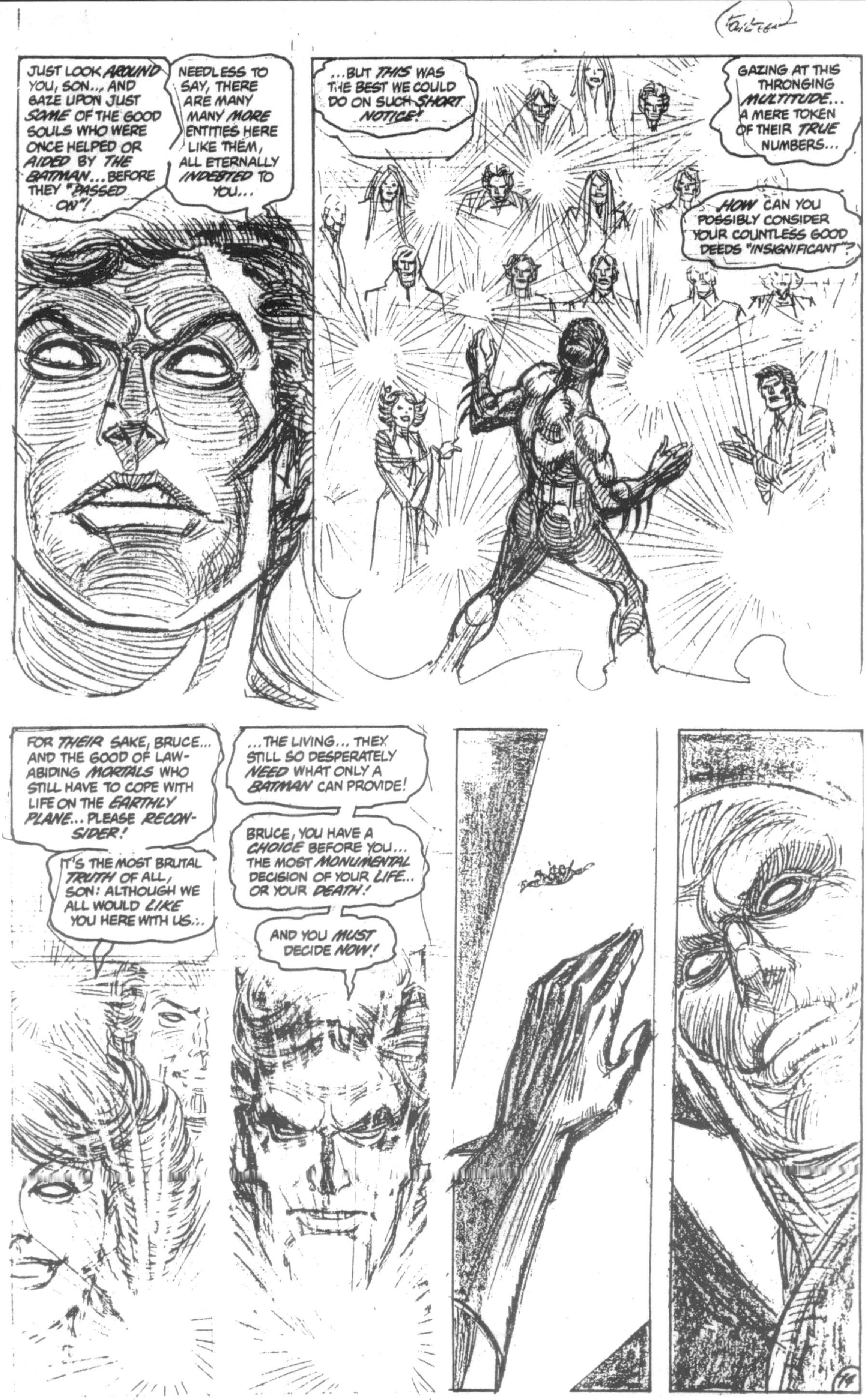
JUST LOOK AROUND YOU, SON... AND GAZE UPON JUST SOME OF THE GOOD SOULS WHO WERE ONCE HELPED OR AIDED BY THE BATMAN... BEFORE THEY "PASSED ON"!
NEEDLESS TO SAY, THERE ARE MANY MANY MORE ENTITIES HERE LIKE THEM, ALL ETERNALLY INDEBTED TO YOU...
...BUT THIS WAS THE BEST WE COULD DO ON SUCH SHORT NOTICE!
GAZING AT THIS THRONGING MULTITUDE... A MERE TOKEN OF THEIR TRUE NUMBERS...
HOW CAN YOU POSSIBLY CONSIDER YOUR COUNTLESS GOOD DEEDS "INSIGNIFICANT"?
FOR THEIR SAKE, BRUCE... AND THE GOOD OF LAW-ABIDING MORTALS WHO STILL HAVE TO COPE WITH LIFE ON THE EARTHLY PLANE... PLEASE RECON-SIDER!
IT'S THE MOST BRUTAL TRUTH OF ALL, SON: ALTHOUGH WE ALL WOULD LIKE YOU HERE WITH US...
...THE LIVING... THEY STILL SO DESPERATELY NEED WHAT ONLY A BATMAN CAN PROVIDE!
BRUCE, YOU HAVE A CHOICE BEFORE YOU... THE MOST MONUMENTAL DECISION OF YOUR LIFE... OR YOUR DEATH!
AND YOU MUST DECIDE NOW!

CI: I don't recall that. Isn't that funny? I'm connected with all of that, but I don't remember it. I vaguely remember drawing *Arak*... well, it wasn't something I stayed with.

JA: *You also did the* Legion of Super-Heroes.
CI: I did not enjoy that at all. Too many characters there. It was very boring, although I didn't mind it when I did *Star Wars*.

JA: *I also have you as doing a little bit of the* V *comic book.*
CI: Yeah, I remember that one. That was based on a TV series. I never saw the show. They hardly gave me any reference for it, either. Anything I did in that whole period was not interesting at all. It was just pure work, nothing else.

JA: *Once you lost the artistic spirit, you just weren't able to get it back, were you?*
CI: Right, and I think it showed in the work, too. Don't you think so?

JA: *Well, sometimes yes, sometimes no. There was that one Batman story I mentioned that I liked quite a bit. Your pacing, your storytelling is as good as ever during this period.*

CI: Well, that's instinctive, I think, as much as I hated what I was doing.

JA: *Maybe what joy you managed to find was in telling a story, rather than the actual craft of making lines, because I still don't think that work is as bad as you think it is.*
CI: That's true, Jim. But it was just a matter of turning out pages. Isn't that awful? Like that *Red Tornado* mini-series. You know me: if I didn't enjoy something, I think it showed.

JA: *Did anybody ever say anything to you? Did anyone ever notice?*
CI: No, no one ever said a word, but I felt it.

JA: *This is the one thing that I particularly wanted to ask you about, because I thought this was odd. DC, in the mid-'80s, licensed their super-heroes for a line of action figures called "Super Powers." Jack Kirby did some of the comics that promoted the toys, and then you did a few issues after Kirby. The thing that was weird was Pablo Marcos' inks. Frankly, I was never a Marcos fan, but I saw Kirby squiggles in your figure work, and I'd never seen you do that. It looks like there was a little of an attempt to be Kirbyish.*

(below) *V* was a huge television event in 1983, and it spawned not only a second mini-series and a year-long regular series, but an 18-issue comic book series, of which Carmine penciled 14 issues under the heavy inks of Tony DeZuñiga. This two-page spread is from *V* #1 (Feb. 1985), written by Cary Bates.

Somewhere, deep in space, circling stars too distant to be seen from Earth with even the most powerful of telescopes, is a place...

...A place where evil lives, secluded in a tower of darkness...

M-Master...! Darkseid! S-S-stop this agony that tears at your faithful servant! P-please! *Sob!* Have m-mercy...! *Sob!*

Silence, Desaad! Your torment no longer amuses me! The price of treachery is high, my loyal one...

...Particularly the treachery that led to my ignoble defeat at the hands of inferiors... and to my imprisonment here upon this desolate and forsaken piece of cosmic debris!

You are responsible! You have betrayed me!

PAUL KUPPERBERG
WRITER
CARMINE INFANTINO
PENCILLER
PABLO MARCOS
INKER
ALBERT T. DE GUZMAN
LETTERER
JOE ORLANDO
COLORIST
BARRY MARX
EDITOR

THRESHOLD

(left) In 1986, Carmine penciled the third *Super Powers* mini-series. Since Jack Kirby had penciled the first two, it is quite possible that inker Pablo Marcos was instructed by the editor to give Carmine's work a similar look. This two-page spread featuring two of Kirby's creations, Darkseid and Desaad, come from issue #1 of the series.

COURTESY OF WWW.ANTHONYSNYDER.COM

DARKSEID, DESAAD ™ AND © DC COMICS.

(below) Detail from Eclipse's *Airboy* #38 (Apr. 1988), which featured the first of a three-part "Heap" back-up story written by Len Wein and inked by Mark Pacella.

©1988 CARMINE INFANTINO AND MARK PACELLA. HEAP ™ AND © TODD MCFARLANE.

CI: Really? Is it possible I didn't do it? I don't think I did it. I wouldn't attempt to be Kirby.

JA: *I had wondered because Kirby was involved in that series. Would they have dared to ask you to keep his look?*

CI: No, they wouldn't, but I may have let myself be influenced. That's possible. I won't deny it, I just don't remember.

JA: Super Powers *was written by Paul Kupperberg, who also wrote* Supergirl.

CI: He was a friend of Paul Levitz, I understand. That's why he got all that kind of work he was doing. He just mailed me the scripts. No further contact there.

JA: *In the 1990s, you did a Web and Crusaders story for DC's* Impact Christmas Special. *They were licensing the characters from Archie Comics.*

CI: That stuff was nothing.

JA: *You did a couple of Heap stories for Eclipse. Was it strange drawing that character again?*

CI: I'm sure it must have been, but I don't remember a thing about it.

JA: *Why did your DC work dry up?*

CI: I had no more interest in doing it. I began turning work down. I think I turned down some Batman stuff, if I'm not mistaken.

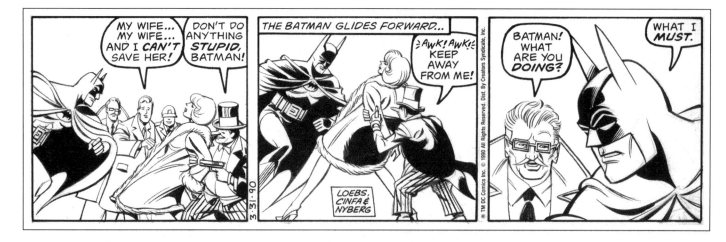

(above) The March 31, 1990 *Batman* newspaper strip, written by Bill Messner-Loebs and inked by John Nyberg.

JA: *But you did draw the* Batman *newspaper strip for a couple of years.*

CI: And those were boring, too. It was lousy writing. You know I never liked Batman. Never, at any point! And that's because of Bob Kane. He was a total pain in the ass. I told you he used to go to Jack Liebowitz and complain about my artwork constantly. And then one time I passed an art store on Madison Avenue and saw a cover of mine there. Kane had copied it directly, painted it, and sold it.

JA: *Well, he probably had somebody else paint it. He had ghost painters as well as ghost pencilers.*

CI: Probably, but he had his name splashed all over it.

JA: *When they contacted you to do the* Batman *newspaper strip, it was Creators Syndicate who distributed that strip.*

CI: But DC was in control of it. I worked for DC, not the syndicate.

JA: *Did drawing a newspaper strip mean anything to you at all at this point?*

CI: No, my interest in comics had failed completely. I couldn't have cared less for anything or anyone. Just like that, anything connected with comics — people or comics — I no longer was interested in.

JA: *Why do you think that* Batman *strip failed?*
CI: Bad writing, simple as that. It was boring.

JA: *After that, you essentially quit doing comic books, but you were still doing some licensing stuff for Joe Orlando.*
CI: Yes, but it dried up for me. I didn't walk away from it.

JA: *I remember you did some Captain Action drawings for the toys.*

CI: I penciled those for the people who owned Captain Action. They contacted me. It nothing to do with DC.

JA: *And you haven't done much stuff since then, except for that one Batman story, which was a Julie Schwartz tribute after he died. Is there anything that would turn you on to want to do a story now?*

CI: No, absolutely nothing. I've no interest in it. My time has come and gone, and it doesn't bother me one bit. In fact, I'm happy I'm out of it. [*Jim laughs*] How's that grab you? I really don't know the people at the companies anymore, either.

JA: *The industry has changed, and you don't feel connected to it.*

CI: True. There was a long documentary on the History Channel about super-heroes, and when they talked about the Flash, I was never mentioned. They forgot about me. I was told they didn't have the room.

JA: *The* Flash *TV show upset you, too.*
CI: Yes. That was not the Flash. That was a Batman in disguise. In one episode, they had a hotel called the Infantino Hotel, but it was a small, throwaway thing.

JA: *When you see an homage like that, does that mean anything to you?*

CI: Not any more. I think of all the people, not only in comics, but in all businesses... the little guy gets screwed. The corporations take everything they want. And this is normal for business, period. There's very little respect for the creative people and what they have to offer, except to exploit them.

Look what DC did with the Elongated Man. He and his wife Sue were a nice, loving couple. Their stories were fun. So DC had his wife raped and murdered. Then he commits suicide! Can't they create anything positive? It's an old gimmick now. Kill the characters and bring them back later like Marvel did with Captain America. And now I understand they've brought back my Flash. They said they'd never do that. Yeah, right. I've no respect for that kind of thinking. The people I had the respect for — the Eddie Herrons, the Bill Fingers — these were writers. The books the companies turn out now are all sex and violence.

There's one guy now, I can't stand his stuff at all, and he's a big name. He lives on sex and violence, and even the critics say his last DC project was the worst series they've ever seen. And he makes movies with the same mindset. I can't watch that kind of thing.

JA: *Sex and violence has permeated all media, not just comic books. Don't you think comics are only reflecting what's in the other media? They're imitating a low, common denominator.*
CI: But that's not good, is it? It's the lower caste imitating the lowest common denominator.

JA: *But it's that way in the movies, it's that way in television. Why do you think our culture has embraced the darkness?*
CI: In my opinion, I think they stretched things out to beyond Beyond. What have they left of them — characters like The Elongated Man — they milk it to death, then they kill it off. Then they go to something else and kill that off. So that's the gimmick now: kill them off. Well, Superman's carried on forever. They can't kill that man off, you know. But even then, they pretended to once, just to make money. Those characters they care about, they can't fool with them. The people who are writing this stuff have no respect for the industry. I really believe that.

JA: *When you drew comic books — I mean the '40s, '50s, and '60s, before you were a publisher — what did you think the average age of your average audience was? Would you say between ten and 15?*
CI: Yeah. It went up a little bit higher, because when we did *Bat Lash* the audience was there, but not in big enough numbers. But overseas, in Europe, they loved it. I hear they brought it back.

JA: *When you became publisher, why did you think the average audience was a little older?*
CI: Because *I* was a little older. I was expecting them to visit the people I grew up with, and they were there. They were getting older, too,

so I figured let's cater to them, and they worked with me.

JA: *The reason I'm asking is I think that's partly why you're seeing what you're seeing now, because the average comic book reader is in his 20s now.*
CI: I think you're right. Those are the only ones who come to the conventions, by the way — 20s, 30s, 40s, you know?

JA: *How many young kids do you see?*
CI: Never! Not one. Like Julie Schwartz said to me one day at a convention in New York, "Look around us. What do you see?" I said, "I don't know." "You don't see many young kids," he said, "do you?" I said "No." He said, "That was the audience years ago," and he was right. He hit it right on the button.

(above) In issue #200 of *Justice League of America*, a laundry list of great artists were brought in to draw chapters featuring the Leaguers they are most closely associated with — Jim Aparo drew Batman and the Phantom Stranger; Gil Kane drew Green Lantern and the Atom; and Carmine, of course, drew the chapter featuring the Flash and Elongated Man, with inks by Frank Giacoia.

COURTESY OF ARNIE GRIEVES.

ELONGAGED MAN, FLASH ™ AND © DC COMICS.

JA: *Because Marvel and DC do comics for an older audience, do you feel like they've missed the mark by leaving the kids out of it?*

CI: Yes, absolutely, although I tried that with Captain Marvel and failed. The mistake there was putting Julie on it. He was not the right editor for that book.

JA: *But that was a deliberate attempt to go after a younger audience. It was not an attempt to get the Superman readers.*

CI: No, it was an attempt to go to a younger audience. But Julie couldn't understand the character. I blame him just as much as I blame myself. But we did do the *Super Friends* comic, and that brought in a younger audience. Ramona [Fradon] drew that one. She was good. She had just the right style.

JA: *Except for Archie Comics and a few DC titles, I think comics have lost that.*

CI: Absolutely, I think so, too. The challenge is to get younger readers and girls to read comics again. I'd like to see them do that, instead of all this vulgar stuff. I challenge them to do that, to do something positive. Comics have lost their entertainment value and sense of fun. When people read the comics of my day, they felt good when they were done. Does anyone feel good when they kill off this guy and that guy? I just don't see it. We wanted our readers to enjoy what we did, to be entertained, and to come back for more. That was the key to our success. If their ideas are that good, and ours so bad, then why are their sales so low in comparison?

JA: *Well, there are more things competing for their money, like the Internet and video games.*

CI: Yeah, but comics are getting slaughtered now. We had competition for the audience, too, but we worked to interest them. I tried new characters, new formats... and I never resorted to disrespecting the characters. Well, I said what I have to say. Let's move on.

(below) One of Carmine's many commission sketches of the Flash.

(above) Carmine sketching at the 2008 New York Comic-Con.

PHOTO BY JIM AMASH.

JA: *Since you've retired, you've spent a decent amount of time doing commissions. Do you enjoy that?*
CI: Sometimes I enjoy them, not always. It depends on which characters they're looking for and what they want me to do with them.

JA: *Most people want the Flash, I assume.*
CI: Yeah, and Adam Strange is very popular, too. Batman, too, of course.

JA: *Do you prefer doing recreations or new compositions?*
CI: No, I do my own compositions. I won't copy anything.

JA: *But at times, you've recreated your old covers.*
CI: Yeah, that's true.

JA: *That seems a little bit less interesting than doing something new.*
CI: I know, but that's what some fans want. That's what they pay for. I was paid very well for them, so that's why I did them.

JA: *What is your preference?*
CI: I prefer to draw something original.

JA: *Okay, if I handed you a canvas, paints, and brushes, and told you to paint something, and you wanted to, what would you paint?*
CI: Oh, that's interesting. I was going to say a seascape, not people. Or if I did people, you'd see them from the back. You would figure that one out... [*Jim laughs*] people walking away towards the distance and never seeing their faces. Isn't that strange? But that's what I would paint.

JA: *Knowing you, I would imagine you'd do something Expressionistic.*
CI: Yes, it would be very much so. That's what I prefer. Modigliani's my favorite painter. You know his work because he's sheer genius. And Degas, of course. The Impressionists of France were my favorite people and artists.

(above) Carmine and Jim Amash mug for the camera at the 2008 New York Comic-Con.

JA: *I'm still trying to get you to do non-comics art, on anything you want, any style you want.*
CI: I know. You're not going to get your way, though. [*laughter*]

JA: *I haven't given up.*
CI: I have no desire anymore. If I feel it one day, I'll do it.

JA: *I just think it would be interesting for you to do something non-comics and not worry about what anyone else thinks but you.*
CI: I know what you're saying. I did that sketch — very Impressionistic — of all the DC characters I'd done... a very strange drawing. It's very different from my usual stuff. It was really the outline of my face and head, and the characters were in and out, around the shapes. It was very interesting, and I enjoyed doing it.

JA: *I still want to see you push yourself in that direction. I think it would be interesting to see what you came up with.*
CI: Well, I can't be pushed. We'll just have to see. Maybe someday, if I'm ever motivated, I'll do something, and maybe it'll surprise you.
    You know, I loved the phrase from *The Tale of* *Two Cities*. I think my whole life in comics was like the best of times and the worst of times.

JA: *When were the best times for you?*
CI: When I was in charge of DC. I'll tell you one of the best times, when we won all those awards. We made a lot of money then. One year, we created $900,000, and that was without advertising. But the following year, because I had to push Marvel on the stands, we lost some money, but they lost, too. They lost twice as much as we did, but the guys upstairs didn't want to hear that. They knew nothing about the publishing business, those guys, and they couldn't have cared less.

JA: *They just knew bottom line, right?*
CI: Right. My bottom line is that I did the very best I could under the circumstances. I took some hits, and I hit back. I got a lot of respect from some people and none from others. But that's life. I made an impact on this business as an artist, as an editor, and as a publisher. I've gotten some flack, but I've received a lot more praise. I know I sound bitter at times, but I can't pretend I didn't have down times, so I won't act like I didn't. But no matter what, I'm proud of what I accomplished.

Art Gallery

(above) These and the following sketches were done throughout the early to mid-'50s on the backs of pages of comic book artwork. Carmine, like many other artists before and since, would often sketch in this manner as a warm-up, or to work out a problem, or to simply take a break from what he was working on.

(right) These sketches were done in 1960.

COURTESY OF HERITAGE AUCTIONS (WWW.HA.COM).

©2010 CARMINE INFANTINO.

(above) Sketches from 1955.

COURTESY OF DAVID ARMSTRONG.

©2010 CARMINE INFANTINO.

(left) Sketch from the mid-'50s.
COURTESY OF FRANK GIELLA.
©2010 CARMINE INFANTINO.

(below) Sketches from 1955.
COURTESY OF GARY LAND.
©2010 CARMINE INFANTINO.

(above) More sketches done sometime in the early to mid-'50s.

COURTESY OF FRANK GIELLA.

(above) There was only one issue of *Star Studded Comics* released by Cambridge House Publishers, but it does contain some of Carmine's earliest comic book work. He penciled and inked the six-page "Jiu Jitsu Joe," the opening page of which is shown here.

COURTESY OF KEN QUATTRO.

(above) *Real Clue Crime Stories* #139 (Jan. 1949). Inks by Bernard Sachs.

(facing page) Carmine didn't draw very many covers for DC before 1950, but he did get the chance with *Flash Comics* #99 (Sept. 1948).

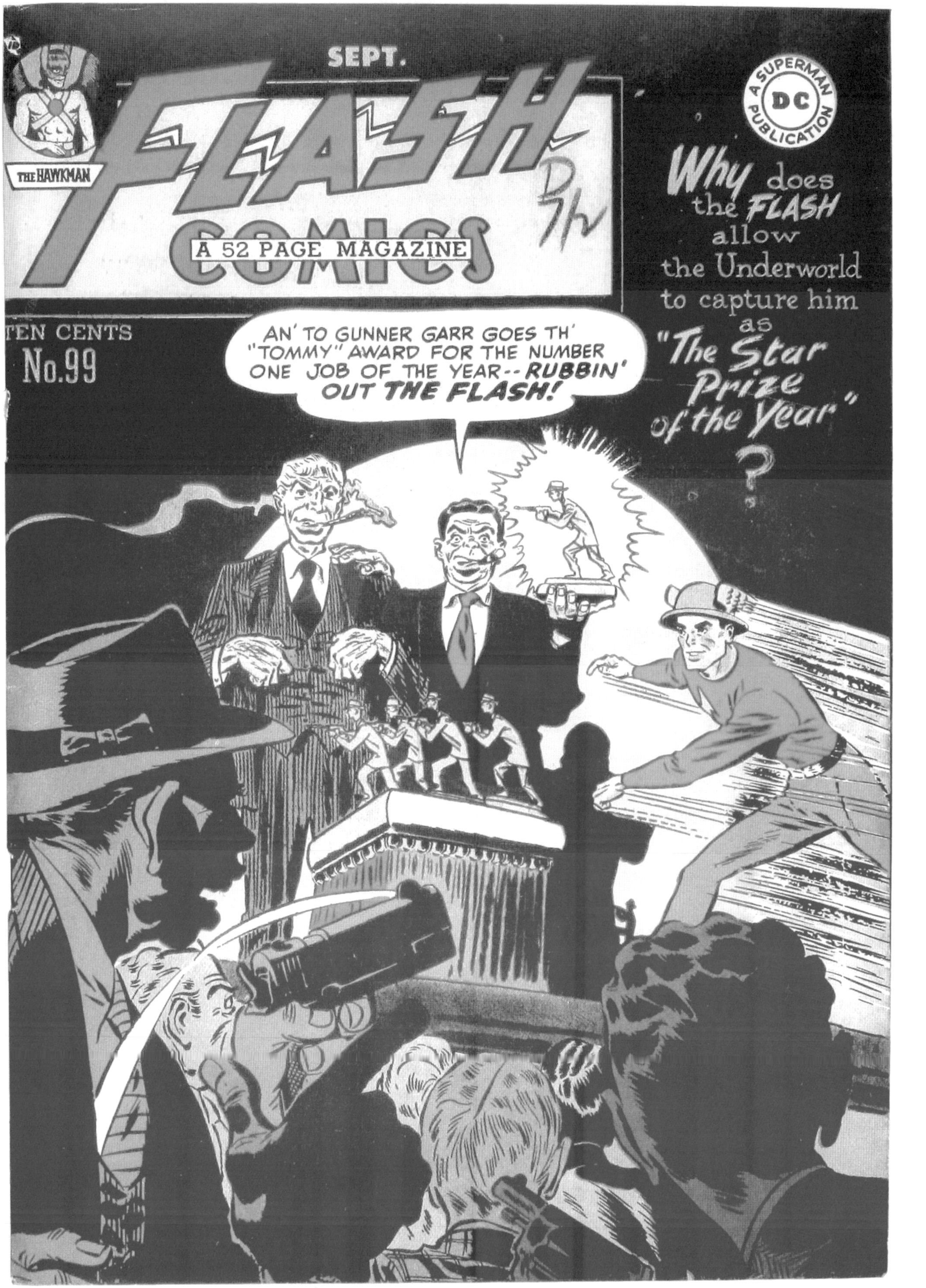

SEPT.
FLASH COMICS
A 52 PAGE MAGAZINE
THE HAWKMAN
TEN CENTS
No.99
A SUPERMAN DC PUBLICATION
Why does the FLASH allow the Underworld to capture him as "The Star Prize of the Year"?
AN' TO GUNNER GARR GOES TH' "TOMMY" AWARD FOR THE NUMBER ONE JOB OF THE YEAR--RUBBIN' OUT THE FLASH!

(above and following twelve pages) In the mid-1940s, Carmine did quite a bit of work for Hillman, publishers of the iconic Airboy and Heap. There he was encouraged not only to pencil and ink, but write as well. We're not absolutely certain Carmine wrote this "Airboy" story from *Airboy Comics* vol. 4, #1 (Feb. 1947), but it's quite possible he did.

COURTESY OF MIKE COSTA.

©1947 HILLMAN PERIODICALS, INC.

OUR STORY BEGINS IN NEW YORK ...IT IS THE SWANK APARTMENT OF "IVORY" ANDERSON.

"IVORY" SURE WILL BE TICKLED TO GET THIS STUFF!

AND HOW!...THESE IVORY CURIOS WILL BE WORTH PLENTY OF JACK!

HEY, "IVORY"... WE GOT ALL THE STUFF YOU SENT US FOR!

YEAH...WE CLEANED OUT EVERY PIECE OF IVORY IN THE STORE!

PUT 'EM ON THE TABLE BOYS!

WELL?..AIN'T'CHA ANY HAPPIER ABOUT IT THAN THAT, IVORY?!

SURE! SURE!..BUT I'VE GOT MY MIND ON SOMETHING BIGGER!..A SOLID IVORY BATH TUB! SWELL? HUH?

LOOK, BOSS! YOU'VE GOT ALL KINDS OF IVORY STUFF HERE...BOOKENDS, SHOE HORNS, CANDLE-STICKS ...EVEN YOUR TOOTH-PICKS ARE IVORY! BUT NOW-AN IVORY BATH TUB!

HEY! WAIT! LOOK HERE... I'LL SHOW YOU SOMETHING!

...THIS REMINDS ME!...I'M GONNA TELL YOU BOYS A LITTLE STORY..

5¢ DAILY LEAD

AIRBOY TO FLY NOTED EXPLORER ON SEARCH FOR AN ELEPHANT WITH FOUR TUSKS....

Will Travel To Elephant Graveyard in India..

...WHEN I WAS A YOUNG PUNK I SAW THAT ELEPHANT WITH FOUR TUSKS.. IN ALLAHABAD, INDIA! IN FACT I'M THE REASON THOSE SCIENTIFIC GUYS HAVEN'T GOT THE ELEPHANT RIGHT NOW!....HERE'S HOW IT WAS..

2

"...THEY HAD THE ELEPHANT CAPTURED AND WERE JUST ABOUT TO SHIP IT TO THE STATES..."

THAT'S THE ONLY ELEPHANT WITH FOUR TUSKS EVER DISCOVERED, ANDERSON!

YEAH! HE'S QUITE A FREAK, EH, PROF!

"WELL, I WAS WAITING TO GRAB A SHIP OUT OF THE DUMP-SO I THOUGHT I WOULD HAVE SOME FUN..."

LET'S SEE HOW ANGRY YOU CAN GET IF I JAB THIS STICK IN YOUR EYE, JUMBO!

"BOY!!..THAT ELEPHANT WENT WILD! HE TORE THE CHAINS FREE, LIKE THEY WERE STRING"...

"...SO THE BEAST DISAPPEARED INTO THE JUNGLE AND THE PROFESSOR WAS PLENTY MAD..."

YOU YOUNG IDIOT! THAT ELEPHANT WAS A SCIENTIFIC PRIZE!

AW, CALM DOWN, PROFESSOR REED! HE DIDN'T HURT YOU, DID HE?

WHAT'S ALL THAT GOT TO DO WITH AN IVORY BATH TUB, BOSS?

JUST THIS, PINKY! THAT OLD ELEPHANT "GARGAN" IS PROBABLY DEAD NOW. SO PROFESSOR REED FIGURES HE'LL GET THE FOUR TUSKS OFF THE BODY IN AN ELEPHANT GRAVEYARD..!

3

...AND IN AN ELEPHANT GRAVEYARD THERE'S PILES OF IVORY! ENOUGH TO MAKE ME A BATH TUB AND MAYBE EVEN A *COFFIN* FOR JUDGEMENT DAY...BOYS, WE'RE GOIN' TO VISIT PROFESSOR REED TONIGHT-AND FIND OUT WHERE THE GRAVEYARD IS!

THAT EVENING, AT PROFESSOR REED'S HOME...

YES! YES! THIS SHOULD BE THE LOCATION OF THE GRAVEYARD! IT'S ALMOST TIME FOR AIRBOY TO ARRIVE!

PLANNING A LITTLE TRIP, PROF?

A HALF HOUR LATER, AIRBOY ARRIVES TO FIND THE PROFESSOR UNCONSCIOUS...

PROFESSOR REED! WHAT'S HAPPENED?

THEY TOOK ALL MAPS! WE'LL NEVER FIND THE GRAVEYARD WITHOUT THEM!

WHO WAS IT, PROFESSOR?

IT WAS THAT GANGSTER IVORY ANDERSON! WE'LL NEVER GET THEM BACK FROM HIM!

MAYBE NOT HERE IN THE STATES! BUT WE'LL GET THEM BACK!

167

IT'S A CINCH HE WANTS THE IVORY IN THE GRAVEYARD. HE'LL HAVE TO GO TO ALLAHABAD FIRST THOUGH, SO WE'LL BEAT HIM THERE!

THE NEXT DAY, BIRDIE WINGS OUT OVER THE ATLANTIC CARRYING AIRBOY AND PROFESSOR REED...

DON'T GIVE UP, PROFESSOR REED! MAYBE WE CAN GET TO THE GRAVEYARD FIRST!

AND NOT MANY MILES AWAY, ANOTHER PLANE IS HEADED TOWARD ALLAHABAD, INDIA!

JUST THINK, PINKY! THE GREAT IVORY ANDERSON BURIED IN AN IVORY COFFIN... SOME CLASS, EH! WHAT A FITTING WAY TO END A GREAT CAREER!

YOU'RE NUTS, BOSS!

SEVERAL DAYS LATER, AIRBOY IS IN THE JUNGLE VILLAGE OF ALLAHABAD...

YES, BWANA! OTHER STRANGERS STAY IN VILLAGE!

THANKS! NOW YOU JUST SHOW US WHERE!

PLEASE BE CAREFUL, AIRBOY! IVORY IS A KILLER!

DON'T WORRY PROFESSOR! I'LL TAKE CARE OF HIM!

AND INSIDE IVORY'S TENT...

WELL, WE START FIRST THING IN THE MORNING, PINKY! I GOT THOSE NATIVE GUIDES EASY!

5

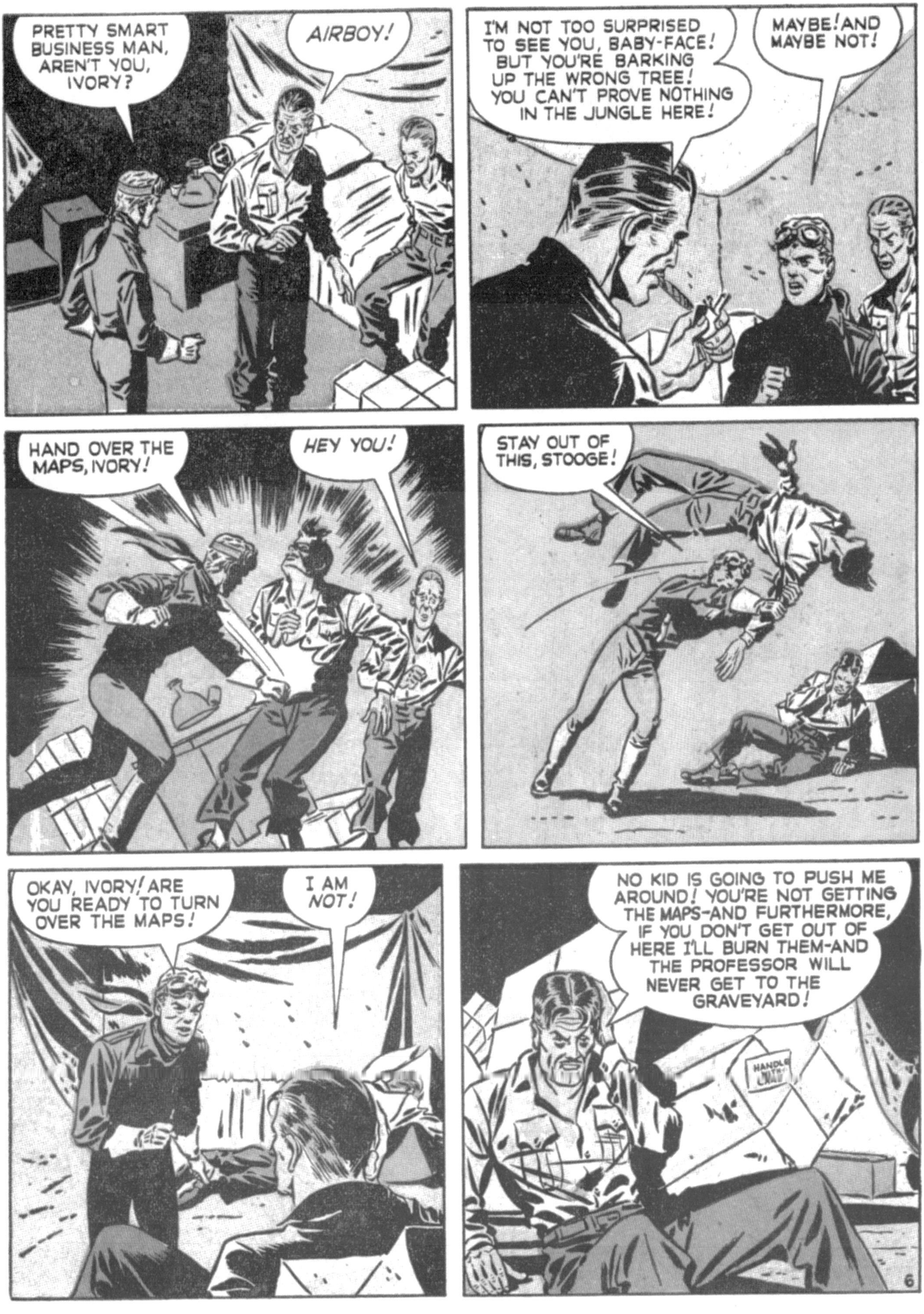
PRETTY SMART BUSINESS MAN, AREN'T YOU, IVORY?
AIRBOY!
I'M NOT TOO SURPRISED TO SEE YOU, BABY-FACE! BUT YOU'RE BARKING UP THE WRONG TREE! YOU CAN'T PROVE NOTHING IN THE JUNGLE HERE!
MAYBE! AND MAYBE NOT!
HAND OVER THE MAPS, IVORY!
HEY YOU!
STAY OUT OF THIS, STOOGE!
OKAY, IVORY! ARE YOU READY TO TURN OVER THE MAPS!
I AM NOT!
NO KID IS GOING TO PUSH ME AROUND! YOU'RE NOT GETTING THE MAPS-AND FURTHERMORE, IF YOU DON'T GET OUT OF HERE I'LL BURN THEM-AND THE PROFESSOR WILL NEVER GET TO THE GRAVEYARD!
6

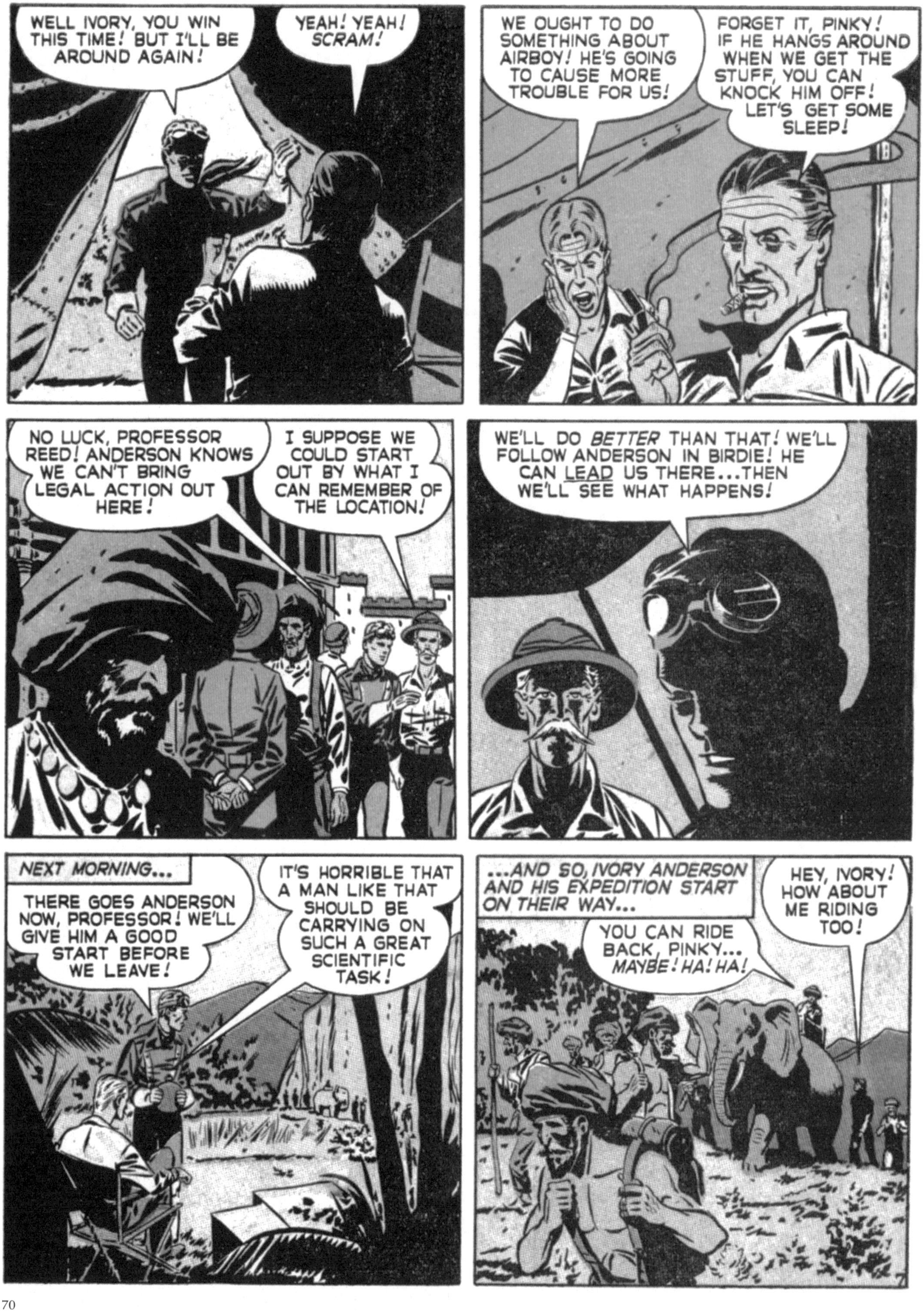

WELL IVORY, YOU WIN THIS TIME! BUT I'LL BE AROUND AGAIN!
YEAH! YEAH! *SCRAM!*
WE OUGHT TO DO SOMETHING ABOUT AIRBOY! HE'S GOING TO CAUSE MORE TROUBLE FOR US!
FORGET IT, PINKY! IF HE HANGS AROUND WHEN WE GET THE STUFF, YOU CAN KNOCK HIM OFF! LET'S GET SOME SLEEP!
NO LUCK, PROFESSOR REED! ANDERSON KNOWS WE CAN'T BRING LEGAL ACTION OUT HERE!
I SUPPOSE WE COULD START OUT BY WHAT I CAN REMEMBER OF THE LOCATION!
WE'LL DO *BETTER* THAN THAT! WE'LL FOLLOW ANDERSON IN BIRDIE! HE CAN LEAD US THERE...THEN WE'LL SEE WHAT HAPPENS!
NEXT MORNING...
THERE GOES ANDERSON NOW, PROFESSOR! WE'LL GIVE HIM A GOOD START BEFORE WE LEAVE!
IT'S HORRIBLE THAT A MAN LIKE THAT SHOULD BE CARRYING ON SUCH A GREAT SCIENTIFIC TASK!
...AND SO, IVORY ANDERSON AND HIS EXPEDITION START ON THEIR WAY...
HEY, IVORY! HOW ABOUT ME RIDING TOO!
YOU CAN RIDE BACK, PINKY... *MAYBE! HA! HA!*

WE'RE GOING TO BE ON A LONG JOURNEY-SO I'M STOCKING UP ON FOOD AND BLANKETS, SIR!

JUST SO WE GET THOSE TUSKS!

ALL THAT DAY AIRBOY HOVERS BIRDIE OVER THE SAFARI OF IVORY ANDERSON...

...AND THE DAYS SLIP INTO A WEEK AS THEY MOVE ON INTO THE DENSE JUNGLE...

WE CAN'T BE FAR OFF NOW, AIRBOY!

I HOPE NOT, PROFESSOR!

FINALLY IVORY ANDERSON GETS GOOD NEWS...

BWANA! BWANA! ELEPHANT GRAVE-YARD IS AHEAD!

YIPPEE!

HURRY UP! HURRY UP!

LOOK, PINKY! IT'S THE GRAVEYARD! IVORY!...TONS OF IT!...I'M RICH!...I'LL BUILD A HOUSE OF IVORY!

GEE!

8

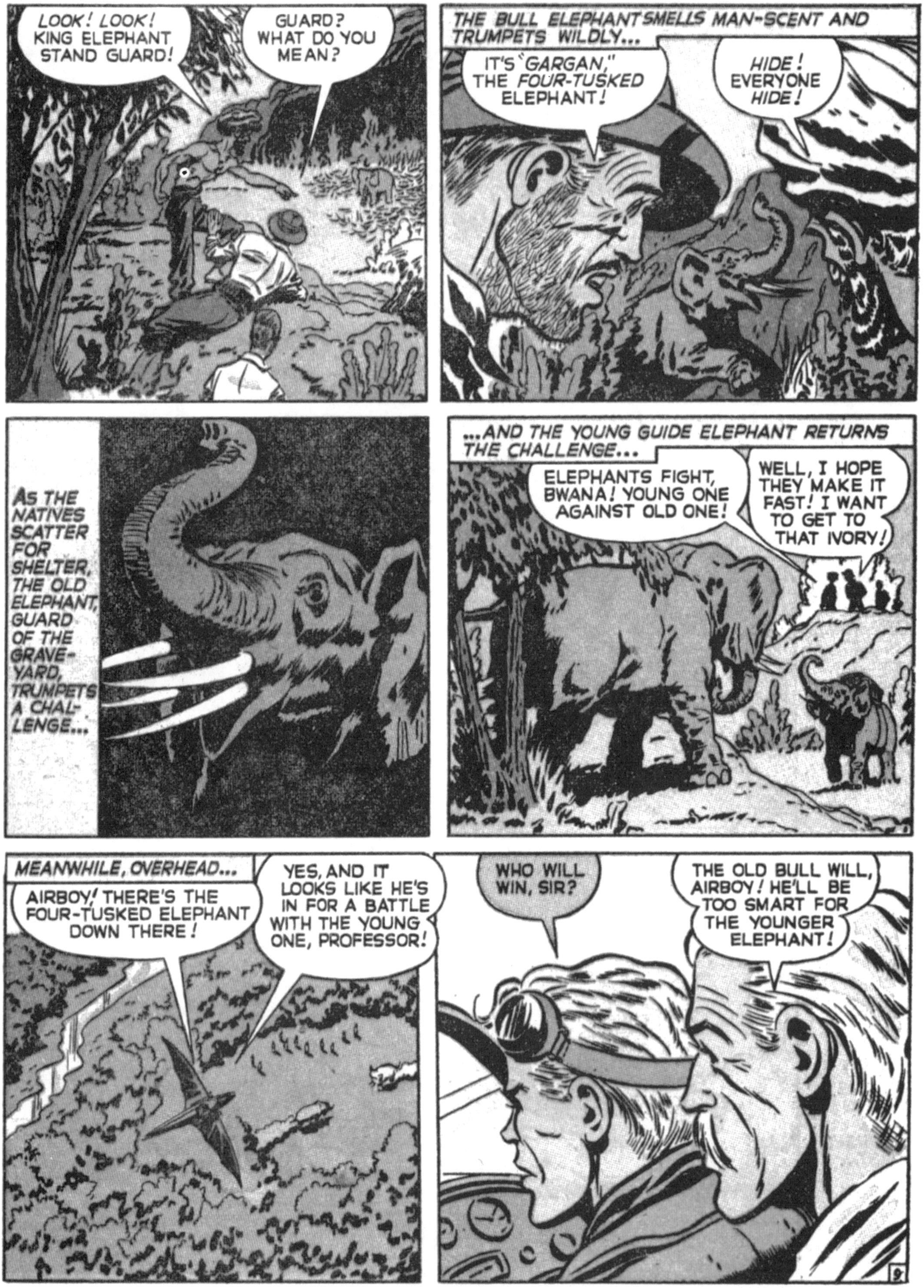
LOOK! LOOK! KING ELEPHANT STAND GUARD!
GUARD? WHAT DO YOU MEAN?
THE BULL ELEPHANT SMELLS MAN-SCENT AND TRUMPETS WILDLY...
IT'S "GARGAN," THE FOUR-TUSKED ELEPHANT!
HIDE! EVERYONE HIDE!
AS THE NATIVES SCATTER FOR SHELTER, THE OLD ELEPHANT, GUARD OF THE GRAVE-YARD, TRUMPETS A CHAL-LENGE...
...AND THE YOUNG GUIDE ELEPHANT RETURNS THE CHALLENGE...
ELEPHANTS FIGHT, BWANA! YOUNG ONE AGAINST OLD ONE!
WELL, I HOPE THEY MAKE IT FAST! I WANT TO GET TO THAT IVORY!
MEANWHILE, OVERHEAD...
AIRBOY! THERE'S THE FOUR-TUSKED ELEPHANT DOWN THERE!
YES, AND IT LOOKS LIKE HE'S IN FOR A BATTLE WITH THE YOUNG ONE, PROFESSOR!
WHO WILL WIN, SIR?
THE OLD BULL WILL, AIRBOY! HE'LL BE TOO SMART FOR THE YOUNGER ELEPHANT!
9

THE YOUNG
ELEPHANT
STOMPS THE
GROUND,
THEN HEAD
LOWERED,
MOVES INTO
BATTLE...

WISE
WITH AGE,
"GARGAN"
AWAITS THE
ATTACK
CALMLY,
THEN
MOVES HIS
GREAT
BULK
ASIDE...

SUDDENLY
"GARGAN"
PUSHES
UPWARD
WITH HIS
FOUR
GREAT
TUSKS
AS THE
YOUNG
BULL
PLUNGES
PAST...

10

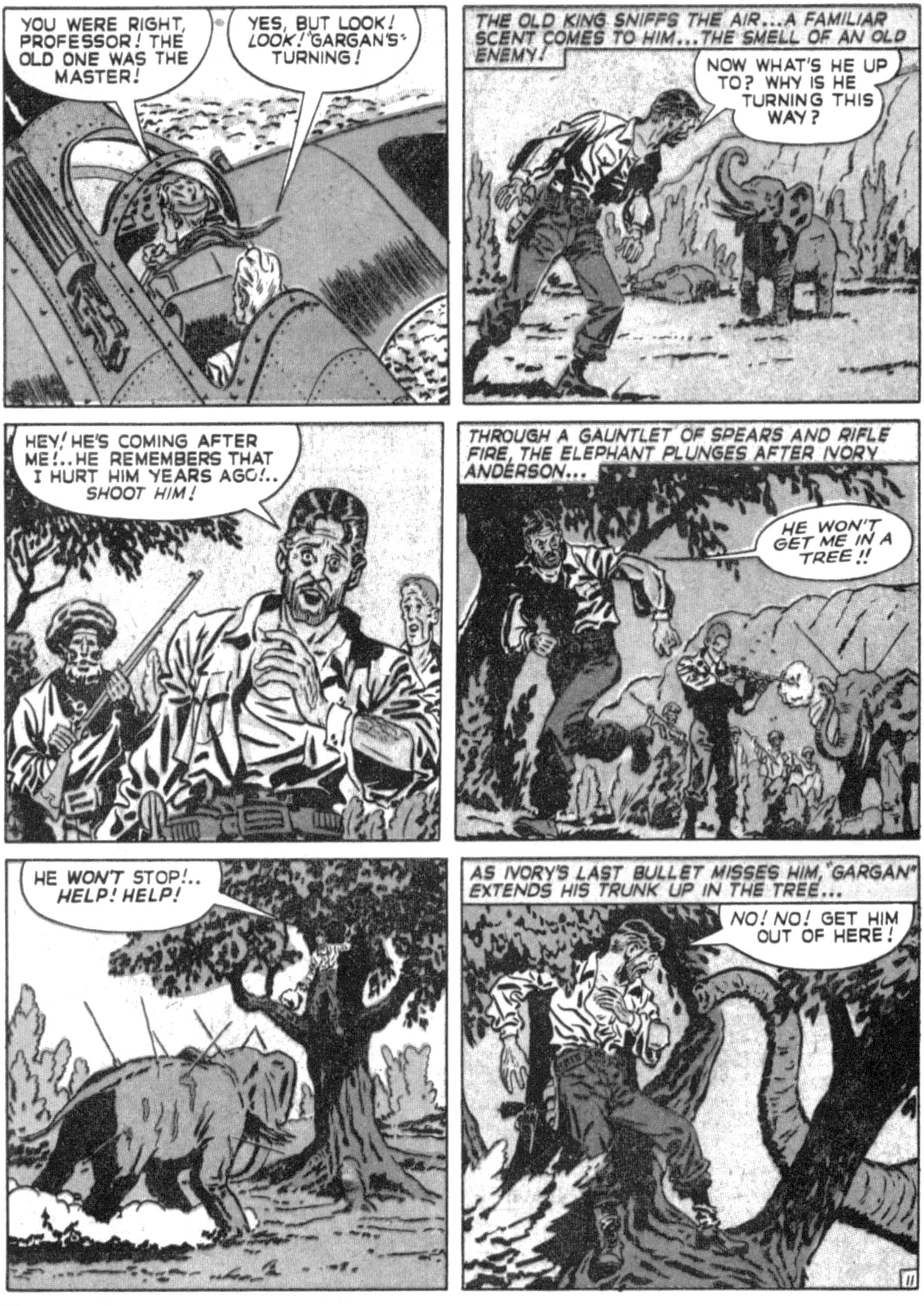
YOU WERE RIGHT, PROFESSOR! THE OLD ONE WAS THE MASTER!
YES, BUT LOOK! LOOK! "GARGAN'S" TURNING!
THE OLD KING SNIFFS THE AIR...A FAMILIAR SCENT COMES TO HIM...THE SMELL OF AN OLD ENEMY!
NOW WHAT'S HE UP TO? WHY IS HE TURNING THIS WAY?
HEY! HE'S COMING AFTER ME!..HE REMEMBERS THAT I HURT HIM YEARS AGO!.. SHOOT HIM!
THROUGH A GAUNTLET OF SPEARS AND RIFLE FIRE, THE ELEPHANT PLUNGES AFTER IVORY ANDERSON...
HE WON'T GET ME IN A TREE!!
HE WON'T STOP!.. HELP! HELP!
AS IVORY'S LAST BULLET MISSES HIM, "GARGAN" EXTENDS HIS TRUNK UP IN THE TREE...
NO! NO! GET HIM OUT OF HERE!
11

YI-I-I-I!!

WITH A GRACEFUL FLING, "GARGAN" TOSSES IVORY INTO THE GRAVEYARD...

"GARGAN" SHRIEKS A VICTORIOUS TRUMPET THROUGH THE JUNGLE

...AND HE LUNGES TO THE GROUND, HIS GREAT HEART FOREVER STILLED...

AND A FEW MINUTES LATER, AIRBOY LANDS...

THE ELEPHANT'S DEAD AND IVORY'S DEAD! ALL THE IVORY IN THE GRAVEYARD IS MINE! ALL MINE!

SUDDENLY!!!

NOT QUITE, PINKY!

12

175

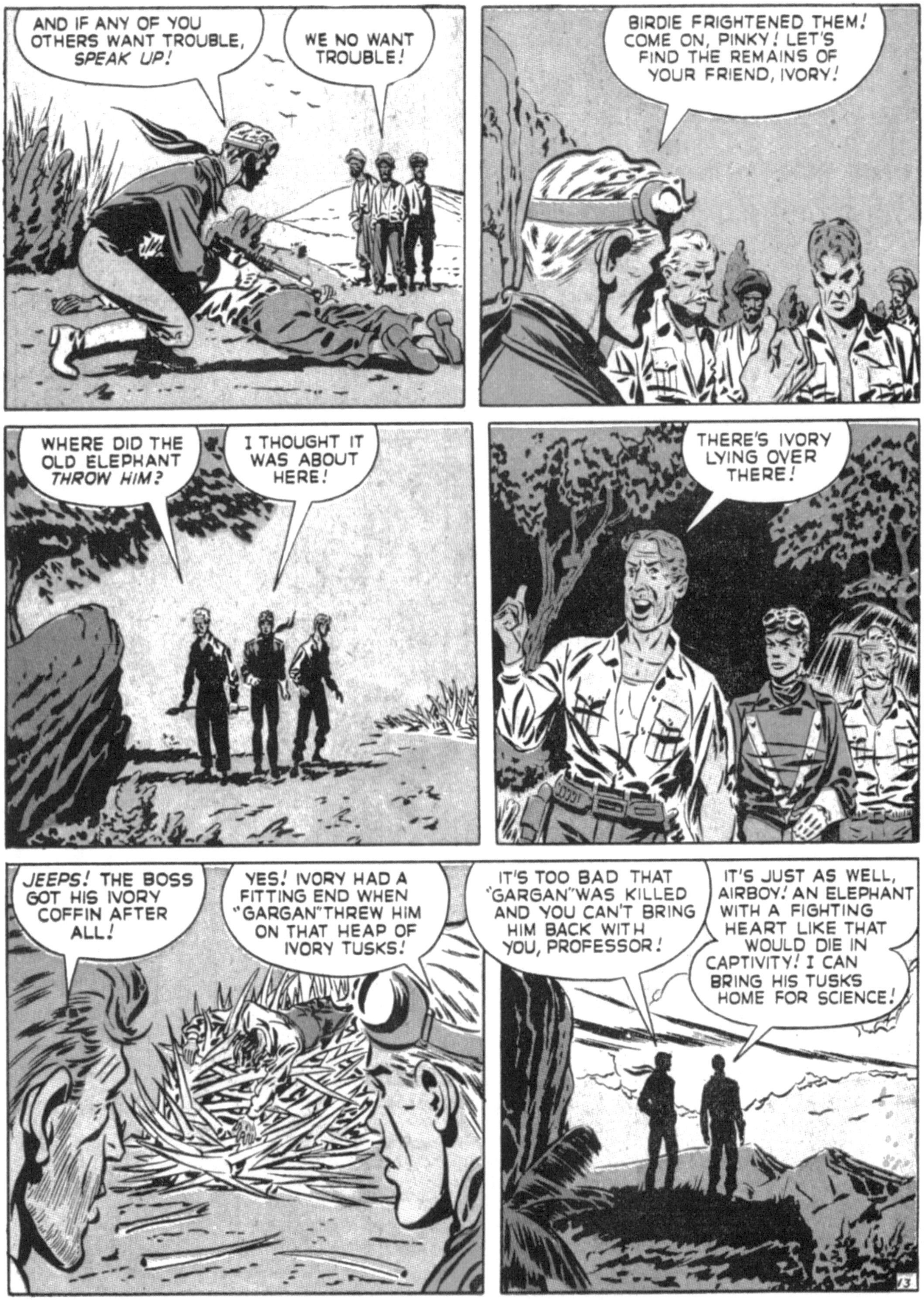
AND IF ANY OF YOU OTHERS WANT TROUBLE, *SPEAK UP!*
WE NO WANT TROUBLE!
BIRDIE FRIGHTENED THEM! COME ON, PINKY! LET'S FIND THE REMAINS OF YOUR FRIEND, IVORY!
WHERE DID THE OLD ELEPHANT *THROW HIM?*
I THOUGHT IT WAS ABOUT HERE!
THERE'S IVORY LYING OVER THERE!
JEEPS! THE BOSS GOT HIS IVORY COFFIN AFTER ALL!
YES! IVORY HAD A FITTING END WHEN "GARGAN" THREW HIM ON THAT HEAP OF IVORY TUSKS!
IT'S TOO BAD THAT "GARGAN" WAS KILLED AND YOU CAN'T BRING HIM BACK WITH YOU, PROFESSOR!
IT'S JUST AS WELL, AIRBOY! AN ELEPHANT WITH A FIGHTING HEART LIKE THAT WOULD DIE IN CAPTIVITY! I CAN BRING HIS TUSKS HOME FOR SCIENCE!
13

(above) More 1950s sketches.
COURTESY OF FRANK GIELLA.
©2010 CARMINE INFANTINO.

(below and facing page)
Sketches from 1955.

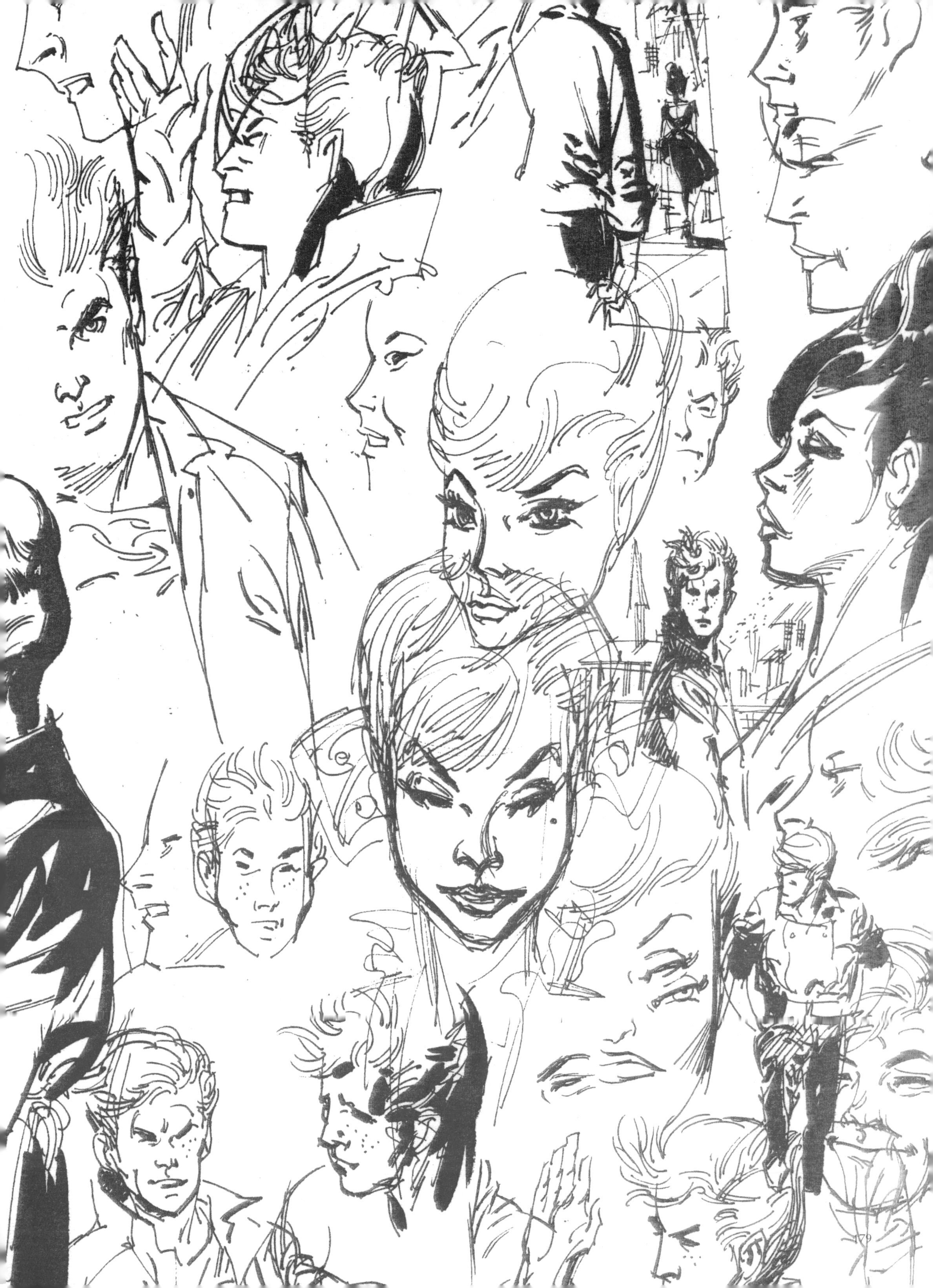

(left and below) More of Carmine's 1950s sketches.

COURTESY OF FRANK GIELLA.
©2010 CARMINE INFANTINO.

(facing page) Page 5 of the "Joe Barton" story from *Wild Boy of the Congo #9* (Oct. 1953), the first issue published by St. John after they took over the title from Ziff-Davis. Carmine penciled this story, and may have inked it as well.

COURTESY OF ROD BECK.
©1953 ST. JOHN PUBLISHING CO.

ONCE AGAIN, JOE FLEES INTO THE JUNGLE...

AT LAST JOE LEAVES THE JUNGLE BEHIND HIM AND EMERGES INTO A CLEARING...

I'M A GONER UNLESS... WAIT! THAT CAVE— GOT TO HAVE TIME TO THINK...

A DEAD END! NOW WHAT?

I'VE TRAPPED YOU IN YOUR LAIR, BARTON— JUST LIKE A BEAST! ARE YOU ANY BETTER OFF?

SUDDENLY, BARTON THROWS A ROCK AT SELENKA, AND CHARGES HIM...

HERE'S SOMETHING YOU DIDN'T EXPECT, SELENKA— THE OBVIOUS!

UGH!

YOU'RE RIGHT, BARTON— ¡PANT!— I WAS EXPECTING SOME TRICK.... UGH...IT'S ALL SO OBVIOUS...

181

(above) A mid- to late 1950s "Pow-Wow Smith" page from *Western Comics*, inked by Joe Giella, who inked most of the "Pow-Wow Smith" stories that Carmine did not ink himself.

(facing page) Opening splash page of the "Detective Chimp" story from *The Adventures of Rex the Wonder Dog* #21 (May-June 1955), written by John Broome with full art by Carmine.

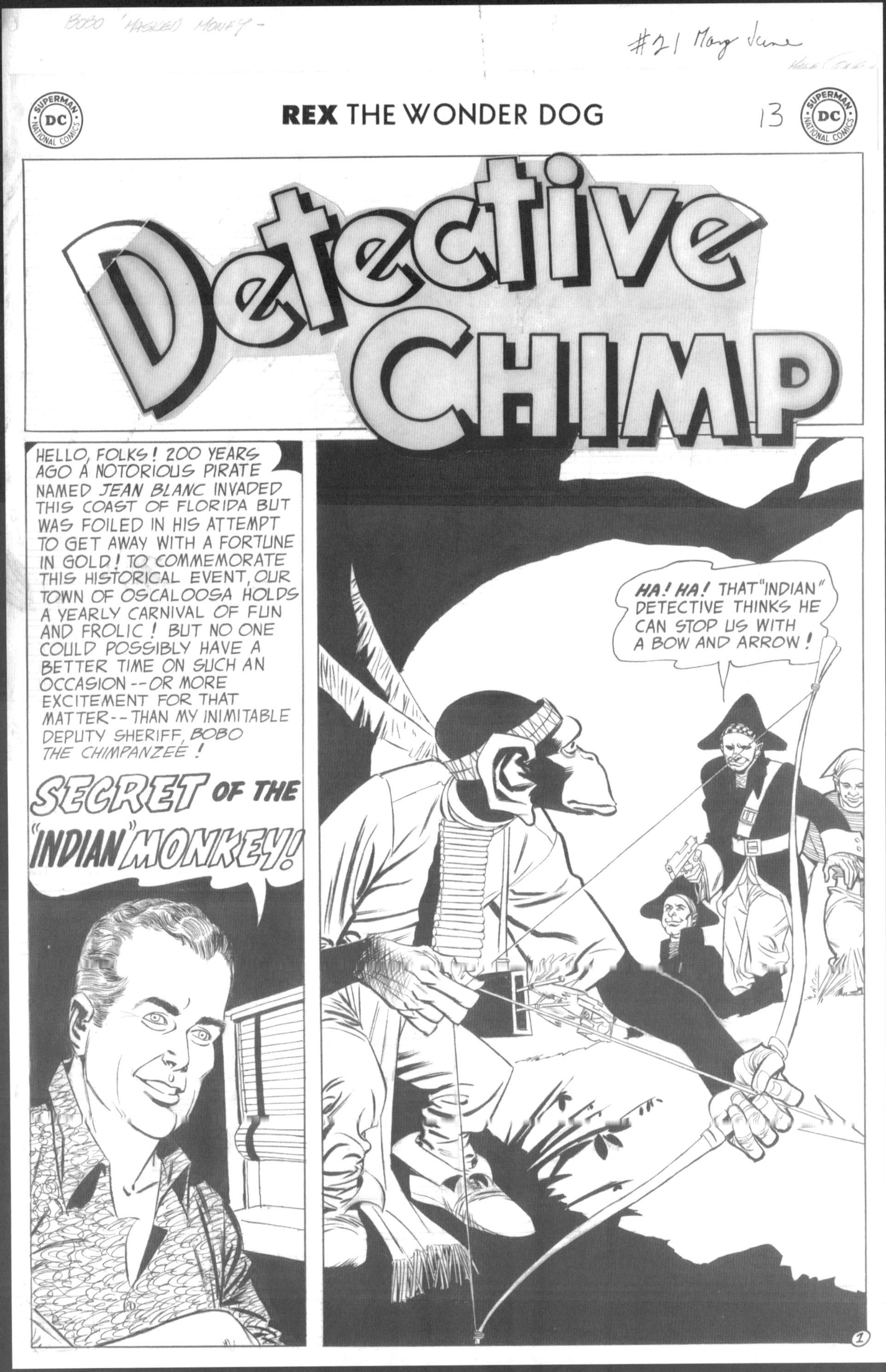
BOBO 'MASKED MONKY -
#21 May June
REX THE WONDER DOG
13
SUPERMAN DC NATIONAL COMICS
Detective CHIMP
HELLO, FOLKS! 200 YEARS AGO A NOTORIOUS PIRATE NAMED JEAN BLANC INVADED THIS COAST OF FLORIDA BUT WAS FOILED IN HIS ATTEMPT TO GET AWAY WITH A FORTUNE IN GOLD! TO COMMEMORATE THIS HISTORICAL EVENT, OUR TOWN OF OSCALOOSA HOLDS A YEARLY CARNIVAL OF FUN AND FROLIC! BUT NO ONE COULD POSSIBLY HAVE A BETTER TIME ON SUCH AN OCCASION--OR MORE EXCITEMENT FOR THAT MATTER--THAN MY INIMITABLE DEPUTY SHERIFF, BOBO THE CHIMPANZEE!
SECRET OF THE "INDIAN" MONKEY!
HA! HA! THAT "INDIAN" DETECTIVE THINKS HE CAN STOP US WITH A BOW AND ARROW!
1

(above) One of the most iconic covers of the Silver Age: *The Flash* #123 (Sept. 1961), inked by Murphy Anderson, introduced the concept of two Earths in the DC universe.

(facing page) The cover of *Superman* #199 (Aug. 1967), inked by Murphy Anderson, announces the first of what would be many races between Superman and the Flash.

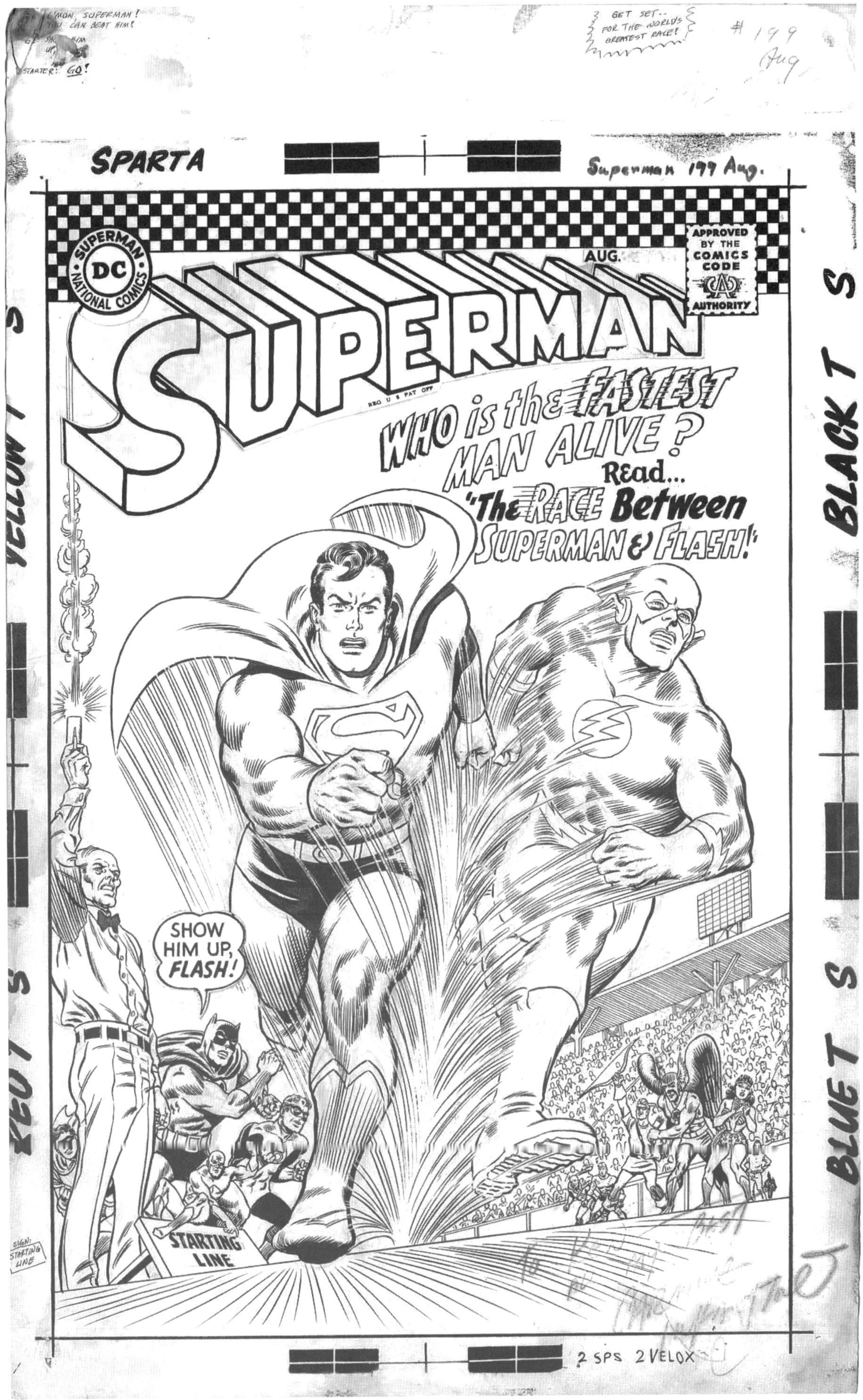
C'MON, SUPERMAN! YOU CAN BEAT HIM!
STARTER: GO!
GET SET... FOR THE WORLD'S GREATEST RACE!
#199 Aug
SPARTA
Superman 199 Aug.
SUPERMAN DC NATIONAL COMICS
AUG.
APPROVED BY THE COMICS CODE AUTHORITY
SUPERMAN
REG U S PAT OFF
WHO is the FASTEST MAN ALIVE?
Read... "The RACE Between SUPERMAN & FLASH!"
SHOW HIM UP, FLASH!
SIGN: STARTING LINE
STARTING LINE
YELLOW T S
RED T S
BLACK T S
BLUE T S
2 SPS 2 VELOX

(above) Elongated Man started out as an adversary of sorts for the Flash, but quickly moved to become one of his closest allies, teaming up with him several times before striking out for his own back-up feature in *Detective Comics*. In *The Flash #124*, written by John Broome and inked by Joe Giella, he — along with Captain Boomerang — help Flash repel an alien invasion.

(facing page) Page 6 of *The Flash #131* (Sept. 1962), written by John Broome and inked by Joe Giella. This story marked the first of many appearances of Green Lantern in the pages of *The Flash*. The two had teamed up in *Green Lantern* earlier in the year and revealed their identities to each other.

THE FLASH

SEPT #131 8

CAPTIVES OF THE COSMIC RAY! PART 2

SWIFTLY EXCEEDING THE *SPEED OF LIGHT* HIMSELF BY MEANS OF HIS AMAZING *POWER RING*, GREEN LANTERN SUCCEEDS IN TRAILING THE MYSTERIOUS VESSEL ACROSS THE VOID OF SPACE AND TO AN UNKNOWN PLANET!

THE STRANGE SPACESHIP DROPPED *FLASH* OFF-- AND THEN TOOK OFF AGAIN! I'VE GOT TO KEEP AFTER IT--FIND OUT WHAT GAME IT'S PLAYING!

LIKE GREEN LIGHTNING, THE *EMERALD GLADIATOR* ZOOMS AFTER HIS QUARRY, RING BLAZING...

SNARED IT! I'M OVERCOMING ITS TREMENDOUS DRIVE-FORCE-- AND BRINGING IT TO A STAND- STILL!

M.O.

THE FLASH

(above) Commission illustration of the Flash, penciled by Carmine and inked by Joe Giella.

(right) A Flash head sketch.
COURTESY OF DR. JEFF McLAUGHLIN.
FLASH ™ AND © DC COMICS.

(below) This Flash commission
piece was penciled by Carmine and
inked by Dick Giordano.
COURTESY OF MICHAEL BROWNING.
FLASH, CAPTAIN COLD ™ AND © DC COMICS.

Commission sketch of the Flash.

Commission sketch of Adam Strange.

(above and right) The cover of *Mystery in Space* #63 (Nov. 1960), inked by Joe Giella, and the final (half-) page of that issue's "Adam Strange" story, inked by Murphy Anderson.

DON'T MISS THE NEXT EXCITING *ADAM STRANGE* ADVENTURE IN THE NEXT ISSUE OF *MYSTERY IN SPACE!*

(above) An early 2000s pencil sketch recreation of the cover of *Mystery in Space* #90 (Mar. 1964).

ADAM STRANGE ™ AND © DC COMICS.

(facing page) Page 9 of "The Powerless Weapons of Adam Strange" from *Mystery in Space* #84 (June 1963).

COURTESY OF MIKE JACKSON.

ADAM STRANGE ™ AND © DC COMICS.

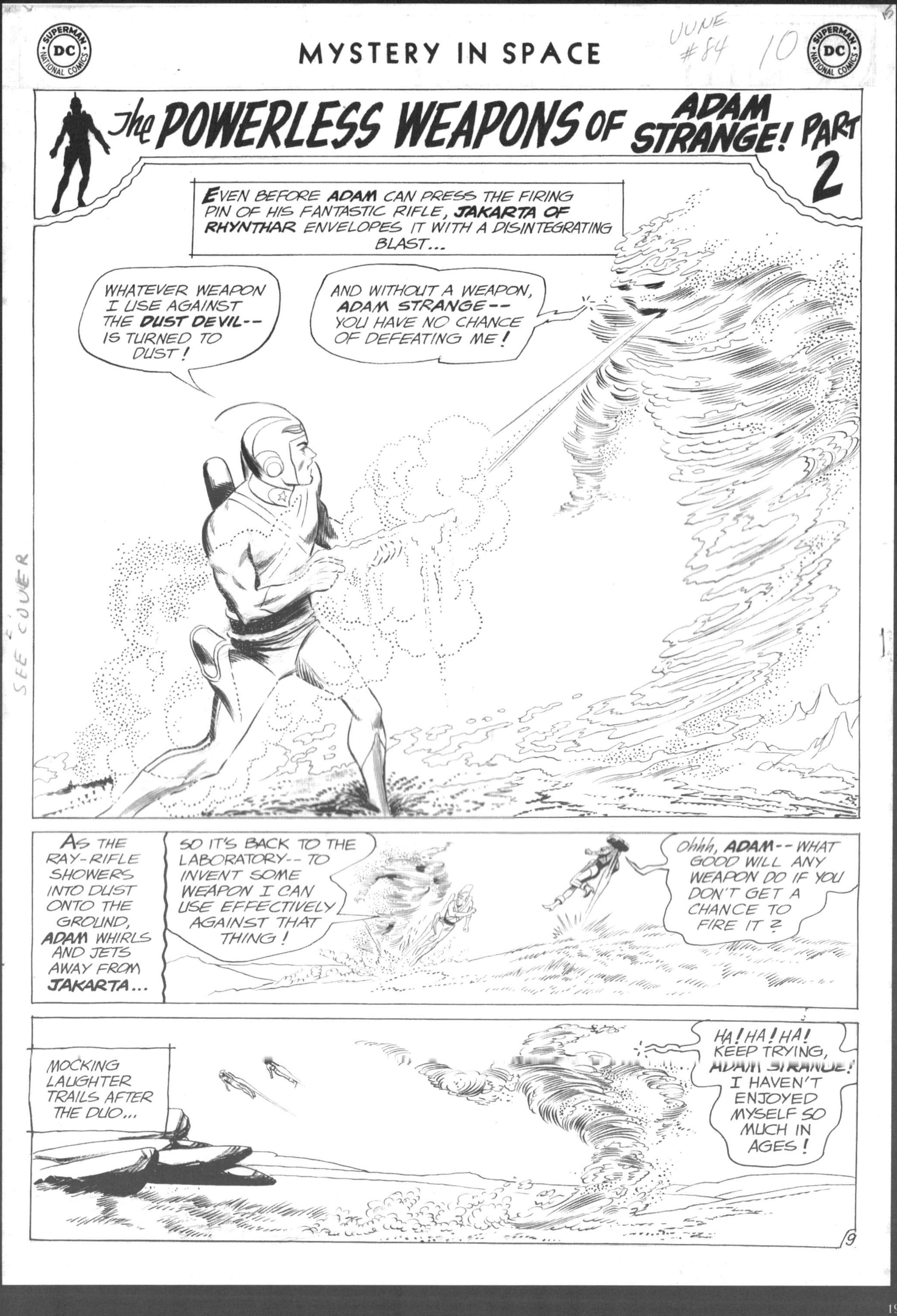

MYSTERY IN SPACE
JUNE #84
10
The POWERLESS WEAPONS OF ADAM STRANGE! PART 2
EVEN BEFORE ADAM CAN PRESS THE FIRING PIN OF HIS FANTASTIC RIFLE, JAKARTA OF RHYNTHAR ENVELOPES IT WITH A DISINTEGRATING BLAST...
WHATEVER WEAPON I USE AGAINST THE DUST DEVIL-- IS TURNED TO DUST!
AND WITHOUT A WEAPON, ADAM STRANGE-- YOU HAVE NO CHANCE OF DEFEATING ME!
SEE COVER
AS THE RAY-RIFLE SHOWERS INTO DUST ONTO THE GROUND, ADAM WHIRLS AND JETS AWAY FROM JAKARTA...
SO IT'S BACK TO THE LABORATORY-- TO INVENT SOME WEAPON I CAN USE EFFECTIVELY AGAINST THAT THING!
Ohhh, ADAM-- WHAT GOOD WILL ANY WEAPON DO IF YOU DON'T GET A CHANCE TO FIRE IT?
MOCKING LAUGHTER TRAILS AFTER THE DUO...
HA! HA! HA! KEEP TRYING, ADAM STRANGE! I HAVEN'T ENJOYED MYSELF SO MUCH IN AGES!
9

(above) A Batman commission piece penciled by Carmine with inks and wash by Joe Giella.

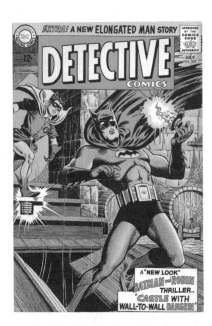

(left and facing page) The cover, inked by Murphy Anderson, and a page from the lead story of *Detective Comics* #329, written by John Broome and inked by Joe Giella, in which the Dynamic Duo skip across the pond to England in order to track down a criminal.

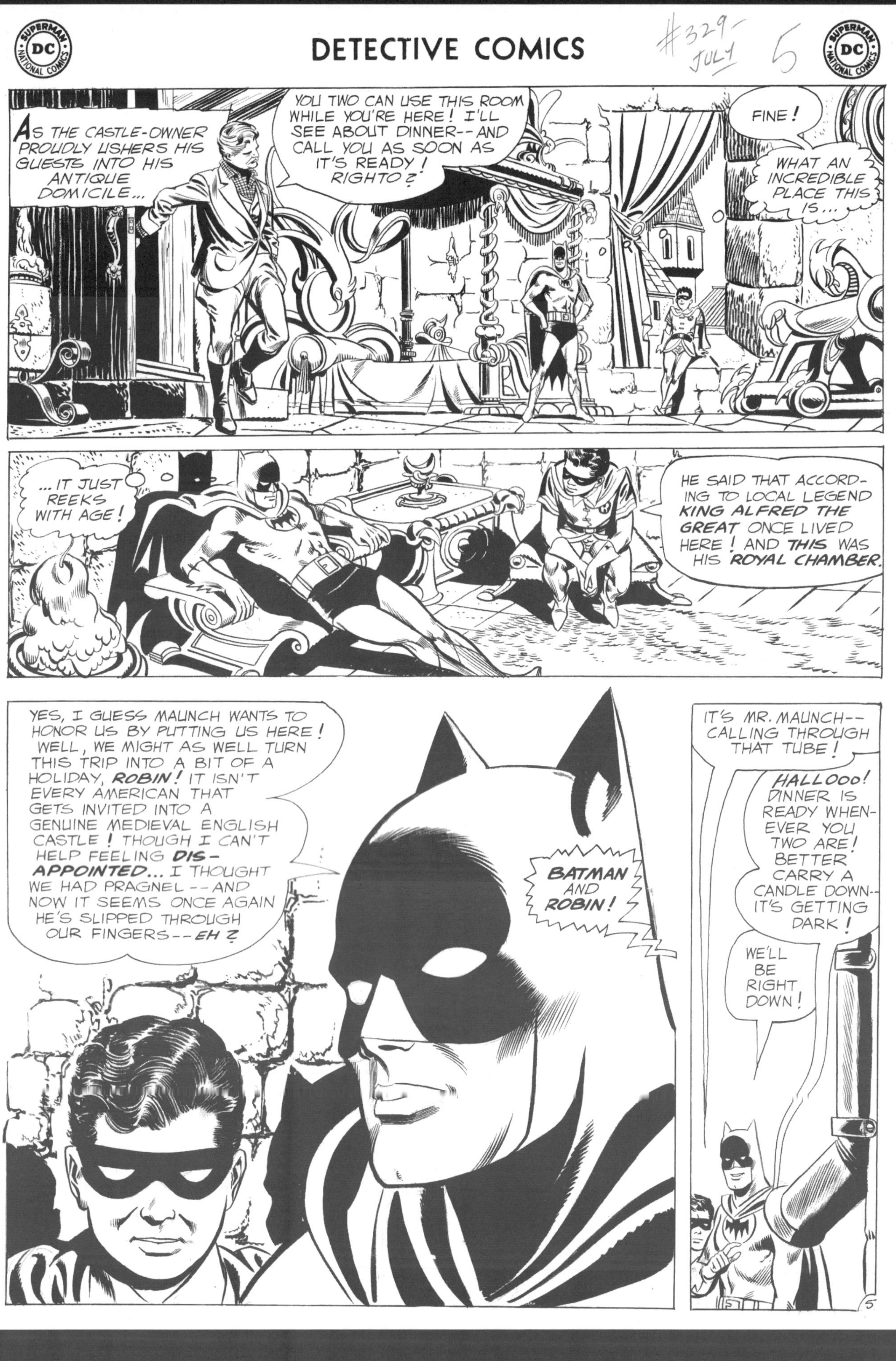
DETECTIVE COMICS
#329- JULY 5
AS THE CASTLE-OWNER PROUDLY USHERS HIS GUESTS INTO HIS ANTIQUE DOMICILE...
YOU TWO CAN USE THIS ROOM WHILE YOU'RE HERE! I'LL SEE ABOUT DINNER-- AND CALL YOU AS SOON AS IT'S READY! RIGHTO?
FINE!
WHAT AN INCREDIBLE PLACE THIS IS...
...IT JUST REEKS WITH AGE!
HE SAID THAT ACCORDING TO LOCAL LEGEND KING ALFRED THE GREAT ONCE LIVED HERE! AND THIS WAS HIS ROYAL CHAMBER.
YES, I GUESS MAUNCH WANTS TO HONOR US BY PUTTING US HERE! WELL, WE MIGHT AS WELL TURN THIS TRIP INTO A BIT OF A HOLIDAY, ROBIN! IT ISN'T EVERY AMERICAN THAT GETS INVITED INTO A GENUINE MEDIEVAL ENGLISH CASTLE! THOUGH I CAN'T HELP FEELING DIS-APPOINTED... I THOUGHT WE HAD PRAGNEL -- AND NOW IT SEEMS ONCE AGAIN HE'S SLIPPED THROUGH OUR FINGERS -- EH?
BATMAN AND ROBIN!
IT'S MR. MAUNCH-- CALLING THROUGH THAT TUBE!
HALLOOO! DINNER IS READY WHEN-EVER YOU TWO ARE! BETTER CARRY A CANDLE DOWN-- IT'S GETTING DARK!
WE'LL BE RIGHT DOWN!
5

(above) Though this appears to be one page of a Batman story, it is actually three. Each tier made up one page of "The Catwoman's Catnapping Caper!" — a 15-page giveaway premium in 1966 for Kellogg's Pop-Tarts. The story was reprinted in a standard comic-book format in the *Batman in the Sixties* collection. Written by E. Nelson Bridwell with inks by Murphy Anderson.

(facing page) Gorillas sell comic books. At least they seemed to in the '60s. So it was only natural that Batman would have to defeat a talking gorilla with a bomb strapped to his chest in *Detective Comics* #339, in a story written by Gardner Fox and inked by Joe Giella.

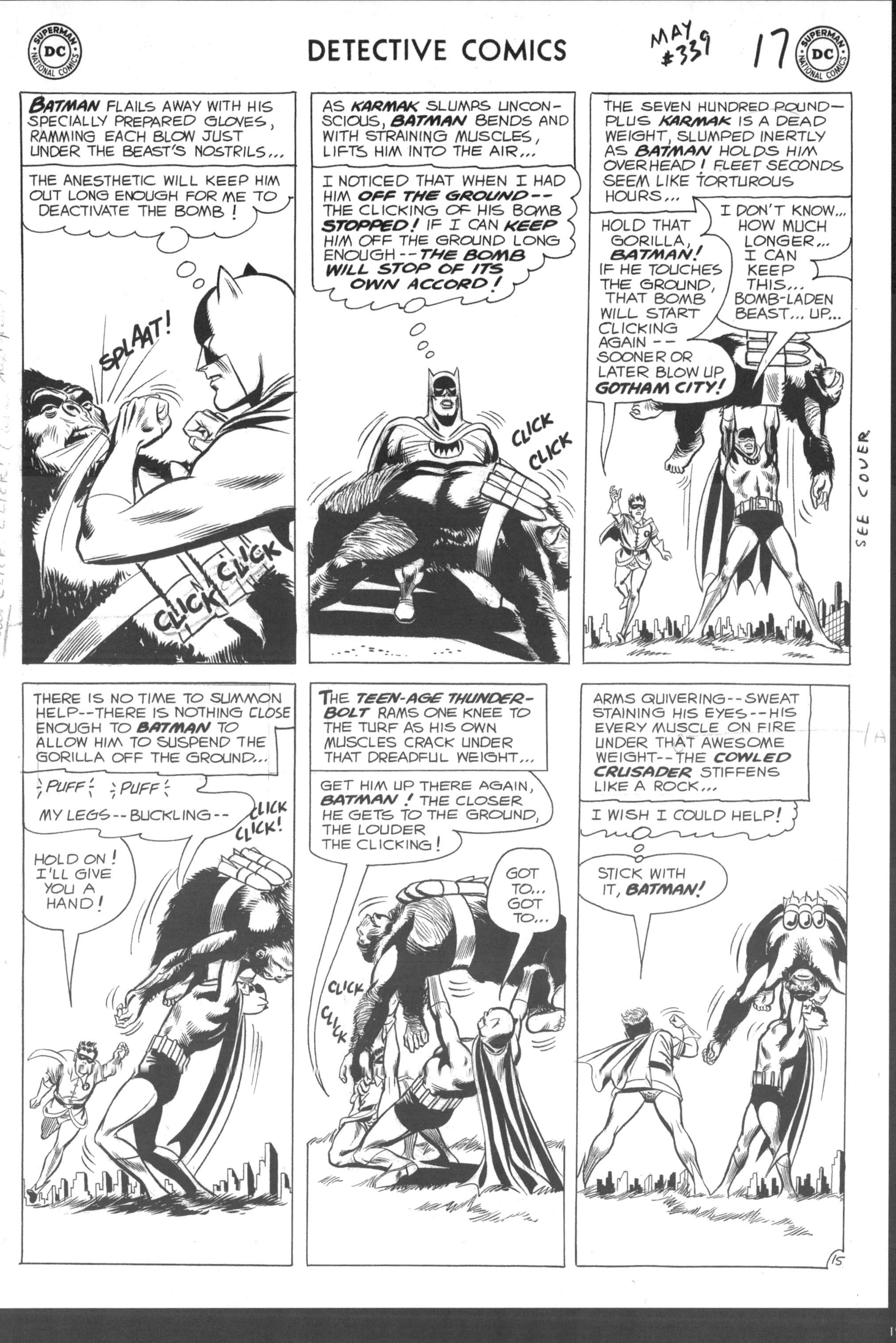

DETECTIVE COMICS
MAY #339
17
BATMAN FLAILS AWAY WITH HIS SPECIALLY PREPARED GLOVES, RAMMING EACH BLOW JUST UNDER THE BEAST'S NOSTRILS...
THE ANESTHETIC WILL KEEP HIM OUT LONG ENOUGH FOR ME TO DEACTIVATE THE BOMB!
SPLAAT!
CLICK CLICK
AS KARMAK SLUMPS UNCONSCIOUS, BATMAN BENDS AND WITH STRAINING MUSCLES, LIFTS HIM INTO THE AIR...
I NOTICED THAT WHEN I HAD HIM OFF THE GROUND-- THE CLICKING OF HIS BOMB STOPPED! IF I CAN KEEP HIM OFF THE GROUND LONG ENOUGH--THE BOMB WILL STOP OF ITS OWN ACCORD!
CLICK CLICK
THE SEVEN HUNDRED POUND-PLUS KARMAK IS A DEAD WEIGHT, SLUMPED INERTLY AS BATMAN HOLDS HIM OVERHEAD! FLEET SECONDS SEEM LIKE TORTUROUS HOURS...
HOLD THAT GORILLA, BATMAN! IF HE TOUCHES THE GROUND, THAT BOMB WILL START CLICKING AGAIN -- SOONER OR LATER BLOW UP GOTHAM CITY!
I DON'T KNOW... HOW MUCH LONGER... I CAN KEEP THIS... BOMB-LADEN BEAST... UP...
SEE COVER
THERE IS NO TIME TO SUMMON HELP--THERE IS NOTHING CLOSE ENOUGH TO BATMAN TO ALLOW HIM TO SUSPEND THE GORILLA OFF THE GROUND...
PUFF PUFF
MY LEGS--BUCKLING--
CLICK CLICK!
HOLD ON! I'LL GIVE YOU A HAND!
THE TEEN-AGE THUNDERBOLT RAMS ONE KNEE TO THE TURF AS HIS OWN MUSCLES CRACK UNDER THAT DREADFUL WEIGHT...
GET HIM UP THERE AGAIN, BATMAN! THE CLOSER HE GETS TO THE GROUND, THE LOUDER THE CLICKING!
GOT TO... GOT TO...
CLICK CLICK
ARMS QUIVERING--SWEAT STAINING HIS EYES--HIS EVERY MUSCLE ON FIRE UNDER THAT AWESOME WEIGHT--THE COWLED CRUSADER STIFFENS LIKE A ROCK...
I WISH I COULD HELP!
STICK WITH IT, BATMAN!
1A
15

(above) A Batman and Batgirl commission piece penciled by Carmine and inked by Joe Giella.

COURTESY OF JEFF HARNETT.

BATMAN, BATGIRL ™ AND © DC COMICS.

(left) The Joker, as drawn by Carmine and inked by Dick Giordano, done for DC's Special Projects arm.

COURTESY OF ARNIE GRIEVES.

JOKER ™ AND © DC COMICS.

(facing page) Page 11 of *Strange Adventures* #205, featuring the origin of Deadman. Written by Arnold Drake and inked by George Roussos.

COURTESY OF EMMANUEL LAPUENTE.

DEADMAN ™ AND © DC COMICS.

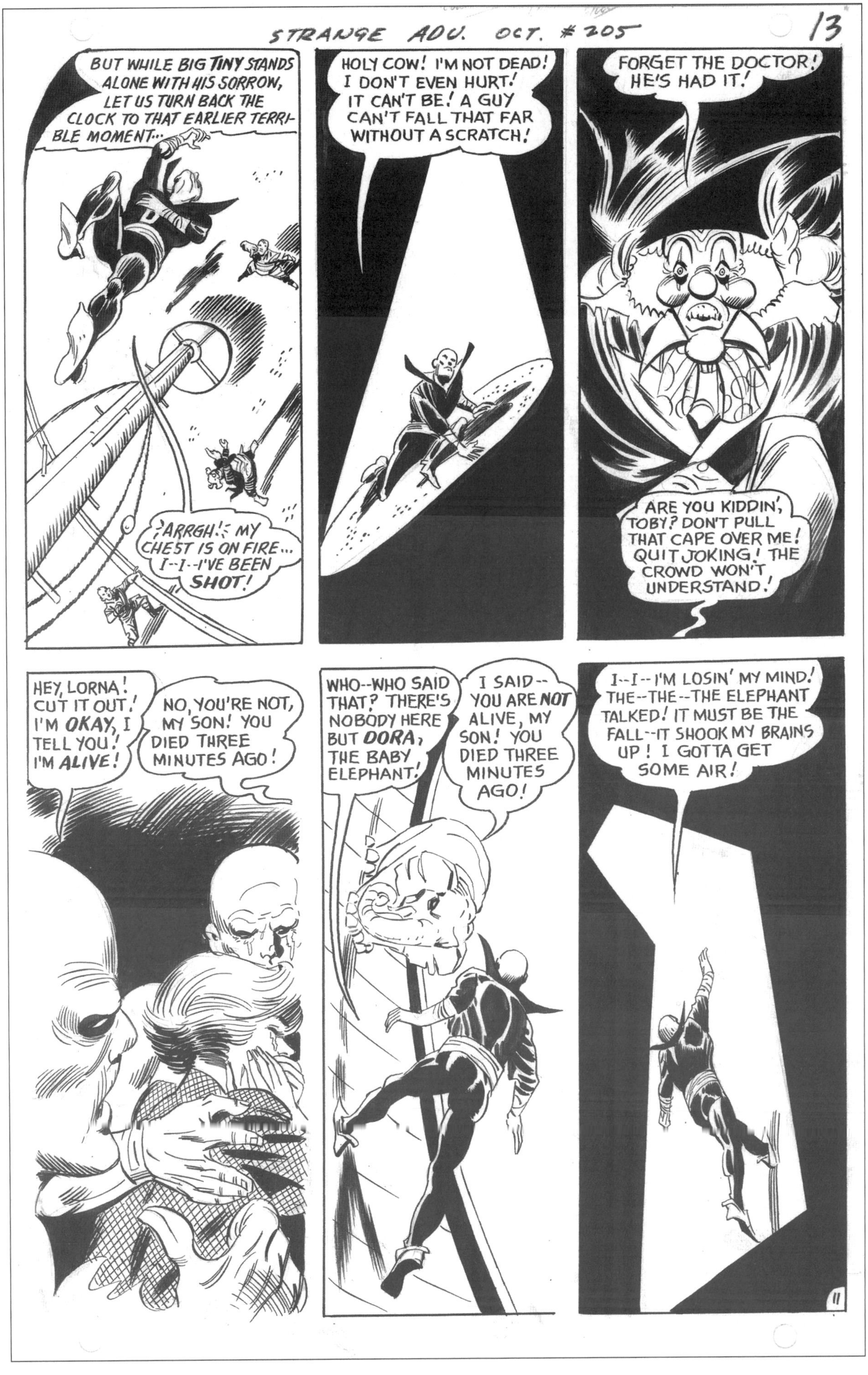
STRANGE ADV. OCT. #205
13
BUT WHILE BIG TINY STANDS ALONE WITH HIS SORROW, LET US TURN BACK THE CLOCK TO THAT EARLIER TERRIBLE MOMENT...
ARRGH! MY CHEST IS ON FIRE... I--I--I'VE BEEN SHOT!
HOLY COW! I'M NOT DEAD! I DON'T EVEN HURT! IT CAN'T BE! A GUY CAN'T FALL THAT FAR WITHOUT A SCRATCH!
FORGET THE DOCTOR! HE'S HAD IT!
ARE YOU KIDDIN', TOBY? DON'T PULL THAT CAPE OVER ME! QUIT JOKING! THE CROWD WON'T UNDERSTAND!
HEY, LORNA! CUT IT OUT! I'M OKAY, I TELL YOU! I'M ALIVE!
NO, YOU'RE NOT, MY SON! YOU DIED THREE MINUTES AGO!
WHO--WHO SAID THAT? THERE'S NOBODY HERE BUT DORA, THE BABY ELEPHANT!
I SAID-- YOU ARE NOT ALIVE, MY SON! YOU DIED THREE MINUTES AGO!
I--I--I'M LOSIN' MY MIND! THE--THE--THE ELEPHANT TALKED! IT MUST BE THE FALL--IT SHOOK MY BRAINS UP! I GOTTA GET SOME AIR!
11

(above and facing page) No, this isn't one of DC's "Strange Sports Stories." Both pages are from "The Replacement," written by Roger McKenzie and inked by Dick Giordano, which appeared in Warren's *Creepy* #93 (Nov. 1977).

"JUST ONE MORE *TRY*, BILLY, BOY AND THAT'S *ALL IT TOOK*. B'AM'S *HOMER*, IN THE BOTTOM OF THE NINTH, *WON* THE GAME AND THE *WHIZZERS* WERE OFF AND *RUNNIN'!*"

YEAH--! WE *DID IT!* WE ACTUALLY *WON!*

HUH-UH, IT WASN'T *US* WHAT WON...

T-THEY'RE CHEERIN'... CHEERIN' ME!

" AN' THAT WASN'T *ALL*, BILLY, BOY. HE HIT *TWO* MORE HOME RUNS THE NEXT DAY AND MADE A GAME-SAVING *CATCH* HIGH OFF THE OUTFIELD *WALL!*"

:OFF!--!

W-WELL, I *GUESS*, IF YA REALLY *WANT* ME TO.

...TA BRING PEOPLE TAGETHER!

(above) A page from *Creepy* #118's "Junior Was a Momma's Boy," written by Gerry Boudreau and inked by Jorge Benuy.

(facing page) Carmine penciled a second story in *Creepy* #93, "The Return of Rah," written by Roger McKenzie and inked by John Severin.

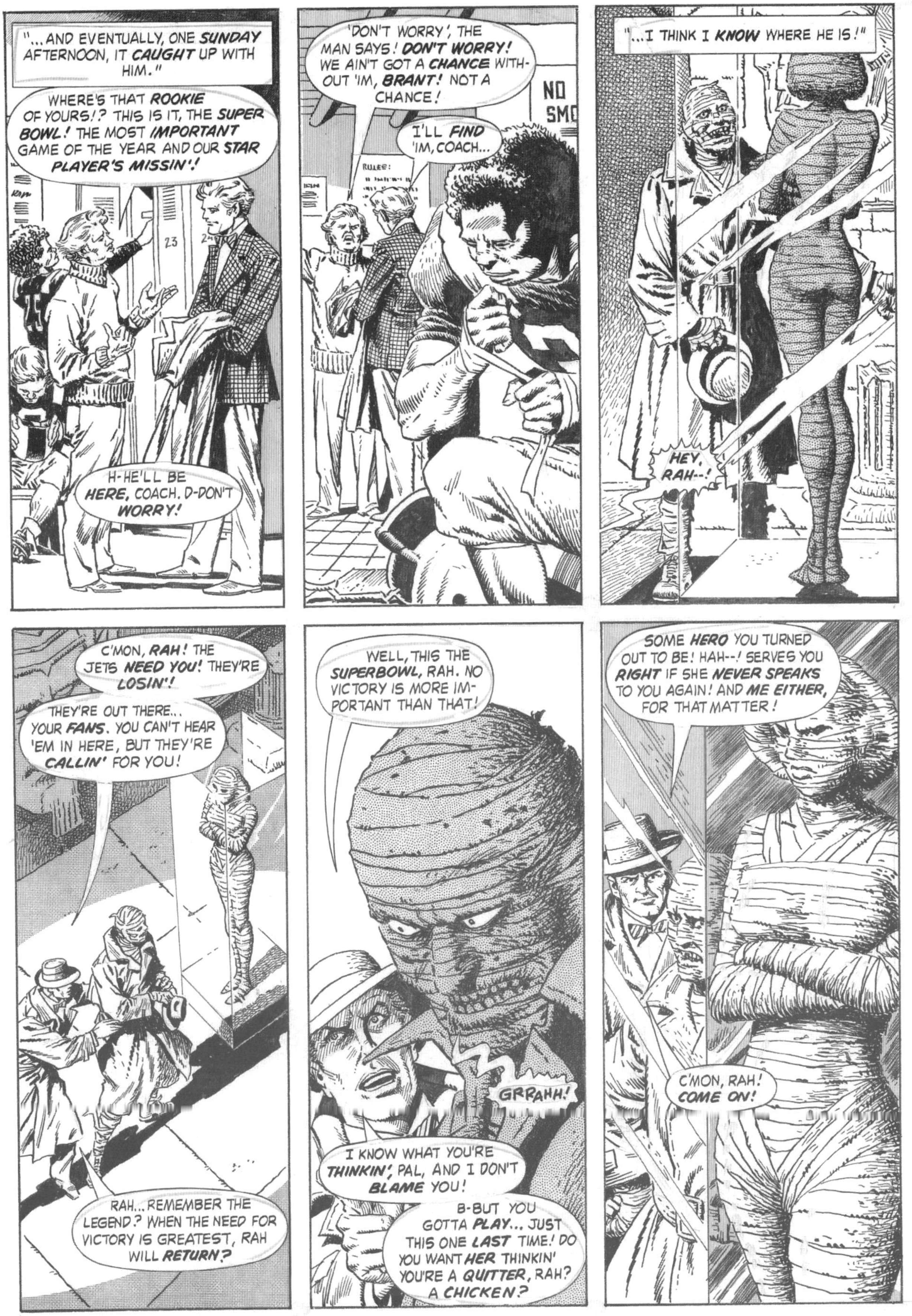
"...AND EVENTUALLY, ONE SUNDAY AFTERNOON, IT CAUGHT UP WITH HIM."
WHERE'S THAT ROOKIE OF YOURS!? THIS IS IT, THE SUPER BOWL! THE MOST IMPORTANT GAME OF THE YEAR AND OUR STAR PLAYER'S MISSIN'!
H-HE'LL BE HERE, COACH. D-DON'T WORRY!
'DON'T WORRY', THE MAN SAYS! DON'T WORRY! WE AIN'T GOT A CHANCE WITH-OUT 'IM, BRANT! NOT A CHANCE!
NO SMO
I'LL FIND 'IM, COACH...
"...I THINK I KNOW WHERE HE IS!"
HEY, RAH--!
C'MON, RAH! THE JETS NEED YOU! THEY'RE LOSIN'!
THEY'RE OUT THERE... YOUR FANS. YOU CAN'T HEAR 'EM IN HERE, BUT THEY'RE CALLIN' FOR YOU!
RAH... REMEMBER THE LEGEND? WHEN THE NEED FOR VICTORY IS GREATEST, RAH WILL RETURN?
WELL, THIS THE SUPERBOWL, RAH. NO VICTORY IS MORE IM-PORTANT THAN THAT!
GRRAHH!
I KNOW WHAT YOU'RE THINKIN', PAL, AND I DON'T BLAME YOU!
B-BUT YOU GOTTA PLAY... JUST THIS ONE LAST TIME! DO YOU WANT HER THINKIN' YOU'RE A QUITTER, RAH? A CHICKEN?
SOME HERO YOU TURNED OUT TO BE! HAH--! SERVES YOU RIGHT IF SHE NEVER SPEAKS TO YOU AGAIN! AND ME EITHER, FOR THAT MATTER!
C'MON, RAH! COME ON!

Spider-Woman was one of Carmine's first regular assignments for Marvel Comics; he penciled the first 19 issues of the series. Shown above is page 22 of issue #1 (Apr. 1978), written by Marv Wolfman and inked by Tony DeZuñiga. In this issue, Spider-Woman appears in a full cowl. Carmine didn't like this aspect of the costume, a carry-over from her debut appearance in *Marvel Spotlight* #32 the year before, and with the next issue Jessica Drew's long, black hair was flowing from her costume, giving her a much more dramatic look. On the facing page is page 23 of Spider-Woman #10 (Jan. 1979), written by Mark Gruenwald and inked by Al Gordon. Gypsy Moth was probably meant to be a one-off villain, but she would return at the end of the series, long after Carmine's departure.

ART COURTESY OF JOE AND NADIA MANNARINO.

SPIDER-WOMAN ™ AND © MARVEL CHARACTERS, INC.

WITH BUT A MOMENT TO REGAIN HER FOOTING, THE SPIDER-WOMAN BOUNDS BACK INTO THE AIR...

CONTINUED AFTER NEXT PAGE

(above) Carmine penciled 31 issues of *Star Wars* over the course of his time at Marvel. Often he was only providing breakdowns, meaning the inkers would spot the majority of the blacks and fill in the technical details so prevalent in the book. This page from *Star Wars* #12 (June 1978), Carmine's second issue, was finished by Terry Austin.

(above) Cover art for *Star Wars* #35 (June 1978), with inks by Bob Wiacek.

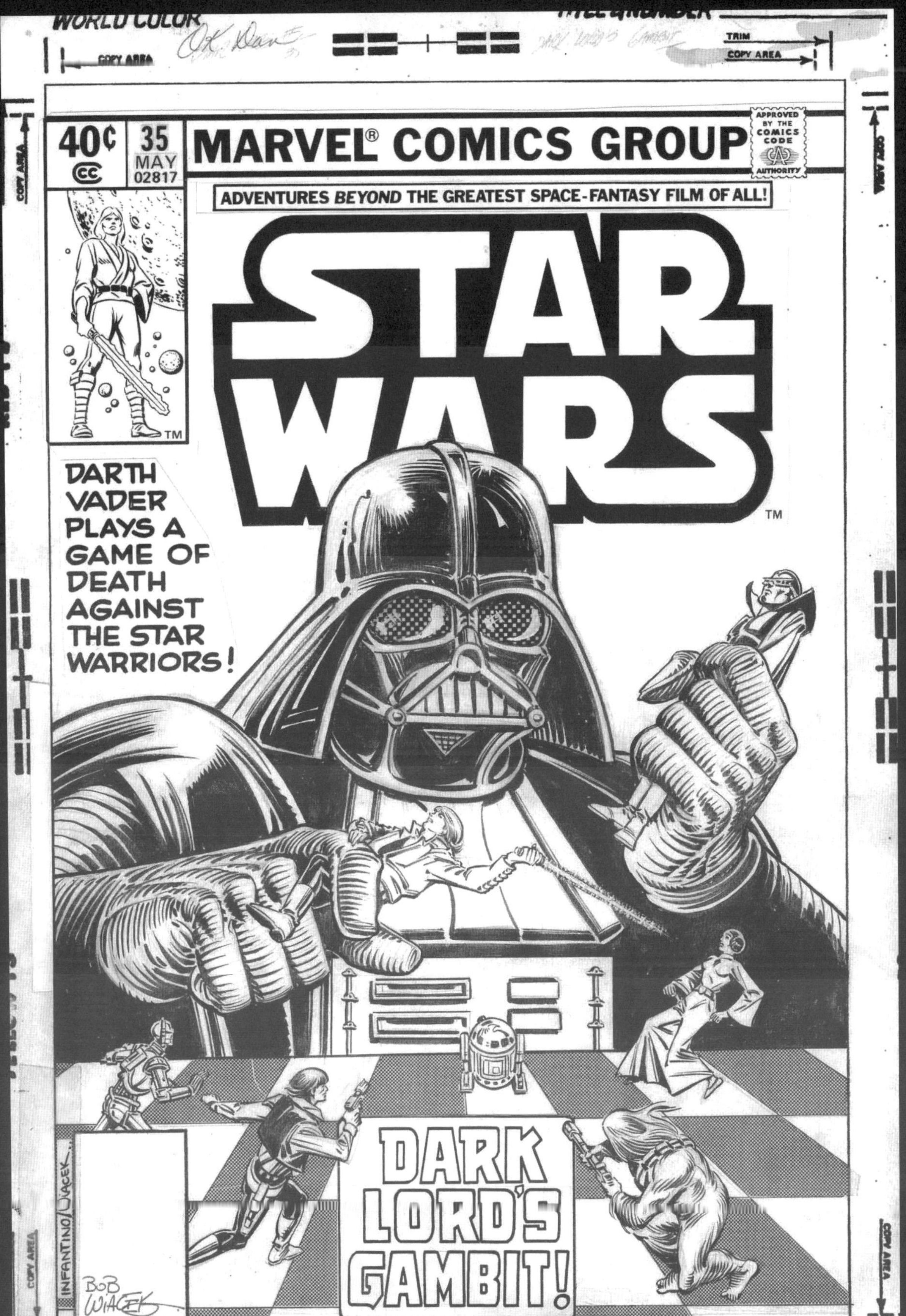
WORLD COLOR
COPY AREA
TRIM
40¢
35
MAY
02817
MARVEL® COMICS GROUP
APPROVED BY THE COMICS CODE AUTHORITY
ADVENTURES BEYOND THE GREATEST SPACE-FANTASY FILM OF ALL!
STAR WARS
DARTH VADER PLAYS A GAME OF DEATH AGAINST THE STAR WARRIORS!
DARK LORD'S GAMBIT!
INFANTINO/WIACEK
BOB WIACEK
TITLE STAR WARS SCHEDULE JAN
NO. 35
MONTH MAY
ARTIST Infantino/Wiacek
XEROX LAWYER DUE DATE STATS NEG POS. CODE

(above and facing page) The cover and a page from *Star Wars* #15 (Sept. 1978). Cover inks and interior finishes by Terry Austin.

FULL ARMOR COULD HIDE ANYTHING FROM A PROTON GRENADE TO YOUR WOOKIEE FIRST MATE--

--THIS LEAVES MUCH LESS TO DOUBT! THE TAPE, PLEASE.

RIGHT! I ASSUME YOU HAVE A CONCEALED MICRO-SCANNER LIKE ME...TO MAKE CERTAIN YOU'RE GETTING THE REAL THING.

PITY WE COULDN'T BE PARTNERS, HAN... WE THINK SO MUCH ALIKE.

WE'D ALWAYS BE WORRIED THAT THE OTHER ONE WOULD THINK OF IT FASTER, JACK--

--LIKE NOW!

AND AS THE PIRATE JABS AT A STUD ON HIS HARNESS...

...HAN KICKS HIM IN THE CHEST AND JETS UPWARD TOWARD THE MILLENNIUM FALCON!

YOU WON'T MAKE IT, SMUGGLER...NOT ALIVE! THAT SIGNALLED FOR THE MAGNETIC FIELD TO BE TIGHTENED--

--NOW THERE'S A VACUUM BETWEEN YOU AND YOUR SHIP!

AND A MAN UNARMORED IN THE VACUUM OF DEEP SPACE WILL FIND HIS BLOOD BOILING IN SECONDS!

AGAINST THAT ALTERNATIVE...THE FALCON'S SKIPPER ELECTS TO MAKE A HEROIC STAND!

LOOKS LIKE JACK CALLED OUT EVERY SPACE RAT WHO COULD CARRY A BLASTER!

NO QUESTION OF ESCAPE NOW, JUST HOW MANY CAN I GET--

--BEFORE THEY GET ME?!

CONTINUED AFTER NEXT PAGE

(above and facing page) Before starting his long run on the *Star Wars* series, Carmine penciled another space epic for Marvel: "Star Lord," which appeared in the pages of the black-and-white *Marvel Preview* magazine. Show here are two pages from issue #14, written by Chris Claremont and inked by Bob Wiacek.

WELL, QUILL, YOU'VE DONE IT *AGAIN.* SOMEONE REACHES OUT TO YOU, AND *ALL* YOU CAN DO IS *BUST* 'EM IN THE *CHOPS.*

DAMN YOU, WOMAN--WHY CAN'T YOU LEAVE ME *ALONE?!*

I DID *ALL RIGHT* TILL I MET YOU! NOW I'M GOING *CRAZIER* BY THE MINUTE.

I HAVE NO *DEFENSES* AGAINST HER, AND PART OF ME ISN'T SURE IT *WANTS* ANY.

STAR-LORD!

CARYTH'S VOICE-- SOUNDS LIKE *TROUBLE!*

HANG ON, LADY! I'M *COMING!*

WATCH YOUR *STEP,* PETER. THE PATH MAKES A SHARP *TURN* UP HERE.

GOOD LORD!

I THOUGHT THIS WAS A *SHALLOW* FISSURE, BUT IT OPENS INTO A REAL *CAVE.*

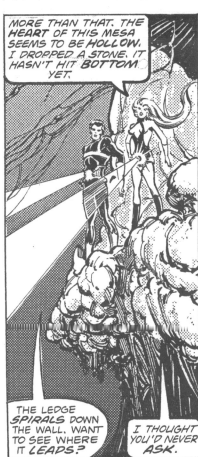

MORE THAN THAT. THE HEART OF THIS MESA SEEMS TO BE *HOLLOW.* I DROPPED A STONE. IT HASN'T HIT *BOTTOM* YET.

THE LEDGE *SPIRALS* DOWN THE WALL. WANT TO SEE WHERE IT *LEADS?*

I THOUGHT YOU'D NEVER *ASK.*

THEY HADN'T GONE *FAR* WHEN...

TREMOR! A BIG ONE!

PETER--THE *LEDGE!* IT'S *DISINTE- GRATING!*

GRAB MY *HAND,* CARYTH! I'LL TRY TO *BRAKE* OUR FALL!

WHOUUFF!

NOT MY *FINEST* LAND- ING, BUT LIKE THE *SAYING* GOES: ANY ONE YOU CAN *WALK* A- WAY FROM...

...HANG ON A MINUTE, I'LL GET US SOME *LIGHT.*

(above) Terry Austin inked this Carmine commission sketch of the Flash
facing off against Gorilla Grodd for its use as the cover to *Alter Ego* #10.

(facing page) Cover art for *The Flash* #301 (Sept. 1981), inked by Dick Giordano.
Carmine returned to the series with issue #296 and remained until the very end with issue #350.

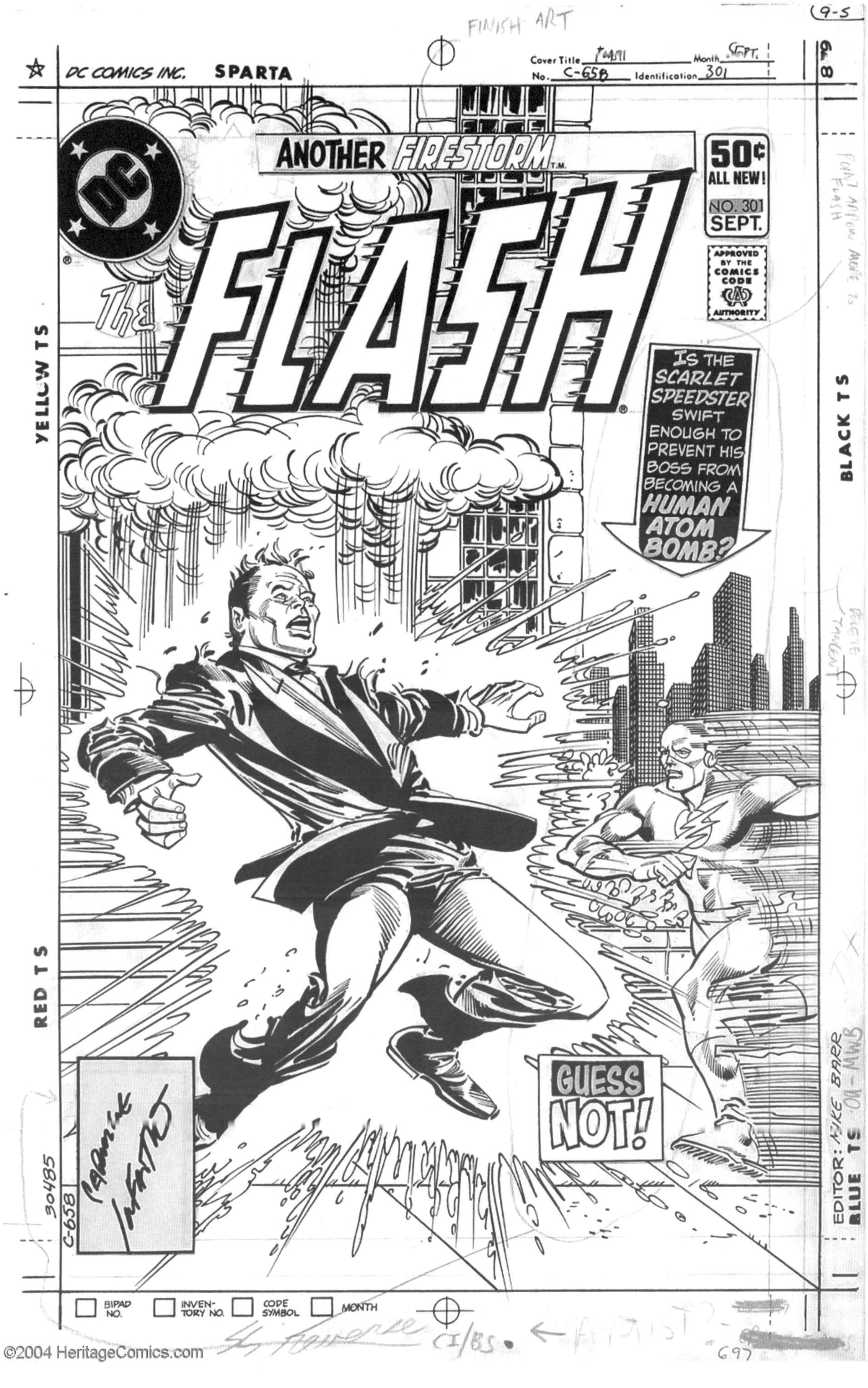
DC COMICS INC.
SPARTA
ANOTHER FIRESTORM
50¢
ALL NEW!
NO. 301
SEPT.
APPROVED BY THE COMICS CODE AUTHORITY
The FLASH
IS THE SCARLET SPEEDSTER SWIFT ENOUGH TO PREVENT HIS BOSS FROM BECOMING A HUMAN ATOM BOMB?
GUESS NOT!
YELLOW TS
RED TS
BLACK TS
EDITOR:
BLUE TS

(above) A Swamp Thing T-shirt design, inked by Alfredo Alcala, done for DC Special Projects.

(facing page) This "cover" (inked by Bob Smith) for the preview of a new "Dial 'H' for Hero" series appeared inside *Legion of Super-Heroes* #272 (Feb. 1981). One would assume it would soon have its own title, but, for whatever reason, a year later "Dial 'H' for Hero" launched as a back-up series in the pages of *The New Adventures of Superboy*, with no further involvement from Carmine.

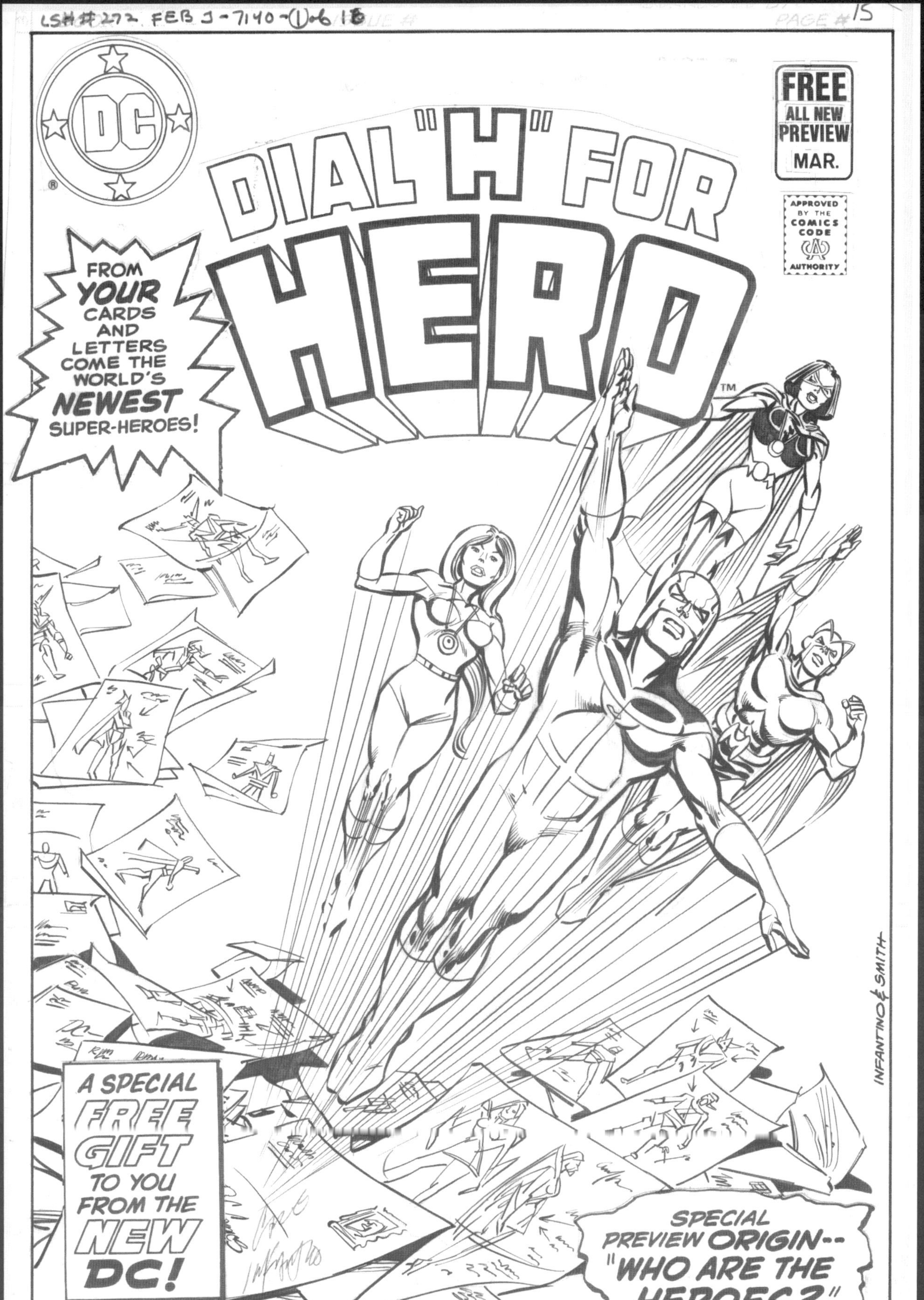
LSH #272 FEB J-7140-①-6 1B
PAGE # 15
DC
FREE
ALL NEW
PREVIEW
MAR.
APPROVED
BY THE
COMICS
CODE
AUTHORITY
DIAL "H" FOR
HERO
FROM YOUR CARDS AND LETTERS COME THE WORLD'S NEWEST SUPER-HEROES!
A SPECIAL FREE GIFT TO YOU FROM THE NEW DC!
SPECIAL PREVIEW ORIGIN-- "WHO ARE THE HEROES?"
INFANTINO & SMITH
J-7074

(above and facing page) Unpublished artwork intended for the second issue of a mid-1980s **Blackhawk** mini-series.
A panel of Carmine's pencils are shown here at full size. The inks for all the artwork are by Pablo Marcos.

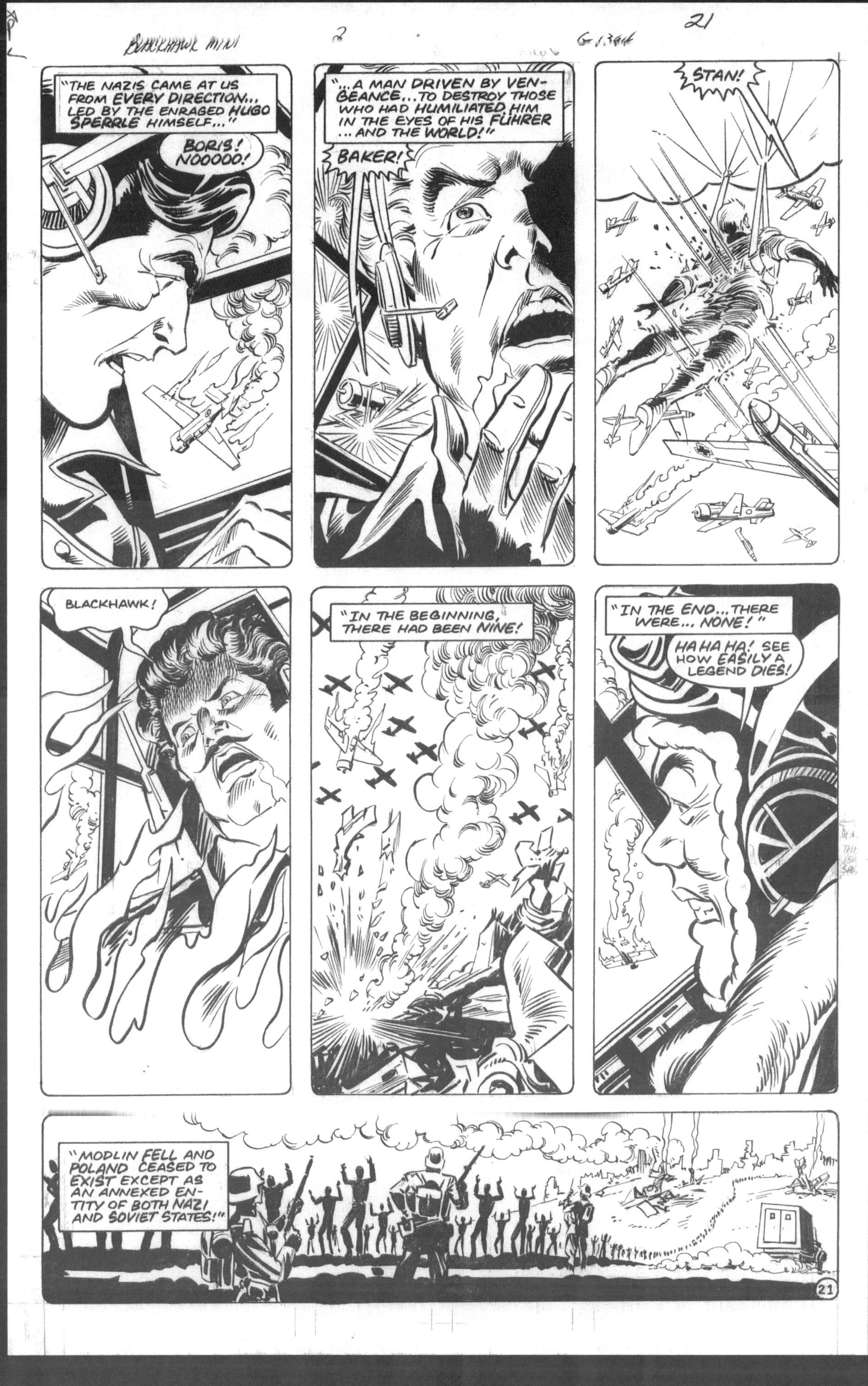
BLACKHAWK MINI
2
21
"THE NAZIS CAME AT US FROM EVERY DIRECTION... LED BY THE ENRAGED HUGO SPERRLE HIMSELF..."
BORIS! NOOOOO!
"...A MAN DRIVEN BY VENGEANCE...TO DESTROY THOSE WHO HAD HUMILIATED HIM IN THE EYES OF HIS FÜHRER ...AND THE WORLD!"
BAKER!
STAN!
BLACKHAWK!
"IN THE BEGINNING, THERE HAD BEEN NINE!
"IN THE END...THERE WERE... NONE!"
HA HA HA! SEE HOW EASILY A LEGEND DIES!
"MODLIN FELL AND POLAND CEASED TO EXIST EXCEPT AS AN ANNEXED ENTITY OF BOTH NAZI AND SOVIET STATES!"
21

(above) Carmine sketching Batgirl for a fan at the 2009 New York Comic-Con. (below right) Carmine yuks it up with Jim Amash.

(left) In 2003, Carmine drew this CD cover for his nephew Jim Infantino's band, Jim's Big Ego. Another of his nephews, John Infantino, inked the piece.

220

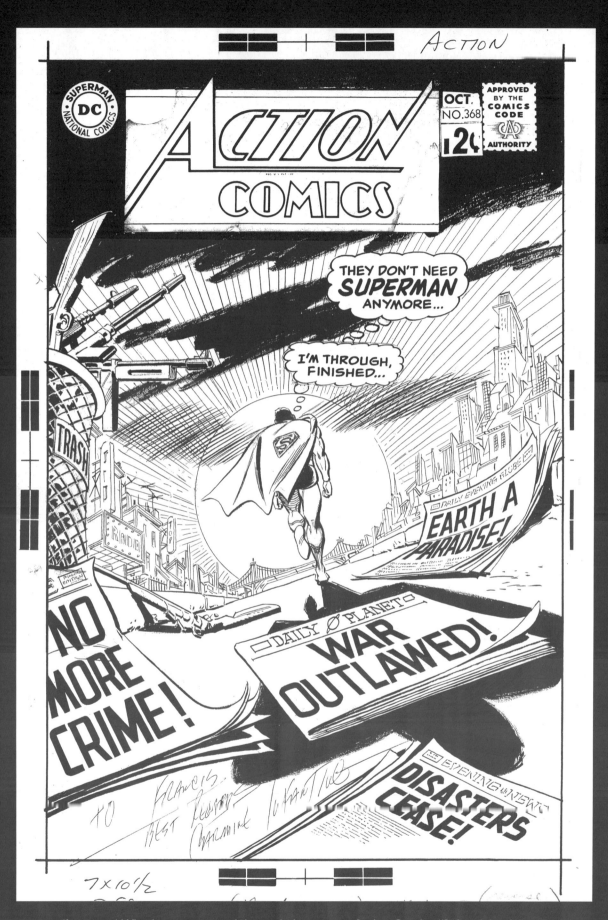

(facing page) What better way to end than with this cover to **Action Comics** #368, with breakdowns by Carmine, finished pencils by Ross Andru, and inks by Mike Esposito.

THE MODERN MASTERS SERIES

Edited by **ERIC NOLEN-WEATHINGTON**, these trade paperbacks and DVDs are devoted to the **BEST OF TODAY'S COMICS ARTISTS!** Each book contains **RARE AND UNSEEN ARTWORK** direct from the artist's files, plus a **COMPREHENSIVE INTERVIEW** (including influences and their views on graphic storytelling),

DELUXE SKETCHBOOK SECTIONS, and more!

And don't miss the companion **DVDs,** showing the artists at work in their studios!

MODERN MASTERS: IN THE STUDIO WITH GEORGE PÉREZ DVD

Get a **PERSONAL TOUR** of George's studio, and watch **STEP-BY-STEP** as the fan-favorite artist illustrates a special issue of **TOP COW's WITCHBLADE!** Also, see George as he sketches for fans at conventions, and hear his peers and colleagues—including **MARV WOLFMAN** and **RON MARZ**—share their anecdotes and personal insights along the way!

(120-minute Standard Format DVD) **$29.95**
ISBN: **9781893905511**
Diamond Order Code: **JUN053276**

MODERN MASTERS: IN THE STUDIO WITH MICHAEL GOLDEN DVD

Go behind the scenes and into Michael Golden's studio for a **LOOK INTO THE CREATIVE MIND** of one of comics' greats. Witness a modern master in action as this 90-minute DVD provides an exclusive look at the **ARTIST AT WORK,** as he **DISCUSSES THE PROCESSES** he undertakes to create a new comics series.

(90-minute Standard Format DVD) **$29.95**
ISBN: **9781893905771**
Diamond Order Code: **MAY073780**

Modern Masters: ALAN DAVIS
by Eric Nolen-Weathington
(128-page trade paperback) **$14.95**
ISBN: **9781893905191**
Diamond Order Code: **JAN073903**

Modern Masters: GEORGE PÉREZ
by Eric Nolen-Weathington
(128-page trade paperback) **$14.95**
ISBN: **9781893905252**
Diamond Order Code: **JAN073904**

Modern Masters: BRUCE TIMM
by Eric Nolen-Weathington
(120-page TPB with **COLOR**) **$14.95**
ISBN: **9781893905306**
Diamond Order Code: **APR042954**

Modern Masters: KEVIN NOWLAN
by Eric Nolen-Weathington
(120-page TPB with **COLOR**) **$14.95**
ISBN: **9781893905382**
Diamond Order Code: **SEP042971**

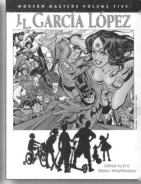

Modern Masters: GARCÍA-LÓPEZ
by Eric Nolen-Weathington
(120-page TPB with **COLOR**) **$14.95**
ISBN: **9781893905443**
Diamond Order Code: **APR053191**

Modern Masters: ARTHUR ADAMS
by George Khoury &
Eric Nolen-Weathington
(128-page trade paperback) **$14.95**
ISBN: **9781893905542**
Diamond Order Code: **DEC053309**

Modern Masters: JOHN BYRNE
by Jon B. Cooke & Eric Nolen-Weathington
(128-page trade paperback) **$14.95**
ISBN: **9781893905566**
Diamond Order Code: **FEB063354**

Modern Masters: WALTER SIMONSON
by Roger Ash & Eric Nolen-Weathington
(128-page trade paperback) **$14.95**
ISBN: **9781893905641**
Diamond Order Code: **MAY063444**

Modern Masters: MIKE WIERINGO
by Todd DeZago &
Eric Nolen-Weathington
(120-page TPB with **COLOR**) **$14.95**
ISBN: **9781893905658**
Diamond Order Code: **AUG063626**

Modern Masters: KEVIN MAGUIRE
by George Khoury &
Eric Nolen-Weathington
(128-page trade paperback) **$14.95**
ISBN: **9781893905665**
Diamond Order Code: **OCT063722**

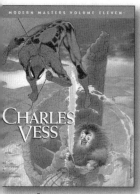

Modern Masters: CHARLES VESS

by Christopher Irving &
Eric Nolen-Weathington
(120-page TPB with COLOR) $14.95
ISBN: 9781893905696
Diamond Order Code: DEC063948

Modern Masters: MICHAEL GOLDEN

by Eric Nolen-Weathington
(120-page TPB with COLOR) $14.95
ISBN: 9781893905740
Diamond Order Code: APR074023

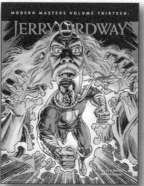

Modern Masters: JERRY ORDWAY

by Eric Nolen-Weathington
(120-page TPB with COLOR) $14.95
ISBN: 9781893905795
Diamond Order Code: JUN073926

Modern Masters: FRANK CHO

by Eric Nolen-Weathington
(120-page TPB with COLOR) $14.95
ISBN: 9781893905849
Diamond Order Code: AUG074034

Modern Masters: MARK SCHULTZ

by Fred Perry & Eric Nolen-Weathington
(120-page TPB with COLOR) $14.95
ISBN: 9781893905856
Diamond Order Code: OCT073846

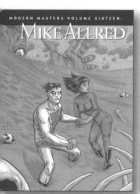

Modern Masters: MIKE ALLRED

by Eric Nolen-Weathington
(120-page TPB with COLOR) $14.95
ISBN: 9781893905863
Diamond Order Code: JAN083937

Modern Masters: LEE WEEKS

by Tom Field & Eric Nolen-Weathington
(128-page trade paperback) $14.95
ISBN: 9781893905948
Diamond Order Code: MAR084009

Modern Masters: JOHN ROMITA JR.

by George Khoury & Eric Nolen-Weathington
(128-page trade paperback) $14.95
ISBN: 9781893905955
Diamond Order Code: MAY084166

Modern Masters: MIKE PLOOG

by Roger Ash & Eric Nolen-Weathington
(120-page TPB with COLOR) $14.95
ISBN: 9781605490076
Diamond Order Code: JAN088704

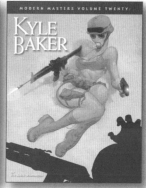

Modern Masters: KYLE BAKER

by Eric Nolen-Weathington
(120-page TPB with COLOR) $14.95
ISBN: 9781605490083
Diamond Order Code: SEP084305

Modern Masters: CHRIS SPROUSE

by Eric Nolen-Weathington &
Todd DeZago
(120-page TPB with COLOR) $14.95
ISBN: 97801605490137
Diamond Order Code: NOV084298

Modern Masters: MARK BUCKINGHAM

by Eric Nolen-Weathington
(128-page trade paperback) $14.95
ISBN: 9781605490144
Diamond Order Code: NOV090929

Modern Masters: DARWYN COOKE

by Eric Nolen-Weathington
(120-page TPB with COLOR) $15.95
ISBN: 9781605490205
Diamond Order Code: MAY091043

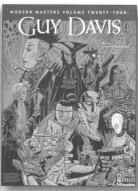

Modern Masters: GUY DAVIS

by Eric Nolen-Weathington
(120-page TPB with COLOR) $15.95
ISBN: 9781605490236
Diamond Order Code: AUG091083

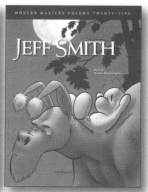

Modern Masters: JEFF SMITH

by Eric Nolen-Weathington
(120-page TPB with COLOR) $15.95
ISBN: 9781605490243
Diamond Order Code: JUN098206

MORE MODERN MASTERS ARE COMING IN 2011! VISIT: www.twomorrows.com

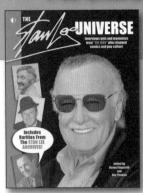